Griswold v. Connecticut

LANDMARK LAW CASES

&

AMERICAN SOCIETY

Peter Charles Hoffer

N. E. H. Hull

Series Editors

JOHN W. JOHNSON

Griswold v. Connecticut

Birth Control and the

Constitutional Right of Privacy

UNIVERSITY PRESS OF KANSAS

Published by the University Press of Kansas (Lawrence, Kansas 66049), which was organized by the Kansas Board of Regents and is operated and funded by Emporia State University, Fort Hays State University, Kansas State University, Pittsburg State University, the University of Kansas, and Wichita State University

Library of Congress Cataloging-in-Publication Data

Johnson, John W., 1946–

Griswold v. Connecticut : birth control and the constitutional right of privacy / John W. Johnson.

p.   cm — (Landmark law cases & American society)

Includes bibliographical references and index.

ISBN 0-7006-1377-3 (cloth : alk. paper) — ISBN 0-7006-1378-1 (pbk. : alk. paper)

1. Griswold, Estelle — Trials, litigation, etc.   2. Trials — Connecticut — New Haven.   3. Birth control — Law and legislation — Connecticut.   4. Privacy, Right of — United States.   I. Title: Griswold versus Connecticut.   II. Title.

III. Series.

KF224.G75J64 2005

342.7308′58 — dc22   2004025497

British Library Cataloguing-in-Publication Data is available.

Printed in the United States of America

10 9 8 7 6 5 4 3 2 1

For thirty years of students

CONTENTS

EDITORS' PREFACE

Do our judges make law, or find it? Should they be allowed to go beyond the letter of constitutions and statutes to create new kinds of rights? One old maxim of American law is that courts should confine themselves to resolving disputes between private parties and avoid engaging in policy making. Indeed, in our system, where the judiciary is presumed the weakest of the three branches of government and the federal bench, which never faces the voters and holds office for life, generally defers to the will of the popularly elected legislative and executive branches, our high court judges are understandably wary about turning their courts into miniature legislatures. This is particularly true of the justices of the highest appeals court in our land, the United States Supreme Court. But there are always exceptions to this rule of judicial restraint, and John Johnson's meticulous yet succinct account of the right to privacy struggle reminds us that our courts can be powerful forces for legal progress.

Today many of us may take the right to privacy as a given of our constitutional regime. In fact, it is nowhere mentioned in the Constitution. It is instead a judicially constructed right, emerging most clearly from the High Court's decision in *Griswold v. Connecticut*. As Johnson explains, privacy had begun its conceptual life as a way of protecting property from intruders and became instead a guarantee that one's person and lifestyle would be safe against the unreasonable intrusion of government agencies. The case itself, concerning Connecticut's outdated and unenforced laws against birth control, would become the basis for even more far-reaching decisions by the court on far more controversial issues like abortion and homosexuality.

In one sense, the High Court was only keeping up with the times, for as attitudes toward personal dignity, agency, and empowerment changed, so the law should follow. But because privacy had no precise textual definition (the Court discovered it in the penumbras of other enunciated rights or in the Ninth Amendment's rights reserved to the people), the decision was both capable of expansion and vulnerable to attack. Advocates of judicial restraint assailed the majority for their activism; defenders of legislative supremacy worried that the Court was setting a precedent for judicial intrusion into the democratic process; social and religious conservatives worried that the Court would undo the very fabric of American family life and open the door to sexual wantonness of all kinds. Even those academics who favored repeal of anachronistic sexual regulations wondered whether the Court had based its decision on poor logic and inept arguments.

The story of the struggle between Connecticut birth control advocates and the Catholic churchmen in the state is a fascinating one in itself, and Johnson is a master of its many twists and turns (including two Supreme Court cases prior to *Griswold*). He shows conclusively that birth control was not an obscure issue arising only in a local context, but a major national question, the resolution of which had far-reaching policy consequences. His discussion of the parallel development of ideas of privacy in Fourth (search and seizure) and First (free speech) Amendment cases during the first half of the twentieth century demonstrates that the Court's decision in *Griswold* was not such a doctrinal novelty as some other historians have proposed. Finally, Johnson carries his story beyond *Griswold* all the way to the current debate over same-sex marital rights, showing how the Court's moral stance in the Connecticut case has become the basis for a new kind of legal world.

This is constitutional history at its best, reaching out beyond text and doctrine to explain how a truly landmark case both reflected and changed its world. As Johnson concludes, "the right of privacy" now touches the "most intimate aspects" of domestic life. Perhaps the men and women who labored so hard to overturn Connecticut's "silly law" did not foresee the revolution their triumph would bring, but such perseverance, courage, and compassion as theirs mark the landscape of our legal history as prominently as the cases themselves.

ACKNOWLEDGMENTS

I have discovered that working on a book about privacy is not a very private matter. Without the help of countless colleagues, professional acquaintances, students, friends, and family members, this book might not have been completed. I am delighted to have the opportunity here to express appreciation to the many individuals who patiently answered my questions, rendered advice, or offered moral support at crucial stages of this effort.

I must begin, however, by thanking an institution — the University of Northern Iowa (UNI). As a faculty member at UNI since 1988, I am well aware that my employer is a comprehensive public university whose principal mission is teaching. But UNI has wisely seen fit in several ways to facilitate faculty research and scholarly publication in support of classroom instruction. In this regard, I was fortunate to have been awarded two "professional development assignments" that provided me with uninterrupted blocks of time to engage this project. The first, during the 2000 spring semester, accorded me the opportunity to begin my research on the law of privacy. The second, during the 2003 fall semester, allowed me to complete the lion's share of the written manuscript. In addition, UNI's Graduate College provided me with a project grant to defray expenses for a research trip to Washington, D.C.

My first exposure to the merits of developing detailed case studies of leading U.S. legal disputes took place in a 1970–71 graduate history seminar at the University of Minnesota taught by the late Paul L. Murphy. In the last thirty years, I have written scores of short essays on leading court cases, edited two editions of a reference work on American court cases, and — counting this effort — published three book-length studies dealing with important cases in U.S. constitutional law. I continue to draw inspiration and insight from Paul's example as a quiet but passionate teacher/scholar. A number of other scholars provided encouragement at critical stages of this project: Kermit L. Hall, Melvin Urofsky, John Wunder, William Lasser, Mary Dudziak, Laura Kalman, and Tinsley Yarbrough.

For assistance in obtaining legal records and other research materials on the right of privacy, I thank the following: Jeff Flannery of the

Manuscript Division of the Library of Congress; Val Russell and Nancy Mashuda-Pohnl of the University of Iowa Law Library; and the Interlibrary Loan staff at the University of Northern Iowa. Thanks also to Paul Springer, a former graduate research assistant, for helping me assemble a bibliography of relevant law review articles.

Once again, I am pleased to extend thanks to UNI History Department colleagues — who I am also privileged to have as friends — for serving as sounding boards for my ideas and for offering encouragement for my scholarship. In particular, I wish to single out Bob Martin, Don Shepardson, David Walker, Roy Sandstrom, Donna Maier, Jay Lees, Wally Hettle, Tom Connors, Chuck Holcombe, and Carol Weisenberger. My academic dean, Julia Wallace, and former dean and now provost, Aaron Podolefsky, have also been unfailing in their support for my research and publication. In addition, both of the UNI History Department's outstanding secretaries, Judy Dohlman and Vickie Hanson, provided invaluable assistance formatting my computer text and producing drafts of the manuscript.

I have been privileged over the last three decades to have taught many bright men and women at three institutions of higher learning. Especially in classes on U.S. constitutional history and American civil liberties, my students have provided me with constant challenges and frequent insights. To single out even a handful of the best of these individuals would be extraordinarily difficult and would likely run the risk of leaving out many worthy of mention. Hence, the words in the book's dedication will have to suffice.

This is my second pleasant experience working with the University Press of Kansas on a book in the Landmark Law Cases and American Society series. Michael Briggs, editor in chief of the Press, once again proved that he is everything a good editor should be — thoughtful and blunt, but always displaying a sincere concern for his authors and their work. Peter Hoffer, the series coeditor, offered trenchant criticism and advice at various stages of this project. An anonymous reader retained by the Press provided incisive guidance in helping me to focus and condense my analysis, and the copyeditor, Karen Hellekson, helped immeasurably to smooth out my prose. Larisa Martin, the Press's production editor, carefully oversaw the mechanics of fashioning this handsome volume. Susan Schott, the Press's assistant director and marketing manager, once again worked assiduously to advertise and promote one of my books.

My personal obligations to friends and family are enormous. My golf buddies — Dick Broadie, Jim Bodensteiner, Dennis Nebbe, Russ Wiley, Lee Luther, Kirk Manfredi, Larry Hamilton, Jack Wilkinson, Laura Strauss, Joe Griffith, Dick Followill, Steve Gaies, Don Wood, and Bill Elder — furnished me with countless hours of pleasant distraction and stress relief. My family — son Matt, daughter-in-law Darcy, son Noah, and grandson Lucas — consistently offered their encouragement and love. As I neared the end of this project, I learned the meaning of the word *serendipity* when I made the acquaintance of Maureen Murphy — a truly wonderful person who, for some unexplained reason, appears to enjoy my company. The better I get to know Maureen, the more I have fallen under her spell.

None of those named above are answerable for any errors, omissions, or dubious conclusions found in the pages to follow. As the person whose name is on the title page, I bear and accept sole responsibility for this book's shortcomings.

In 1953, Estelle Griswold — former office worker, sometime singer, and recently certified medical technologist — returned with her husband to her home state of Connecticut after spending several years abroad. Searching for a job, if not a cause, she learned of the availability of a paid position as executive director of the Planned Parenthood League of Connecticut (PPLC). Although she confessed to her interviewers that she did not know much about birth control, she proceeded to impress those evaluating her candidacy with her varied experiences and willingness to learn about contraception. She was offered the position, and she accepted. Thus began a crusade to furnish Connecticut women with access to birth control information that would occupy much of the remainder of her life. The principal challenge that Griswold faced in her new position was an 1879 Connecticut statute that made it a crime to use contraceptives in the state. Although several other states in the 1950s maintained restrictions on the manufacture and advertising of contraceptives, Connecticut's statute forbidding the "use" and "abetting" in the use of contraceptives was the most restrictive in the country. For almost half a century, pressure on the state legislature to abolish or modify this law had come up empty.

Shortly after accepting the leadership position with the Connecticut Planned Parenthood organization, Griswold met two men who would become allies in the campaign of the PPLC to do battle with the state's anticontraception law. The first was Dr. C. Lee Buxton, a scholarly physician and the new director of the Yale University infertility clinic, a project that the PPLC had financially supported for many years. The other was Fowler V. Harper, an outspoken Yale law professor. Together, Griswold, Buxton, and Harper would lead the fight for the legalization of birth control in Connecticut. Their efforts would also prove instrumental in revolutionizing American law by bringing the so-called right of privacy under the protective umbrella of the U.S. Constitution. These objectives were realized in a 1965 decision of the United States Supreme Court bearing the name *Griswold v. Connecticut*.

Griswold quickly became one of the most debated and controversial court decisions of the 1960s. It also came to serve as a litmus test for legal scholars analyzing the Supreme Court under the chief justiceship of Earl Warren. Was this a creative decision fashioned by a forward-looking Supreme Court majority that embraced the spirit of an evolving Constitution? Or was it an instance of a sloppy, activist judicial fiat that violated the intentions of the Constitution's brilliant founders? It is no exaggeration to say that *Griswold* changed the course of American constitutional law. In addition, the *Griswold* decision continues into the twenty-first century to set the agenda for debates about privacy in American life and how the nation's founding document should be interpreted.

The principal definition of the word *privacy* offered by the most recent edition of the *Oxford English Dictionary* is "the state or condition of being withdrawn from the society of others or from public attention; freedom from disturbance or intrusion; seclusion." Supposedly this usage dates to the late Middle English period, 1350–1469. A secondary definition is "absence or avoidance of publicity or display; secrecy" — a usage that arose in the late sixteenth century. The men who wrote the U.S. Constitution and the Bill of Rights in the late eighteenth century did not explicitly posit a constitutional right of privacy in the nation's founding document. Was this an oversight? Or was privacy so well understood and appreciated by the likes of James Madison, George Mason, and Alexander Hamilton that the Constitutional founders did not feel the need to make it explicit? Regardless of the intentions of the framers, privacy issues would be mentioned occasionally in nineteenth-century court decisions. With the advent of the American industrial revolution in the late nineteenth century, opportunities for a clash between technology and individual rights increased, and lawyers and judges began to talk more frequently about the need to protect personal privacy. World War I raised individual civil liberties concerns to a scale heretofore not experienced in American courts. The Bill of Rights, which had lain essentially dormant throughout most of the nineteenth century, finally took on a life of its own. About the middle of the twentieth century, the need to articulate explicitly a constitutional right of privacy began to be suggested in lawyers' appellate briefs and in essays appearing in law journals. Even a few U.S. Supreme Court judges in the 1950s began to sound the clarion call for a constitutional right of privacy. Then came the turbulent 1960s and the *Griswold* decision.

Whatever one's view of the soundness of the legal reasoning in *Griswold*, it would be hard to dispute the contention that, since 1965, the right of privacy has proven to be one of the most protean concepts in American legal history. It has served as the basis for a series of blockbuster court decisions on intimate personal matters, notably the right to die, the rights of homosexuals, and most controversially, the right of a woman to choose an abortion. In addition, the *Griswold* decision and the right of privacy have figured prominently in several recent Supreme Court confirmation hearings. In a broader sense, the issue of privacy remains part of the warp and woof of American life in the new century. When the issue of privacy is broached today, it is usually raised in connection with such important matters as abortion, death, genetic manipulation, sexual activity, national security, criminal justice, workplace rights, Internet practices, credit history, and the collection of data about one's life. It is hard to glance at a newspaper, view a televised news program, or spend more than a few minutes online with your computer without being alerted that your privacy may be in jeopardy because of the activities of a government agency, a large corporation, or some ominous force. Americans, public opinion polls tell us, cherish privacy and resent the prospect that we might be scrutinized or manipulated by forces outside of our control. Yet a few of us are willing to appear on reality TV shows to parade our prejudices, our cute family experiences, and even our bodies. We want our fifteen minutes of fame *and* what was once called the "right to be let alone." We voluntarily proffer intimate personal information to unseen and unmet individuals in online chat rooms and for Internet purchases, but we gladly pay for telephone features to shield our identities and block communications from pestering telemarketers.

Griswold v. Connecticut: Birth Control and the Constitutional Right of Privacy, published on the fortieth anniversary of the Supreme Court ruling in *Griswold*, tells the story of the making of a landmark decision by the nation's highest court. It seeks to ground the account of the case in two contexts: in the specific struggle to establish the right to birth control in Connecticut; and in the debate over the origins, definition, and elaboration of the constitutional right of privacy in American life. This examination focuses on the course of the *constitutional* right of privacy. That is, it probes how the justices of the U.S. Supreme Court—prodded by litigants, and lawyers and other judges—determined, elaborated, and qualified how certain provisions of the federal Constitution came to protect privacy. This treatment does not claim to be a comprehensive study of the law of privacy. *Griswold* and almost all of the cases that the U.S. Supreme Court has used over the last half century to craft the constitutional right of privacy have involved issues of sexual intimacy and family life. Thus, cases on these subjects are the focus of analysis in the pages to follow. There are, of course, many other contexts in which privacy and the law intersect — for example, in the security of one's home, the rights of those accused of crimes, oversight of employees in the workplace, Internet practices, personal credit, and the collection of data about individual lives by business or government. In addition, some provisions of the Patriot Act, passed by Congress in the aftermath of the terrorist attacks of 2001, have also resulted in criticism from civil libertarians that legitimate national security concerns have infringed on personal privacy. These subjects, as important as they are, have generally not figured into the Supreme Court's development of the constitutional right of privacy. Thus, they are outside the scope of this study.

CHAPTER I

The Connecticut Exception to Birth Control in America

Pessaries and Prudes

Although the technology of contraception had improved markedly since 1800, the range of birth control strategies available to Connecticut women in the 1950s had changed very little over the previous 150 years. There were spermicidal suppositories, vaginal sponges, cervical caps, and intrauterine devices. Men, of course, could wear condoms, often called "rubbers," or withdraw before ejaculation (that is, coitus interruptus). Couples could practice one of many versions of the rhythm method — refraining from intercourse during a woman's most fertile period. There were still stories circulating in the 1950s of couples seeking contraceptive potions, peddled almost like the snake oil medicines of rural carnivals or county fairs. Douching with various solutions or engaging in other forms of action after intercourse — such as sneezing or running around in circles — were still occasionally used to prevent conception. In the extreme, couples could forswear sex entirely. Abortion was then an illegal option to end a pregnancy, as, of course, was infanticide.

But the most commonly prescribed form of contraception offered by Connecticut doctors in the 1950s was the diaphragm. A diaphragm is a device inserted into the vagina over the cervix before intercourse and then removed after the completion of the sex act. Diaphragms made of animal skin had been around for thousands of years. Generally called "pessaries" in the nineteenth century, the diaphragm also bore such colorful names as the "womb veil," the "female protector," or "Victoria's Protector." The diaphragm came into relatively widespread use in America after the vulcanization of rubber in the mid-nineteenth century. Poor woman clamored for the diaphragm at early birth control clinics, believing that it was the "rich woman's secret" to preventing the birth of unwanted children. Until the quantum leap in birth control technology offered in the 1960s by drugs such as the Pill that caused the temporary cessation of menstruation, the diaphragm was the preferred form of birth control in America.

The diaphragm and other forms of contraception were sold in Connecticut at the time Estelle Griswold took over the day-to-day leadership of the Planned Parenthood League of Connecticut (PPLC). But Mrs. Griswold had her work cut out for her in her new job because contraception was also illegal in her state. Still on the books in the early 1950s was an 1879 Connecticut statute — codified in the 1958 revision of the General Statutes of Connecticut as Section 53–32 — that held that "[a]ny person who uses any drug, medicinal article or instrument for the purpose of preventing conception shall be fined not less than fifty dollars or imprisoned not less than sixty days nor more than one year or be both fined and imprisoned." In addition, counseling women of the use of the diaphragm, even if performed by licensed physicians, was also proscribed by an "accessory statute," Section 54–196 of the 1958 revision of the General Statutes: "Any person who assists, abets, counsels, causes, hires or commands another to commit any offense may be prosecuted and punished as if he were the principal offender."

In the early 1950s, Connecticut and Massachusetts were the only states in the union that still had anticontraception statutes on the books. These laws were not enforced, except for the legal test cases that will be discussed in this book. Nevertheless, some New England political figures and birth control activists believed that the very presence on the statute books of the Massachusetts and Connecticut anticontraception laws kept some women from seeking reproductive advice from physicians and, in many nonquantifiable ways, discouraged the practice of birth control in the two states.

The Connecticut anticontraception law sprung largely out of the efforts of a small number of influential reformers in late nineteenth-century America. Many of those who had railed against slavery in the late antebellum period were looking for new movements in post–Civil War America to pour their passions into. Among the causes that came to replace abolitionism was the social purity movement. Well-educated and often well-born men and women channeled their reforming ardor into campaigns to clean up America's cities. Among the blights that these reformers came to scorn in the burgeoning urban areas was commercial vice. Prostitution, of course, was a one of the vices targeted by the social purity movement. So was the trade in obscene pictures and literature.

One union veteran, Anthony Comstock, moved to New York City shortly after being mustered out of the Grand Army of the Republic. An intensely religious man, Comstock was scandalized by the trade in human vice that he found on the streets of Gotham. Prostitution and the hawking of obscene writings, drawings, and photographs, together with the general seediness of the saloons and flophouses, proved shocking and repulsive to the young man from the countryside. Comstock ultimately convinced a handful of financial benefactors of the New York YMCA to support him in a full-time campaign to strengthen the nation's obscenity laws, thus allowing him to quit his short-lived job selling dry goods.

Comstock and his supporters incorporated the New York Society for the Suppression of Vice; Comstock served as the society's first director. Among Comstock's claim to fame was the successful lobbying of Congress to pass, in 1873, a bill that strengthened federal law against sending obscene materials through the mails. The amendments favored by Comstock came to be known as the federal Comstock Law. Included among the so-called obscene materials proscribed by the law were information and pictures relating to the "prevention of conception." Placing the literature on birth control under the category of obscenity proved to be a blow from which the early advocates of contraception would take almost a century to recover. Comstock, for reasons that have never been clearly explained by historians, convinced Congress to appoint him as a special agent or "inspector" for the Post Office, with authority to arrest individuals sending obscene materials through the mails. Carrying the imprimatur of federal law, Comstock proceeded to conduct his own raids. In 1873 alone, he logged over 23,000 rail miles with his inspector's pass, arrested fifty-five individuals (twenty of whom were ultimately convicted), and seized over 60,000 "obscene rubber articles" — no doubt condoms and diaphragms.

Many states passed their own "little Comstock laws," proscribing various forms of obscenity, including information about birth control.

The 1879 Connecticut law was one of these. In fact, when the Connecticut law was passed initially as Chapter 78 of the Public Acts of 1879, it was titled "An Act to Amend an Act Concerning Offences Against Decency, Morality, and Humanity." It tracked very closely the language of the original Comstock Act. The legislative committee that succeeded in adding the anticontraception language to Connecticut's little Comstock Act was chaired by P. T. Barnum, a Bridgeport Republican best known for his circus, billed as the "Greatest Show on Earth." In the revision of the General Statutes of Connecticut in 1888, the state obscenity law was broken into multiple sections, and the portion banning contraceptives was placed in a separate section.

Certainly some of the advice and materials being circulated under the umbrella of birth control in the late nineteenth century were of dubious benefit; some were potentially lethal. Medical quackery was endemic in late nineteenth-century America. So Comstock's efforts and his namesake legislation might have kept some dangerous materials out of people's hands. On balance, however, responsible advocates of birth control argued that Comstock's efforts set back for decades the quest for circulating the best contraceptive advice available. Thus it left the field in the 1870s and 1880s largely to druggists, as well as to hawkers of patent medicines and other charlatans.

Margaret and Sadie

Although a handful of physicians advised married couples privately on birth control options in the late nineteenth and early twentieth centuries, they almost universally avoided published distributions of their thoughts on birth control. The penalties of the Comstock laws were simply too chilling. Only a few "sex radicals," as they were then called, had the temerity to advocate for birth control. The most notable of these was a feisty New England woman of Irish descent named Margaret Higgins Sanger.

Born in 1879 to Michael and Anne Higgins of Corning, New York, Margaret was the sixth of her mother's eleven children. The contrast between the lives of her parents had a decided impact on what would eventually become Margaret's lifelong passion: the advocacy of birth control. Anne Higgins had a constant cough and died of tuberculosis in her forties, while Michael Higgins survived to be a garrulous and seemingly happy octogenarian. Could it be that enduring so many pregnancies and bearing so many children limited her mother's choices, the quality of her life, and her very life span?

A year after her mother's death, Margaret left the family home in Corning and entered nursing school in White Plains, New York. While pursuing her nurse's training, Margaret met her future husband, William Sanger. Within months of her marriage, she was pregnant and afflicted with tuberculosis. Following an unhappy period of confinement in a sanatorium, she returned to the family home in Hastings-on-Hudson and through a difficult delivery gave birth to a son.

After the birth of their child, the Sangers moved to a Manhattan apartment, which soon became a gathering place for some of the most colorful political radicals of the World War I era. Regular guests included Alexander Berkman, the infamous anarchist and editor of *Mother Earth;* William D. Haywood, the leader of the International Workers of the World (the "Wobblies"); John Reed, an American poet who would later participate in and write glowingly of the Bolshevik Revolution; and last, but certainly not least, Emma Goldman, the ubiquitous women's rights activist. Relieved from much of the moment-to-moment demands of child rearing by the babysitting provided by Bill's mother, Margaret was freed to accept work as a private nurse and began to dabble in political causes.

In 1912 Sanger began writing a series of articles on female sexuality for *The Call,* a socialist daily. The series was cut short, however, in February 1913, when one of Sanger's articles was found to be obscene and therefore unmailable under the Comstock Act. In the course of her travels around New York City, Sanger was touched — and outraged — by the scores of poor women who assembled each Saturday night outside the office of Lower Manhattan's five-dollar abortionist. After their abortions, many of the women voiced pleas for the "secret [that] rich people have to stop babies from coming."

The event that Sanger claimed turned her into a full-time birth control advocate was a self-administered abortion that went tragically wrong for a young woman named Sadie Sachs. When Sanger first met Sadie Sachs, the woman was already the mother of three small children and married to a man who persisted in demanding his marital rights, no matter how tired or sick his wife might be. Summoned to administer to the infection accruing from a self-induced abortion, Sanger spent three weeks in a hot, squalid tenement tending to Sadie's needs. A few months later, Sachs fell into a coma from another botched — probably self-induced — abortion. This time she died. Sanger's Sadie Sachs story may have been apocryphal or a composite of several emotionally charged stories. Regardless of its authenticity, Sanger used it over the years to good emotional effect to stir her listeners and readers.

As the Sadie Sachs narrative suggests, for Sanger at this time in her public career, birth control was a feminist issue: women needed to practice birth control in order to circumvent male tyranny and to afford themselves control over their bodies and their very lives. This message meshed more smoothly with the goals of women's rights in the early twentieth century than it did with that of the agenda of the medical profession. In fact, Sanger and other advocates of contraception believed that more reliable information on birth control in the World War I era could be obtained from anarchist leaflets than from medical journals.

Just before the onset of World War I, Sanger visited England and the European continent to study the practice of birth control. She returned to the United States with scores of French pessaries and formulas for contraceptive douches and suppositories. She also began to challenge the Comstock Act by publishing a pamphlet called *The Woman Rebel* that championed a woman's right to seek birth control information and to put that advice into practice. Facing prosecution under the Comstock Act, Sanger fled the country, returning to Europe to continue her study of birth control. This experience convinced her that contraception, to be effective for the masses, demanded more than informative articles in a few pamphlets; it required the medical services that could only be delivered through a network of clinics. Returning to America in 1916, Sanger renewed her lectures and writing. Arrested for violating a New York law that made it a misdemeanor to sell or otherwise dispense contraceptive information, Sanger spent thirty days in a New York jail. Upon release from jail, Sanger found that she had achieved the status of a heroine to suffragettes and other advocates of women's rights.

By the mid-1920s, Sanger had opened several birth control clinics, had established a journal titled the *Birth Control Review*, had founded an organization named the American Birth Control League, had written two books, had toured the country and the Far East, and had divorced Bill and married a millionaire. She was an international celebrity—charismatic and hard-working, but generally a pain to deal with. She would remain the most visible advocate for birth control in America, perhaps in the entire world, for the remainder of her long life. Unlike her mother, who died as an invalid in her early forties, Margaret lived—like her father—to be an octogenarian. She died in 1966.

Eugenics and One Package

The identification of Margaret Sanger—the leading advocate for contraception—with various radicals and radical causes may have afforded the birth control movement its initial impetus. However, in the aftermath of the Red Scare after the Russian Revolution, the connection of the struggle for contraception with the activities and lifestyles of, for example, Emma Goldman and Margaret Sanger did the cause no favor. Throughout the early twentieth century, Sanger resisted making overtures to physician organizations because she perceived them, quite correctly, to be unsympathetic to women's rights. No better indication of this is the fact that the American Medical Association, as part of its campaign to "professionalize" the business of medicine in the early twentieth century, sought to make it almost impossible for women to become doctors. Hence, it is not surprising that doctors, either singularly or in the context of their professional bodies, refused to accept the advice from laywomen when it came to the need for contraception. The intransigence of the medical profession against women on the issue of birth control was only strengthened because the leading advocate of the cause was an intemperate political radical.

The person who would bridge the gap between Margaret Sanger and the medical profession was a Brooklyn gynecologist named Robert Latou Dickinson. Commencing his practice around the turn of the century, Dr. Dickinson was presented with enough sad cases of women in trouble to become skeptical of the Victorian belief that sex should be engaged in only for the propagation of the race. In fact, it was not long before Dickinson took a further step. He began to advise his patients that sex was essential to a good marriage and that sometimes unplanned or unwanted pregnancies could get in the way of marital happiness. Hence, he encouraged his patients to practice birth control. Moreover, he took it on himself to engage in research on the practice of birth control, to publish findings in consonance with those favoring contraception, and to lobby his fellow practitioners as to the virtues of sex without procreation.

Possessing an upper-class pedigree, Dickinson was a "safe" champion for contraception. He personally insisted on fitting diaphragms for married women through the outpatient departments of hospitals. Although he did not practice in the clinics that catered to poor women, he recognized the value of the data that Margaret Sanger and her associates were gathering through her Clinical Research Bureau. By the late 1920s Dickinson was lobbying the city of New York to license the clinics of Sanger and her associates. For her part, Sanger was becoming increasing willing to soft-pedal the feminist rhetoric in the clinics. More importantly, Sanger bowed to the supervision of certified physicians in the dispensing of contraceptive information and devices in her clinics. By the 1930s, Sanger, who had long preferred the terms "voluntary motherhood" or "birth control" for contraceptive practices, grudgingly acquiesced to the ascription favored by the medical profession, "family planning."

From the modern perspective, one distressing aspect of the uneasy accord between Sanger and the medical community was their coming together over eugenics. Defined by one authority as "the branch of biology concerned with the genetic basis of racial diversity," eugenics was a widespread article of faith for many Americans in the period between the world wars. In practical terms, believers in eugenics wanted to devise ways to minimize the impact of "bad genes" on the country's population. Social reformers, intellectuals, and informed members of the general population believed that the "controlled breeding" touted by eugenicists was a way of improving the racial stock.

The medical profession of the early twentieth century generally drifted within the eugenics mainstream. For most physicians who specialized in obstetrics and gynecology, certain racial stocks were "better" than others. So if fertility could be enhanced among, for example, the preferred Nordic women, that would be all to the benefit of America's genetic health. Correspondingly, if fertility could be reduced among those women of southern or eastern European stock through birth control, the men of medicine might be willing to give contraception their support. Given this logic, playing the eugenics card became a way to mitigate — even obliterate — the historic reluctance of the medical profession toward birth control.

Margaret Sanger accepted the position of the orthodox eugenicist that unrestrained breeding boded ill for the genetic health of the population. But for her, no particular racial genes were ideal in propagation. The problem with unrestrained breeding, she believed, was that racial decay had been taking place for millennia because of the "sexual enslavement" of women. She put it thusly: "Abused soil brings forth stunted growth. An abused motherhood has brought forth a low order of humanity." Sanger saw racial deterioration as a direct outcome of the "repressive Victorian class and sexual order." Sanger targeted lower-class women in her birth control clinics, not because they were racially inferior, but because they were the most sexually subordinated. Middle- and upper-class women deserved contraceptive counseling as well, but many were already receiving it.

Following these two different strings of logic, eugenics served as a key link in the alliance between the Sangerists and the American medical profession. Sanger supported birth control for all women in order to lessen sexual enslavement. The doctors, being especially interested in cutting into the bulk of the racially unfit lower classes, were willing to allow the Sanger-founded birth control clinics to continue to operate as long as they were staffed by certified medical personnel. Conversely, the doctors generally wanted to encourage fertility among upper- and middle-class women. Yet they recognized that this battle had already been fought and lost: the women in the comfortable classes — many of them the wives and daughters of physicians — were already practicing birth control. Thus, the medical profession by the late 1920s had arrived at the position of supporting the spread of birth control information to all American women, primarily because it wished to encourage the curtailing of fertility where most needed: among the lower classes. Although the alliance over eugenics between the Sangerites and the medical profession provided the theoretical basis for advancing the cause of birth control, it would take a court decision to provide the practical impetus.

On December 7, 1936, the U.S. Court of Appeals for the Second Circuit issued its ruling in a decision known as *U.S. v. One Package*.

The case arose as a consequence of the federal government's seizure of a package of pessaries mailed from Japan to Dr. Hannah Stone, a licensed physician and director of Margaret Sanger's Birth Control Research Bureau in New York. The government claimed authority to confiscate the diaphragms as "obscene articles" pursuant to the Tariff Act of 1930, an outgrowth of the original Comstock Act of 1873. Dr. Stone and her attorneys maintained that she had a legal right to import these birth control materials for the legitimate medical purposes of saving lives and promoting the welfare of patients. The federal district court agreed with Dr. Stone, but the federal government appealed the case to the Second Circuit.

In arguing for affirmation of the district court ruling, Morris Ernst, the attorney for Dr. Stone (and Margaret Sanger), presented an appellate brief containing a massive amount of medical and sociological evidence in support of the proposition that birth control devices were necessities for many women, especially those of lower socioeconomic status. Ernst's tactic proved successful in the Second Circuit. The appellate court opinion, written by Judge Augustus Hand, avoided the question of whether the articles were obscene. But Hand did hold that the 1873 Comstock Act could not be construed in such a way as to deny to physicians the articles that were mailed for the purpose of enhancing public health. And who would determine whether particular materials were essential to public health? Why, doctors, of course. The broad ruling of the Second Circuit in the *One Package* case has generally been interpreted by judges, lawyers, and legal scholars as effectively ending the reign of Comstockery. The holding in *One Package* paved the way for the receipt and deployment of more birth control materials to married couples. Sanger and her colleagues met shortly after learning of the ruling in *One Package* to discuss the implications of the decision for birth control in the country in general and Connecticut in particular. Sanger saw the decision as "an emancipation proclamation to the motherhood of America." Equally as important, Dr. Dickinson and other pro–birth control physicians on the American Medical Association's (AMA) Committee on Contraceptive Practices, used the *One Package* decision as a vehicle to prevail on the AMA's House of Delegates to adopt, in the summer of 1937, a committee report favorable to the "dissemination and teaching of the best methods of birth control."

By the middle of the 1930s a number of Connecticut physicians were offering birth control information and granting married couples prescriptions for contraceptives. But these doctors were acting illegally. They were in violation of the abetting feature of the state's 1879 anti-contraception law. To the best of anyone's memory, this law had never been enforced. However, its continued presence on the statute books likely had a chilling effect on the provision of birth control information by some Connecticut physicians, and, perhaps, kept some of the state's women — particularly those of lower socioeconomic status — from realizing that contraceptive counseling was available.

Reluctant Legislators, Intransigent Priests

For over a decade before the Court of Appeals' decision in *U.S. v. One Package*, groups and individuals wishing to make birth control information available to married couples had attempted to lobby the Connecticut state legislature to abolish the 1879 ban on birth control. The campaign to effect a legislative burial of the anticontraception law would redouble in strength after the *One Package* decision and would continue into the 1950s. In addition, on several occasions between 1920 and 1960, various versions of a "doctors' bill" were proposed that would grant an exception to physicians counseling women on birth control for medical rather than family planning purposes.

The story of the legislative drive to change Connecticut's anticontraception law has an ironic beginning. In draft form, the so-called Comstock Act of 1873 contained a physicians' exemption to the section banning the possession, sale, or mailing of contraceptive devices. However, when discussion began in the U.S. Senate in February 1873 on the bill that would become the Comstock Act, a Republican senator from Connecticut, William A. Buckingham, presented an amendment that struck out the medical exemption for birth control. Senator Buckingham's amendment benefited from only a minimum of discussion on the floor of the Senate. Senators may have been confused about what the amendment was attempting to accomplish. In any case, the amendment was approved, and a few days later, the Senate passed the amended bill and delivered it to the House of Representatives. With absolutely no substantive discussion, the House on March 1, 1873, approved the entire bill. It was signed into federal law shortly thereafter. Had the Buckingham amendment never been proposed, and had the Comstock Act been enacted in its original form, the struggle to make birth control information and technology available to American women and men would have been essentially a private medical matter rather than what it actually became: a very public battleground for morals, religion, and governmental policy that would last almost a century until its resolution in the *Griswold v. Connecticut* decision of 1965.

The Comstock Act, complete with the Buckingham amendment, was on the minds of Connecticut's legislature when it approved the state anticontraception bill a few years later in 1879. The Connecticut law was part of a plenary statute that attempted to single out for prosecution several "offenses against decency, morality and humanity." It had been introduced just two days after an almost identical bill had been presented to the Massachusetts legislature. Both bills were strongly endorsed by the New England Society for the Suppression of Vice, a regionally based Comstock organization.

The first attempt to repeal the Connecticut anticontraception law was mounted in early 1917 by Henry F. Fletcher, a follower of Margaret Sanger. Fletcher apparently prevailed on a member of the Connecticut legislature to introduce a bill to repeal the 1879 anticontraception law. Fletcher's linkage with Margaret Sanger, who was burdened then by legal problems and an identification with international radicalism in the World War I era, spelled a quick and decisive defeat for the repeal bill that he championed.

A campaign to modify the 1879 anticontraception statute would next be advanced in the 1923 session of the Connecticut legislature. In the previous year, supporters of birth control had established the Connecticut Birth Control League (CBCL), a state affiliate of Sanger's American Birth Control League (ABCL). A member of the state legislature, Samuel Sisisky, introduced a bill to furnish a medical exception to the 1879 ban on birth control in the state. The Sisisky measure provided that "giving of information or advice or medicine or articles for prevention of conception by a doctor or nurse" would not be considered a violation of the abetting portion of the 1879 law. Although such a "doctors' exception" was not as thoroughgoing a reform of the law as a total repeal, it was considered more politically feasible at the time.

The foremost resistance to the Sisisky bill came from leaders of the

Roman Catholic clergy. Auxiliary Bishop John G. Murray of Hartford challenged Sanger and the supporters of the pending Connecticut legislation at the joint committee hearing. He maintained that contraception is "a violation of natural law." He submitted that "the Creator gave the sex function for just one purpose and to exercise it for any other purpose is a perversion of that function." He also presented an interesting twist on the eugenics argument by claiming that "the races from northern Europe," which he saw as genetically superior to all other races, "are doomed to extinction, unless each produces at least four children." Sanger had the last word at the hearing: she countered Bishop Murray's assertion that birth control violates natural law by pointing out that, according to Murray's own logic, the practice of celibacy by Catholic churchmen was unnatural. Sanger may have scored the most debating points at the 1923 Judiciary Committee hearing, but she did not convince the joint committee of the merits of her position. The Judiciary Committee recommended against the endorsement of a doctors' exception to the 1879 statute. Shortly thereafter, without a word of floor debate, the two houses of the Connecticut legislature rejected the Sisisky bill.

The experience in 1923 was repeated again and again in other biennial sessions of the Connecticut legislature. Between 1923 and 1963 there were twenty-nine bills introduced to modify or repeal the 1879 anticontraception law. Every legislative session from 1923 to 1935 saw at least one such bill proposed — and defeated. Between 1935 and 1941, the advocates of birth control in Connecticut attempted another strategy: defying the law by opening birth control clinics in key Connecticut cities. After a court decision that found such clinics in violation of the 1879 law, the CBCL returned to its strategy of attempting to secure sympathetic legislation. Between 1941 and the early 1960s, the forces wishing to modify the anticontraception law introduced sixteen more modification bills. As in the 1920s and 1930s, all of the proposed modification enactments failed at one stage or another of the legislative process.

Session after session, the pattern was repeated: Proponents of a repeal bill or a doctors' exception bill would offer drafts of legislation to modify the 1879 anticontraception law. The bills would be referred to the state legislature's joint Committee on the Judiciary. Hearings would be held. Generally the strongest voices in favor of the legislation would be members of the national or state birth control leagues. Some-times Margaret Sanger would be present herself. More often, sympa-thetic physicians would testify as to their reasons for favoring a modification of the law. Occasionally there would be testimony from women in childbearing years, frustrated by the ban on medical advice about birth control in the state of Connecticut. Criticisms of the modification proposals would be spearheaded by Catholic priests and bishops and by representatives of a legion of Catholic organizations. Sometimes the bills would receive a majority endorsement of the Judi-ciary Committee, sometimes not. If the repeal or doctors' exception bills did make it to the state's lower house, the same pro and con voices heard before the Judiciary Committee would once again be heard on the floor of the legislature.

Sometimes the lower house of the legislature would vote in favor of a modification bill. Generally this was the case when the Republican majority in the legislature was the greatest. By the 1920s the Protes-tant zeal of the Comstockians that birth control information was obscene had faded; in its place was a staunch Roman Catholicism that was adamantly opposed to birth control because it was said to violate God's law that procreation should not be disrupted by artificial means. In Connecticut, Republicans tended to be Protestant, while the more ethnically diverse Democrats were heavily Catholic. The membership in the lower house of the Connecticut legislature was, for the first half of the twentieth century, disproportionately rural and Protestant. The Senate, by contrast, was divided into thirty-six districts, many of them heavily urban and Catholic. On those occasions when a repeal or doc-tors' exception bill would be voted favorably on by a majority of the lower house, it would be rejected by Democrats in the state senate. During the entire period from 1920 to 1950 Democrats controlled the Connecticut senate. If all other hurdles standing in the way of modi-fying the 1879 anticontraception statute were surmounted, the heav-ily Democratic/Catholic state senate remained as an immutable barrier to the movement toward birth control in Connecticut.

Statements by activists before the Judiciary Committee hearings or quoted in the press illustrate the often harsh tenor of the debates over the modification bills. For example, in the 1927 Judiciary Com-mittee hearing, Hannah Stone testified thusly in favor of that session's repeal bill: "Contraception is distinctly a medical problem," she maintained; "it should be the duty and privilege of the physician to advise his patients in regard to it." In support of a doctors' exception bill pending in the 1933 legislative session, a pro–birth control physician, Dr. James Raglan Miller, reported that in just the last six months of 1932, fifty-seven Connecticut women had died during pregnancy. At least nine of these unfortunate women had died as a result of illegal abortions. A doctors' exception to the 1879 law that would permit physicians to offer contraceptive counseling, he argued, would prevent such tragic and preventable human losses. In support of this reform bill, another Connecticut doctor presented a petition bearing the signatures of five thousand Connecticut doctors, more than half of the doctors then practicing medicine in the state.

The arguments raised by the critics of modifying the anticontraception law tended to reflect religious or moral concerns of the Catholic Church. Typical of the Catholic interest groups arguing against amending the 1879 law was Mrs. Louise Fisher, a mother of five who represented the Connecticut Council of Catholic Women. Mrs. Fisher expressed concern that the proposed 1925 repeal of the 1879 statute would "increase the trend toward evading of responsibilities on the part of married people." She cautioned that "persons shouldn't enter into married life unless they are willing to accept the obligation of children." She concluded her testimony by proclaiming that "there is already too much love of luxury and . . . this bill would encourage that very thing." Representative Caroline T. Platt supported some modification of the law to benefit women with serious health problems. But she raised the fear of many eugenicists that legalized birth control would mean that future population growth would accrue only in immigrant families. She urged defeat of the measure in order to keep up growth in the population among "the proper element." Another type of concern expressed by those against modification of the 1879 law was that repeal or a doctors' exception would send the wrong message to the young people of Connecticut. A physician named David A. Fox, in speaking against the doctors' exception under consideration in the 1931 session of the legislature, submitted that the passage of this measure would be like sanctioning young people to have "a bottle of gin in one hand and a birth control certificate in the other."

The failure to get the Connecticut legislature to support any modifications of the 1879 anticontraception law contrasted with perceived public sentiments on birth control. The rudimentary survey research of the 1930s indicated substantial support for birth control among the American population as a whole. For instance, to the question "Should the distribution of information on birth control be made legal?," posed by the American Institute for Public Opinion in 1936, fully 70 percent of those adults expressing an opinion were in the affirmative. In 1943 various national public opinion polls revealed that support for making contraceptive information available had increased to 85 percent for women generally and a remarkable 69 percent for Catholic women. Evidently, the Catholic hierarchy had more influence on Catholic legislators than among the general Catholic population of the country.

By the mid-1930s, perhaps out of frustration with the intransigence of the Connecticut legislature and perhaps because of the public groundswell for birth control, the Connecticut Birth Control League gambled on a new approach: opening clinics to dispense birth control information and devices. Margaret Sanger and her associates had operated successful birth control clinics in New York since the World War I era. Other states had positive experiences with them. Why not Connecticut? The state's 1879 anticontraception law, of course, appeared to make clinics patently illegal. But no Connecticut woman or physician had been prosecuted under the law before the mid-1930s. So for leaders of the Connecticut birth control movement, public defiance of a state statute seemed a risk worth taking.

The first birth control clinic in the state of Connecticut was founded in Hartford, the state capital and largest city, in July 1935. It provided birth control services for married women who could not afford to seek the professional counsel of a private gynecologist. Over the next four years similar clinics were established in Waterbury and several other Connecticut cities. What cut short the effort to provide contraceptive counseling to poor women in Connecticut was the state's attempt in 1939 to enforce the 1879 anticontraception statute by seizing records of clients of the Waterbury clinic. While the case concerning the seizure of birth control records was being litigated, the leaders of the CBCL assessed the risks of arrest to clients and staff of the clinics to be too significant to justify keeping the clinics open. Nevertheless, the short experiment with birth control clinics would occasion the first judicial test of the old law.

CHAPTER 2

Judicial Challenges to
the Connecticut Ban on Contraception

The Waterbury Bust

On June 8, 1939, the Connecticut Birth Control League (CBCL) held its annual luncheon and meeting at the Farmington Country Club. In the course of her remarks to the assembled members, League President Sallie Pease characterized the opening of a birth control clinic in the Chase Dispensary of the hospital at Waterbury, Connecticut, as one of the League's most important achievements of the previous year. The Waterbury clinic, she noted, brought convenient and inexpensive reproductive services to the women of Waterbury, the most ethnically diverse, most blue collar, and probably the poorest of Connecticut's large urban areas. Approximately 70 percent of Waterbury's 100,000 residents were either first- or second-generation Americans, predominantly Irish and Italian. Virtually all of these new Americans were practicing Catholics. In practical terms, however, the importance of the Waterbury clinic was more symbolic than real. The majority of patients coming to the Waterbury clinic had been previously fitted for diaphragms at clinics in Hartford or New Haven. During its eight months of operations, the Waterbury clinic generated only $97 in total income, with a mere $10 coming from patients themselves. Clearly the folks who established the facility to provide contraceptive services in Waterbury were not in it for the money.

On the day after Sallie Pease's remarks, the *Waterbury Democrat* carried a story bearing the front-page headline, "Birth Control Clinic Is Operating in City." It quoted a dispensary supervisor who confirmed what Pease had announced at the CBCL meeting. However, some Waterbury doctors, quoted in a story in another local paper, pointed out that the "Waterbury clinic" did not offer birth control counseling or provide birth control devices to just any woman dropping in from the street. Its contraceptive services were limited to women referred to the dispensary by physicians — and then only for health reasons. The doctors emphasized that a healthy woman stopping by the clinic without a referral would not be permitted to receive birth control advice, let alone be fitted for a diaphragm.

The distinction as to who could receive reproductive services and why was lost on much of the public. Catholic clergy were particularly incensed. Father Eugene P. Cryne, president of the Catholic Clergy Association of Waterbury, took it on himself to call a special meeting of the association for a Saturday morning to consider taking steps against the clinic for its apparent threat to traditional Catholic morality. Father Cryne, described by fellow clergymen as a "very forceful" individual with "a definite sense of right and wrong," took control of the meeting and led those assembled to draft the following strong resolution against the Waterbury birth control clinic:

Whereas, it is the teaching of the Catholic church that birth control is contrary to the natural law and therefore immoral, and

Whereas, it is forbidden by statue law to disseminate birth control information for any reason whatsoever or in any circumstance, and

Whereas, it has been brought to our attention that a so-called birth control clinic, sometimes called a maternal health center, is existing in Waterbury as admitted by the superintendent of Chase Dispensary, accord to the papers, therefore, be it

Resolved, that this association go on record as being unalterably opposed to the existence of such a clinic in our city and we hereby urge our Catholic people to avoid contact with it and we hereby publicly call the attention of the public prosecutors to its existence and demand that they investigate and if necessary prosecute to the full extent of the law.

The next day, a Sunday, the text of this resolution was read from the pulpit in every Catholic church in Waterbury and several nearby towns.

One of those sitting in a Waterbury church pew on June 11, 1939, who paid special attention to the association's resolution was William Fitzgerald, the state's attorney for Waterbury. Described by contemporaries as a devout Catholic, Fitzgerald was regular in his attendance at mass and a volunteer in several church groups. Although possessing no personal animus against birth control, he felt that it was his duty to enforce the law. He promptly applied for a search warrant for any "books, records, registers, instruments, apparatus and appliances used and kept for the purpose of violating the criminal law" that might be "kept, deposited, stored and used" at the Chase Dispensary. The judge who was approached for the warrant was Frank P. McEvoy, a Waterbury native, a Catholic, and a member of the advisory board of the Diocesan Bureau of Social Service. Judge McEvoy's wife had been a leader in blocking a pro–birth control statement by the Connecticut League of Women Voters several years earlier. Not surprisingly, after hearing only a few sentences of explanation from Fitzgerald, Judge McEvoy granted the warrant to search the premises and seize birth control materials and patient records. Shortly after receiving authorization to conduct a search of the Waterbury clinic and to confiscate birth control devices and clinic documents, Waterbury's deputy sheriff and a county detective served the appropriate papers to a clinic staffer and expropriated "several bags and boxes of articles." The raid, from start to finish, took less than an hour.

Bill Fitzgerald and his office engaged in a good deal of discussion over the next few days as to who to charge with violations of the 1879 anticontraception statute. His choices included members of the following groups: the patients themselves, officers of the clinic, the leaders of the CBCL, or the doctors dispensing contraceptive advice and fitting women for diaphragms. After interviewing a number of individuals from each of these categories of potential malefactors, Fitzgerald elected to file charges against the clinic's two staff physicians, Roger B. Nelson and William A. Goodrich, and against Clara Lee McTernan, the founder and director of the clinic, who was a certified nurse. As one of the coincidences of litigation in a small community, it happened that Fitzgerald and McTernan were next-door neighbors and friends. Fitzgerald, however, had not been aware of McTernan's role in the clinic until he stumbled across her name in the records his office seized from the dispensary.

The Legislature Knows Best

The CBCL needed a lawyer to represent Drs. Nelson and Goodrich and Clara McTernan. After a brief search and some discussion, Sallie Pease and her associates at the CBCL retained the services of J. Warren Upson, a thirty-five-year-old graduate of Yale Law School and a junior partner in one of Waterbury's top law firms. Upson's first task was to represent the interests of his clients and the Waterbury clinic before Superior Court Judge Frank McEvoy in a hearing concerning the fate of the seized contraceptive supplies. State's attorney Fitzgerald moved to have the contraceptives destroyed because their very existence violated the laws of Connecticut. Upson resisted the motion, arguing that the materials had been illegally seized. Judge McEvoy scheduled a hearing on this matter for early July 1939. At that hearing, after reviewing the briefs of counsel and listening to the entreaties of the lawyers, he ruled in favor of the state's attorney. Upson appealed the seizure ruling to the Connecticut Supreme Court of Errors. The state supreme court would make its ruling on the validity of this point at the same time it handed down a decision on the broader statutory and constitutional issues in the case against McTernan, Goodrich, and Nelson.

The next court appearance for Upson was before another judge of the Superior Court, Kenneth Wynne, to learn what charges would be levied against his clients for operating the clinic in the Chase Dispensary. This appearance took place in mid-June. At this time, arrest warrants were formally served against the three defendants, Clara McTernan, William Goodrich, and Roger Nelson. They all pled not guilty and were released without bail to their lawyers' custody to await their day in court. The three defendants, as they expected, learned that they were being accused of violating the 1879 anticontraception statute on a number of counts. They were charged with providing birth control counseling and devices to six specific women.

The main legal argument that Upson presented on behalf of McTernan and the other defendants before Superior Court Judge Wynne was a demurrer. A demurrer is a legal claim in which a lawyer admits the truth of the matters of fact alleged in the complaint against his client but argues that, even if those facts are true, there are legal reasons why his client is not guilty. The reason identified by Upson was that the abetting portion of the Connecticut anticontraception statute violated the constitutional liberty of the defendants guaranteed by provisions of the Fourteenth Amendment to the U.S. Constitution and analogous provisions of the Connecticut constitution because it did not grant an exception for duly licensed medical professionals to render their best professional advice based on the health of the women visiting the Waterbury clinic.

State's attorney Fitzgerald argued against the demurrer, relying principally on a decision handed down the previous year by the Supreme Judicial Court of Massachusetts, *Commonwealth v. Gardner.* Massachusetts had on its books in the late 1930s an anticontraception law similar to that of Connecticut. The *Gardner* case arose when medical personnel in the offices of the North Shore Mothers' Health Office in Salem, Massachusetts, were arrested for providing contraceptive services. In their challenge to state law, they argued for a medical exception. If the legislature had wished to specify a health exception, the Massachusetts court concluded, it would have said so in clear terms. The proximity of the Bay State, the similarity of the anti–birth control statute to that of Connecticut, and the historically high reputation of the Supreme Judicial Court of Massachusetts throughout New England made the *Gardner* precedent a particularly strong one in the eyes of the Connecticut prosecutor.

Notwithstanding the *Gardner* precedent, Judge Wynne saw the matter as did Upson and his clients. On August 7, 1939, he upheld Upson's demurrer to the charges filed against McTernan, Goodrich, and Nelson. The effect of his ruling was to hold that the 1879 anticontraception law was in violation of the U.S. Constitution — at least until his decision was reviewed by a higher court. In his written opinion, Judge Wynne paraphrased the dilemma of Connecticut physicians attempting to come to terms with their role as the providers of advice and proper care to women of childbearing age:

> The unaided language of the statute would offer no defense to a doctor facing prosecution for a violation of it. Thus the question which must be determined is this: Is a doctor to be prosecuted as a criminal for doing something that is sound and right in the best tenets and traditions of a high calling, dedicated and devoted to health? Should he be forced to practice furtively and in stealth

rather than give up what his conscience and his honest professional judgment dictates?

Judge Wynne indicated his reluctance to read exceptions into the 1879 anticontraception statute. Nevertheless, he concluded that without proper safeguards for women's health, the law "is defective on the broad constitutional grounds set up in the demurrer."

In the parallel matter in the state Superior Court concerning the confiscation of contraceptive materials, Upson and his clients came up short. On August 23, Judge Frank McEvoy filed an opinion in which he held that the raid on the Chase Dispensary on June 12, 1939, was legally justified, and thus that the materials seized should be "condemned and destroyed." Judge McEvoy apparently saw *Gardner* much more in point with the situation in Connecticut than did Judge Wynne.

Both Judge Wynne's ruling to uphold the demurrer and Judge McEvoy's ruling to permit destruction of the seized contraceptive materials were appealed to the Connecticut Supreme Court of Errors, the highest court of the state. Upson was not particularly optimistic about prospects for success of his clients when he argued his case before the justices of the Connecticut Supreme Court on January 4, 1940. Three of the five justices were former Connecticut legislators, and a fourth had served as a staffer in the state legislature for several terms. This "legislative bias" of the court worried him because he and his clients were making the case that the legislature should not be taken literally at its words when it came to contraception. They were arguing for appending a medical exception to the 1879 anticontraception statute, an exception that the legislature had explicitly rejected on several occasions in the 1920s and 1930s. Could this court be convinced to make that exception now?

The answer was no. In a 3–2 decision in the case of *Connecticut v. Nelson, Goodrich and McTernan*, issued on March 20, 1940, the majority of the state supreme court refused to read the old statute in such a way as to grant a medical exception. Writing for the court majority, Justice George E. Hinman made specific reference to the many failed attempts between 1923 and 1935 to repeal the anticontraception law or to provide for a doctors' exception. In his words, "rejection by the Legislature of a specific provision is most persuasive that the act should not be construed to include it." The various court decisions of other state and federal courts cited by Upson as justifying a medical exception, Justice Hinman regarded as interesting but "not persuasive."

Hinman then maintained that the 1879 anticontraception law was permitted under the state's "police power." In constitutional law and public policy, the police power refers to the right of a state legislature to enact legislation for the benefit of the health, welfare, safety, and morals of the people of the state. He noted that it was reasonable to infer from the clear language that the Connecticut legislature wrote into its anticontraception law that the members of the assembly saw "grave dangers" that would result to the public good from the practice and advocacy of birth control in the state. Even if a majority of the state supreme court had seen merit in a physicians' exception, Judge Hinman ruled that it was not incumbent on the courts to read such an exception into the law. For those who felt strongly that a physicians' exception was called for, the state Supreme Court of Errors directed them to make their case to the General Assembly of the state legislature rather than the courts.

Although Justice Hinman did not feel that it was his place to second-guess the motives of the Connecticut legislature for proscribing contraception in the state, he did submit that the legislators might have reasonably believed that outlawing contraceptives would encourage moral behavior, especially among married individuals. In an orderly society, Justice Hinman maintained, liberty must be subjected to limits. Just as adultery and fornication were still listed as crimes against public morality on the Connecticut statute books of 1940, the state legislature had every right to place contraception in a similar forbidden category. Hinman thus set aside the lower court judgment and remanded the case to the Superior Court, instructing it to overrule the demurrers. The two dissenting judges filed no opinion.

The only matter remaining for the state supreme court to dispatch in the dispute stemming from the June 1939 raid on the Waterbury clinic was the disposition of the confiscated contraceptives. In a separate action before the Supreme Court of Errors, with the inelegant title *State of Connecticut v. Certain Contraceptive Materials*, Justice Hinman threw a bone to the clinic: he ruled that the statute under which the state's attorney seized the clinic's accouterments of birth control was actually written to apply only to the expropriation of gambling materials — that is, lottery tickets, slot machines, and the like. So the court ordered the return of the confiscated contraceptive materials to Mrs. McTernan and Drs. Goodrich and Nelson. This judicial gratuity was small consolation to the personnel at the Waterbury clinic.

On the same day that the state's highest court rendered its opinion, Sallie Pease sent a telegram to all birth control clinics in Connecticut recommending that they close their doors. All complied. The public defiance of the 1879 anticontraception statute had thus failed in the late 1930s; it would not be repeated in Connecticut until the early 1960s.

One Doctor and Three Women Spurned

Local papers, like the *Waterbury Democrat*, which had supported the raid on the Chase Dispensary and the prosecution of the three defendants, editorialized that the state's highest court had adopted a "very defensible position that legally and morally birth control cannot be countenanced through the instrumentality of the medical profession . . . for the dissemination of such information and aid as would defeat the very purpose of matrimony." By contrast, newspapers outside the region were almost universally critical of the decision. The *News and Courier* of Raleigh, North Carolina, for example, summed up the general national sentiment by excoriating the Connecticut court for its "backwardness."

The effort that the BCLC and the Connecticut activists had poured into the *Nelson* case had taken its toll. Bill Goodrich, Roger Nelson, and Carla McTernan lacked the stomach for further litigation, let alone direct action. All three willingly accepted state's attorney Bill Fitzgerald's offers of nolle prosequi (that is, proposals not to prosecute them as individuals for violating the 1879 anticontraception law). In addition, after the muddled resolution of the *Nelson* case, Goodrich, Nelson, and McTernan appeared to lose interest in the cause of birth control reform.

Losing also spawned second-guessing and recriminations. Margaret Sanger blamed a "weak" Connecticut leadership for failing to carry the day. She reportedly said that "something certainly went wrong . . . to have lost that case and to have . . . [generated] so adverse and medieval an opinion." A few national activists, such as Morris Ernst, a lawyer for the Birth Control Federation of America (BCFA), argued that birth control interests in Connecticut should not close clinics in the wake of the *Nelson* decision but should actually open more such facilities and even consider placing clinics within the protective walls of church buildings. These criticisms and suggestions did not go down well with local birth control activists such as Sallie Pease and her associate Katharine Hepburn. They took it on themselves to journey to New York and give the movement's national leadership a piece of their mind.

The Connecticut Birth Control League changed its name in the early 1940s to the Planned Parenthood League of Connecticut (PPLC). The change in nomenclature at the state level mirrored the change nationally: the Birth Control Federation of America became the Planned Parenthood Federation of America (PPFA). The name changes reflected the belief of the procontraception movement's leadership that the phrase "family planning" was more palatable to a wide audience than the stark term "birth control." Regardless of what they called themselves, most of the Connecticut activists favored a return to legislative lobbying after the judicial failure in the *Nelson* case.

Despite two decades of inability to convince the Connecticut assembly to modify its nineteenth-century anticontraception law, local activists made new attempts at repeal or the passage of a doctors' exception at every biennial session from 1941 to 1963. These legislative campaigns were no more successful than those of the interwar years. In spite of public opinion polls that continued to show that a substantial majority of residents of Connecticut, even Catholics, favored birth control, the leaders of the anti–birth control movement seemed to be more aggressive and ultimately more effective in lobbying the legislature than were the advocates of reform. Among the most strident voices against legislative reform was Father Andrew J. Kelly of Hartford. In opposing the 1941 doctors' exception bill, Father Kelly labeled as "pagan" and "agnostic" the advocates of birth control. Given comments such as these, the proponents of legislative repeal or modification of the 1879 law continued to face an uphill battle. In session after legislative session, repeal or doctors' exception bills went down to defeat in the Democrat-dominated state senate. Republican candidates for office who appeared to embrace contraception risked defeat or, at best, bruising campaigns.

A few of the pro–birth control activists in Connecticut in the early 1940s kept reminding the others that the vote in the Connecticut Supreme Court of Errors in the *Nelson* case had been a bare three to two against reading a health exception into the 1879 statute. Perhaps a better-staged judicial test case would have a chance of capturing one more procontraception vote on the state's highest court. So while activists continued their uphill legislative battle, a parallel judicial initiative was being mounted.

By early 1941 a critical mass of the Connecticut pro–birth control activists were convinced of the appropriateness of a return to the state courts to challenge the ban on contraception. Warren Upson was no longer interested in representing those interests, so the leadership of the movement secured the services of an experienced and well-regarded New Haven attorney, Frederick H. "Fritz" Wiggin. A former president of the state bar association, Wiggin had more standing in the state's legal community than did Upson. The approach proposed by Wiggin was to identify a licensed physician who could apply to the state courts for a "declaratory judgment" as to whether the 1879 Connecticut state law against offering contraceptive counseling prohibited him from prescribing the use of contraceptives for married women in situations where pregnancy would imperil their health or even their lives. An application for a declaratory judgment may be sought in situations where an individual or organization is unsure of his/her/their legal rights and consequently asks a court for guidance. One advantage of a doctor seeking legal advice in this fashion is that he does not expose himself to legal liability or professional sanctions if the courts should not furnish him with the advice he desired.

The doctor who agreed to allow his name to be used for this legal maneuver was Wilder Tileston, then a sixty-five-year-old professor of medicine at Yale University who maintained a private obstetrics and gynecology practice in New Haven. Dr. Tileston was able to identify three married women who resided in or near New Haven. Each had documented health risks that, in his professional judgment, would be exacerbated by pregnancy. The women's real names were not provided in the court proceedings. Hence they were referred to by pseudonyms. "Jane Doe" was a mother of five, over forty years of age, who had been advised that her high blood pressure could lead to toxemia and a 25 percent chance of death should she again become pregnant.

"Mary Roe" was a recently married twenty-two-year-old who had experienced lung problems as a result of tuberculosis and had to be institutionalized in a sanatorium for four years; a pregnancy, she was informed, could set her recovery back several years and might even lead to her death. And "Sarah Hoe" was a twenty-five-year-old who had been weakened by three pregnancies within a period of twenty-seven months; she was told that a fourth pregnancy might result in permanent disability. All three women wished to continue to have sexual relations with their husbands without incurring the health dangers posed by pregnancy. Dr. Tileston, through his attorney Fritz Wiggin, claimed that the 1879 anticontraception statute, if applied so as to deny him the ability to prescribe contraceptives to these three women, violated his right to "due process of law" under the Fourteenth Amendment to the U.S. Constitution and parallel provisions of the Connecticut Constitution. The defendant in the action by Dr. Tileston was the recently appointed state's attorney for New Haven Country, Abraham S. Ullman.

Wiggin filed the action in the New Haven County Superior Court in late 1941. A panel of physicians was charged by the Superior Court with evaluating Jane Doe, Mary Roe, and Sarah Hoe. The panel agreed with Dr. Tileston's medical assessment that pregnancy would be medically perilous to each of the three women. Essentially, then, the facts in the case were not in dispute. The next step in the proceeding saw Superior Court Judge Earnest C. Simpson refer the questions of law regarding the 1879 statute to the Supreme Court of Errors.

The oral argument before the highest court of Connecticut on February 4, 1942, was a quiet affair. Wiggin succeeded in keeping members of the PPLC from turning up in large numbers. He feared that the presence in court of a contingent of birth control activists might irritate the five members of the supreme court. State's attorney Ullman presented a simple but powerful legal argument: the words of the 1879 statute did not permit any physicians' health exception to the ban on contraception; had the legislature been so inclined as to amend the statute, it had declined to do so, despite having been presented with numerous opportunities over more than sixty years of lobbying, hearings, and floor debate. In his argument to the court, Wiggin pointed out that the *Gardner* precedent from Massachusetts that had been so telling in the *Nelson* case had been qualified by a recent decision in the Bay State, *Commonwealth v. Corbett*. In that case, the highest court of Massachusetts had reversed the conviction of a Boston pharmacist who had sold condoms to an undercover policeman. The Massachusetts court found it significant that the condoms at issue in *Corbett* were marketed for the prevention of disease, not for contraception. In the absence of any evidence that the pharmacist believed the buyer would be using the condoms for contraception rather than disease control, the court determined that the seller had not violated the statute. In Wiggin's view, the Massachusetts decision in *Corbett* should be read to permit a women's health exception to a statute very similar in letter and spirit to the one in Connecticut.

The Connecticut Supreme Court handed down its decision in *Tileston v. Ullman* on May 22, 1942. As in *State v. Nelson*, it split 3–2. Once again the court majority, in an opinion written by the court's newest member, Arthur F. Ells, paid great attention to the legislature's unwillingness to modify the old anticontraception law. In Ells's words, "in the consideration of these bills year after year there was ample opportunity for the legislature to accept a compromise measure. . . . Its refusal to make any change, in the light of its opportunity to do so, impels us to the conclusion that not even in such situations as are presented in the instant case did the legislature wish to permit exceptions."

The court majority next addressed the relevance of the Massachusetts struggle with contraception to the situation in Connecticut. In *Commonwealth v. Gardner*, the highest court of Massachusetts had ruled that it could not read a physician's exception into its state's anti–birth control statute to permit the prescription of contraception for the preservation of life or health of a woman. The fact that an appeal of the *Gardner* decision to the U.S. Supreme Court was dismissed "for want of a substantial federal question" indicated that the nation's highest court did not see any constitutional problems with a statute very much like the law in Connecticut. For Justice Ells and the court majority, the prosecution in *Corbett* had not proven that the condom sold by the pharmacist was vended for the purpose of preventing contraception. If the three unidentified women in the *Tileston* case were really concerned about the adverse consequences to their health from pregnancy, Ells submitted that there is a course of action that affords greater safety than contraception: abstention from sexual intercourse.

In contrast to their silent action in *Nelson*, the dissenters in *Tileston* put their thoughts in writing. A long opinion of Justice Christopher Avery was more willing to find persuasive authority in a handful of federal decisions and the Massachusetts decision in *Corbett* than was the majority. Justice Avery and his codissenter Newell Jennings gave much less weight to the Connecticut legislature's unwillingness to alter the state's anticontraception law than did their brethren in the majority. But Avery did point out a curious and disturbing contradiction in Connecticut statutory law. The absolute ban on the use of contraceptives, once again reiterated by the majority in *Tileston,* appeared to him to contradict in spirit the state's antiabortion law, which granted an exception to physicians if, in their judgment, a woman's life was in jeopardy. To him, there was a logical disconnect after the majority ruling in *Tileston:* the relatively unobtrusive use of contraceptives, supported by the majority of Connecticut adults, was banned even if a physician believed that the life of a woman was jeopardized by pregnancy; but the more invasive and generally unpopular practice of abortion was explicitly countenanced by state law if a woman's life hung in the balance.

The PPLC, perhaps taking heart from the strong dissenting opinion, chose to appeal the ruling in *Tileston* to the U.S. Supreme Court, alleging constitutional defects in the statute and its interpretation. The principal role in coordinating the appeal for the PPLC was assumed by Morris Ernst, the lead attorney for the national birth control organization, the Planned Parenthood Federation of America. Abraham Ullman continued to represent the interests of the state of Connecticut in defending its anticontraception statute. The U.S. Supreme Court announced in November 1942 that it would entertain the appeal from the PPLC and scheduled oral arguments for January 1943.

Warren Upson reappeared at this point in the battle over contraception by preparing an amicus curiae brief on behalf of 541 Connecticut doctors who supported a woman's health exception to the anticontraception statute. Although not directly a party to the litigation at hand, a group or individual requesting Supreme Court permission to argue as an amicus curiae maintains that it possesses an interest in the outcome of the case and thus may be able to offer a perspective on the dispute that might be of interest to the court. The amicus brief from the Connecticut physicians contended that Dr. Tileston was confronted by a Hobson's choice, either "failing in his duty as a physician or subjecting himself to a criminal penalty in the event that this statute is found to be constitutional." Another amicus brief, in support of Dr. Tileston and in the striking down of the 1879 Connecticut anticontraception law, was filed on behalf of 166 physicians in thirty-six states and the District of Columbia. It maintained that "medical opinion with substantial unanimity supports the prescription and use of contraceptives" in instances such as those that predicated Dr. Tileston's request for a declaratory judgment.

The task before Morris Ernst in preparing his Supreme Court brief challenging the constitutionality of the 1879 Connecticut anticontraception law was a daunting one. He was alleging that the three patients of his client, Dr. Tileston, faced possible deprivation of their lives in the event that they would become pregnant. He based this claim principally on the Fourteenth Amendment to the U.S. Constitution, which holds in part that "No State shall . . . deprive any person of life . . . without due process of law." The original PPLC attorney, Fritz Wiggin, had not seen fit to incorporate the three pseudonymous women as plaintiffs. This would prove to be a critical shortcoming in this legal challenge to the anticontraception law. Ullman, in his brief opposing the claims of the PPLC, pointed out quite correctly that the 1879 Connecticut statute did not place Dr. Tileston himself in peril of his life. For Ullman, the "real parties in interest" were Jane Doe, Mary Roe, and Sarah Hoe. Their absence from the original complaint, Ullman maintained, meant that Dr. Tileston did not have legal standing to raise the constitutional issues in the U.S. Supreme Court.

Notes kept by U.S. Supreme Court justices on the pending case of *State v. Tileston* indicate that Ullman's arguments on standing were telling. One of Associate Justice William O. Douglas's clerks, Vern Countryman, wrote a memo to the justice to the effect that Dr. Tileston lacked standing to sue because the constitutional rights that he claimed were transgressed "belong not to him but to his patients." At the oral argument on January 13, 1943, Morris Ernst was challenged by Chief Justice Harlan Fiske Stone and other members of the Court on just this issue. Ernst tried to argue in the presence of the justices, just as in his appellate brief, that Dr. Tileston's "liberty and property" were protected along with "life" by the Fourteenth Amendment and thus were threatened by strict enforcement of the 1879 statute. But the chief justice reminded him that the nation's highest court was limited in its review only to those issues that the Connecticut Supreme Court has ruled on. Even if Dr. Tileston might himself have faced prosecution under the ruling in *State v. Nelson* by prescribing contraceptives to the three women in the case, the chief justice pointed out that the original complaint had not presented the argument that the *Nelson* precedent was a threat to Dr. Tileston himself.

At the conference held on January 16, Chief Justice Stone spoke first and longest. He emphasized the point he made in the oral argument, namely that the petitioner, Dr. Tileston, had failed to argue that there was any injury to his own property or his practice. He had only alleged that there was an injury to "life" — but not his own life. In Stone's words, Tileston "need not have limited his constitutional claim in this way, but he did." This, in Stone's mind, was a fatal flaw: Dr. Tileston had not established that there was a constitutional question. All the other justices speaking at the conference on *Tileston* agreed with the chief justice. Accordingly, on February 1, 1943, in a two-page per curiam opinion — an unsigned statement for the whole Court — the Supreme Court ruled that Dr. Tileston lacked standing to challenge the constitutionality of the Connecticut anticontraception statute. The Court accepted the Connecticut state's attorney's argument that the original complaint failed to contain allegations regarding possible deprivation of Dr. Tileston's liberty or property rights, and that the potential dangers to "life" were to the doctor's patients, not to himself.

A little over two months after the Supreme Court's per curiam opinion in *Tileston*, the Connecticut state senate, in a fitting denouement to the early 1940s battle to give birth control legal standing in Connecticut, defeated, by a vote of 24 to 11, a bill that would have permitted hospitals and physicians to prescribe contraceptives for married women. All fourteen senate Democrats voted against the measure, as did ten Republicans. Although efforts to achieve legislative reform of Connecticut's anticontraception law would continue during each two-year session of the assembly into the mid-1960s, there would not be another judicial test of the law for almost twenty years.

CHAPTER 3

More Judicial False Starts

The Singer, the Doctor, and Several Lawyers

In large part because of the frustration of having the substance of its case rejected by the U.S. Supreme Court in *Tileston v. Ullman*, the Planned Parenthood League of Connecticut (PPLC) in 1943 turned its attention back to the Connecticut legislature and yet another pending bill to modify the 1879 anticontraception law. The PPLC's efforts on behalf of this bill were for naught. It passed the Connecticut house by a vote of 155 to 84, but it went down to an overwhelming defeat in the senate. Other modification bills proposed in the late 1940s and early 1950s met similar fates. If anything, the antagonism toward family planning by the Catholic church and other anti–birth control interests intensified as the World War II era receded. One of the most bitter characterizations of birth control came from William J. Kenealy, dean of the Boston College of Law. Dean Kenealy testified before a Connecticut legislative hearing in 1948 that birth control was no better than "mutual masturbation" and constituted "pleasure by means of an unnatural act." If such views continued to receive a sympathetic ear from legislators, the PPLC reasoned, maybe a second attempt at judicial reform made more sense.

One judicial option considered by the PPLC shortly after World War II was a suit in the federal courts to enjoin enforcement of the 1879 statute. However, after a brief exploration of this approach, the PPLC and its consulting attorneys determined that the procedural hurdles were just as daunting as through the state courts. Another alternative the League looked into was to mount a test case to see if the infamous nineteenth-century law could be enforced against a vendor of contraceptives. Vern Countryman, a former law clerk to Supreme Court

William O. Douglas and, by 1953, a professor at the Yale Law School, purchased a box of condoms from a Hamden, Connecticut, drugstore. Countryman went to the local police station, showed his purchase to the officer on duty, and indicated that he wished to file a complaint against the druggist for selling products that could be used to violate the 1879 anticontraception law. Countryman was referred to the county prosecutor, who, being familiar with the Massachusetts decision of *Commonwealth v. Corbett* (1940), noted the difference between prophylactic and contraceptive uses of condoms, thus suggesting that the druggist could avoid the thrust of the old law by arguing that the condoms he marketed were intended to prevent disease rather than to prevent conception. In addition, once Countryman learned that the drugstore that sold him the condoms was a locally owned business, he lost interest in his gambit. He did not want to try to demonstrate his point at the expense of a struggling small-town druggist.

The legal option that would ultimately be implemented by the PPLC in the 1950s was yet another effort to seek a declaratory judgment from the Connecticut courts regarding the constitutionality of the 1879 anticontraception law. This time, rather than having physicians as the sole complainants and thus likely dooming their test cases to defeat on the grounds of standing, the members of the group vowed that they would secure as principal litigants actual Connecticut married women who, because the medical risks to them of pregnancy were quite substantial, sought prescriptions for contraceptives. The hope of the PPLC leadership was that the state courts, or, if necessary, the U.S. Supreme Court, would realize that these women actually faced real health risks if they followed the letter of the 1879 law and were not permitted to use birth control. Before the female plaintiffs could be identified, however, some new players for the PPLC entered the fray.

Estelle T. Griswold was interviewed in 1953 for the open position of executive director of the PPLC. She had attended Hartford public schools, where she had been a good but difficult student, skipping two grades but being suspended on one occasion for playing hooky. After high school she studied for three years at a nearby school of music. From the 1920s to the 1950s she sang professionally in the United States and France, worked a series of clerical jobs, trained as a medical technologist, and volunteered for a variety of human rights causes.

In her travels to Latin America and Africa, she saw firsthand the problems caused by overpopulation and the absence of family planning. She and her husband relocated to New Haven in the early 1950s and took up residence in a house very close to the headquarters of the PPLC. The League board, impressed by Griswold's "phenomenally interesting" life experiences, hired her to direct the PPLC for a yearly salary of $5,000. Although not a lawyer or a physician, she would turn out to be an excellent fund raiser and administrator for the PPLC.

Griswold, described by friends as "dynamic" and "vivacious," exhibited a great capacity to work and an ability to focus on key strategic issues to advance the cause of family planning. In the often fractious world of not-for-profit groups, however, her take-charge style occasionally rubbed board members and coworkers the wrong way. Significantly, however, Griswold would take a leading role in, and lend her name to, the Supreme Court case that would finally bring about the demise of the old Connecticut anticontraceptive law.

Another key player in the upcoming judicial tests of the nineteenth century anticontraceptive statute was Dr. C. Lee Buxton, a recently appointed director of the Yale University infertility clinic, a project for which the PPLC had provided partial funding for many years. Lee Buxton was born in Superior, Wisconsin, and had spent much of his youth in St. Paul, Minnesota. He then went east for prep school and college. He received his undergraduate degree from Princeton and his MD from Columbia University. Dr. Buxton developed a medical research specialty in female infertility. After service in the navy in World War II, he held a professorship of medicine at Columbia University and had a remunerative New York City private gynecological practice. In the 1950s he came to New Haven to assume the chair of the Obstetrics and Gynecology Department in the Yale Medical School. Soon after relocating to Connecticut, he became a leading advocate of contraceptive services in the state. It was Dr. Buxton who identified the women who would be the plaintiffs in the next action to test the constitutionality of the 1879 anticontraception statute, and he would later share billing with Estelle Griswold in the case in the 1960s that would get the two of them arrested and, after a long legal fight, succeed in bringing down the state's ban on birth control. In the late 1950s and early 1960s, Buxton received countless obscene letters and crank phone calls and endured numerous bad jokes, all because of his advocacy for birth control.

Then there were the lawyers. Fowler Harper, who would become a principal legal strategist for the PPLC in the 1950s and early 1960s, grew up in Ohio in the early twentieth century. Harper passed the Ohio bar even before graduating from law school at Ohio Northern University. He taught at several midwestern law schools and was one of the bright young liberal lawyers attracted to President Franklin Roosevelt's New Deal administration. In Washington he served as general counsel of the Federal Security Agency, deputy chairman of the War Manpower Commission, and solicitor for the U.S. Department of the Interior. After the war he returned to the midwest to become a professor of law at the University of Indiana. Harper had been an active member of the leftist Lawyers Guild in the 1930s and was more than willing to stand up for unpopular causes. In 1947 Harper joined the faculty of the Yale Law School and quickly became a popular teacher and enhanced his reputation as an expert on tort law. Harper was also an inveterate gambler and heavy drinker.

How Harper and Buxton met is subject to some debate. One account has it that Estelle Griswold invited Buxton and Harper to her home for cocktails in the fall of 1957 with the express purpose of getting the two of them to join forces with her and the PPLC to bring down the infamous state anticontraception law. A more likely story is that Harper and Buxton had encountered each other at New Haven social functions a number of times before Griswold invited them for drinks. Regardless of how they first met, it is not at all surprising that Buxton and Harper would agree to do battle together against the 1879 anticontraception Connecticut statute, a law that they both felt violated the constitutional rights of residents of the state.

Another lawyer who would take a leading role in the contemplated PPLC litigation was a young woman named Catherine Roraback. After receiving her degree from Yale Law School in 1948, Roraback had practiced for a few years in the Washington, D.C., area. She had returned to New Haven sometime in the early 1950s and began volunteering for the New Haven Civil Liberties Council. There she renewed acquaintances with some of her former law professors, including Fowler Harper, Thomas Emerson, and Fred Rodell. When asked for her help with the planned PPLC litigation by her old friend and professor, Fowler Harper, she readily signed onto the crusade against the 1879 anticontraceptive law.

Anonymous Plaintiffs and Another Test Case

After having assembled its medical and legal teams for the contemplated assault on the 1879 anticontraceptive law, the next step was to identify plaintiffs who could meet the requirements of legal standing to sue. Sometime in late 1957 or early 1958, Dr. Buxton agreed to be one of the plaintiffs himself. He and Roraback began to keep their eyes open for young married couples with medical situations that would benefit from contraception and were willing to serve as anonymous litigants.

By May 1958 Buxton and Roraback had located five married couples who seemed appropriately qualified to test the constitutionality of the nineteenth-century anticontraception statute. One couple, Jean and Marvin Durning, would almost immediately leave the New Haven area and thus drop out of the case. They were to have been known as "Rena and Ralph Roe." Three of the remaining four couples wished to remain anonymous. Ruth O., a married woman twenty-five years old and a patient of Dr. Buxton, had had a stroke during the late stages of a pregnancy and had delivered a stillborn child. The stroke left her with slurred speech and partial paralysis in one leg. She wanted to continue having sexual relations with her husband but be spared the dangers of pregnancy, so she desired to be prescribed contraceptives. In the litigation she was assigned the name "Jane Doe." Elizabeth and David O., also patients of Buxton, were a married couple who had borne three abnormal children, none of whom lived more than a few weeks; they too wanted to benefit from birth control and not have to undergo another pregnancy. For the test case, they became "Pauline and Paul Poe." Anne and Hector Kinloch, a married couple then in their late twenties who had consulted Dr. Buxton, had Rh blood incompatibilities and thus would likely not be able to have normal children; they too sought the right to practice birth control. They were assigned the names of "Harold and Hannah Hoe." The final couple, Yale law students David and Louise Trubek, were essentially replacements for the Durnings. The Trubeks had no health abnormalities that would complicate pregnancy and did not insist on anonymity. Their wish was to be able to complete their legal education and adjust to married life with protected sexual intercourse before confronting the prospect of child rearing. All the couples alleged in the complaints filed by Roraback that the Connecticut anticontraception law denied to them their rights to liberty as guaranteed by the Fourteenth Amendment to the U.S. Constitution.

The cases involving Dr. Buxton and the anonymous plaintiffs would be consolidated and treated in the same proceeding; the Trubek complaint, which was filed a bit later, would be dealt with in a separate action. In December 1958 Roraback asked the Connecticut Superior Court for a declaratory judgment determining the constitutionality of the Connecticut state law that, she argued, kept her clients from realizing their constitutional rights. Ray Cannon, for the office of the State Attorney General, demurred. In other words, he accepted the facts in Roraback's complaints — that the medical condition of the women involved prevented them from having safe pregnancies or bearing normal children, and that Dr. Buxton was legally prevented from rendering advice on birth control by Connecticut law — but maintained that the legal precedents of *Nelson* and *Tileston* upholding the constitutionality of the 1879 statute were clear. Superior Judge Frank Healy sustained the demurrer and rendered judgment in favor of Abraham Ullman, the state's attorney in New Haven. From this order Roraback appealed. The Trubek case, despite the slightly different factual situation, suffered the same fate a few months later. It was argued before another superior court judge, a judgment was entered in favor of the state's attorney, and the matter was appealed to the state supreme court.

During the time that Roraback was preparing the PPLC brief to the Connecticut Supreme Court, she was confronted with pressure from the national organization, the Planned Parenthood Federation of America (PPFA), to get involved in the case. The PPFA, through its attorneys Harriet Pilpel and Morris Ernst, offered harsh critiques of Roraback's legal arguments. Roraback did not appreciate the PPFA's attempt to hijack her case. Eventually things were smoothed over between the national and state planned parenthood organizations, and the PPLC encouraged the national organization to prepare an amicus brief in support of the League's position should the case need to be appealed to the U.S. Supreme Court.

The PPLC appeal before the Connecticut Supreme Court in the cases of Buxton, Doe, Poe, and Hoe was argued on October 7, 1959. The chief justice, Raymond E. Baldwin, was a Republican and former governor who had supported legislation liberalizing the state's anti-contraception statute a quarter century earlier when he had been serving in the state legislature. His previous position on contraception notwithstanding, Justice Baldwin seemed hostile to the PPLC interests during oral argument. The fears of the PPLC were borne out on December 22, 1959, when the state's highest court, speaking through Justice Baldwin, ruled unanimously in favor of the state.

The chief justice acknowledged that the facts were legally different in the case before him when contrasted to the facts in the previous two Connecticut Supreme Court decisions concerning the anticontraception law, the 1940 decision of *State v. Nelson* and 1942 decision of *Tileston v. Ullman*. In the earlier two cases, a physician had been attempting to claim rights on behalf of others. By contrast, in the situation before the state supreme court in 1959, all of the parties — the doctor and his several patients — were asserting their own constitutional rights. Nevertheless, Connecticut's highest court held once again that attempts to claim that the 1879 statute violated anyone's constitutional rights were without foundation. Baldwin and his colleagues concluded that the old anticontraception measure was still fully within the ambit of the state's police power to serve public health, safety, and morals. What persuaded the court once again was the fact that the state legislature had considered, but rejected, bills to institute a doctors' exception to the 1879 statute in every legislative session since the decision in the *Tileston* case. Accordingly, the chief justice wrote: "Courts cannot, by the process of construction, abrogate a clear expression of legislative intent, especially when, as here, unambiguous language is fortified by the refusal of the legislature, in the light of judicial interpretation, to change it."

Near the end of the opinion, the chief justice commended the PPLC and its lawyers by noting that "the claims of infringement of constitutional rights [by the anticontraception statute] are presented more dramatically than they have ever been before." But it quickly added that the claims are "essentially the same" as in *Nelson* and *Tileston*. In all three cases, Baldwin wrote, the problems that might ensue for married couples from a pregnancy could be obviated by an alternative other than contraception — namely, abstinence from sexual intercourse.

The case of David and Louise Trubek did not reach the state supreme court until late 1960. As distinct from the Poes, the Hoes, and Jane Doe, the justices acknowledged that the Trubeks were not claiming any health dangers from a possible pregnancy. Nevertheless, they saw no legal difference. The unanimous court wrote: "We find nothing in the concept advanced by the plaintiffs, or in the facts recited in the complaint in connection therewith, which would warrant a conclusion that the rights and jural relations of parties in the situation of the plaintiffs have not been concluded by previous decisions." So if this young couple wished to postpone having children in order to have time to adjust to their marriage and to complete their education, their legal recourse in Connecticut in 1960 was abstinence rather than contraception.

Guinea Pigs for an Abstract Principle

Given the unwillingness of the state legislature to modify state law on contraception, and given the legislative background of so many of the state supreme court justices, the PPLC didn't expect a sympathetic hearing from Justice Baldwin and his colleagues. The League's real hope lay in an appeal to the U.S. Supreme Court. Harper, who took the leading role in preparing the case for appeal, moved promptly to petition for review by the nation's high court. A Washington attorney and friend of Harper's recommended that the League file two separate appeals, one on behalf of Dr. Buxton and the other on behalf of his patients. The number of patients, however, available to participate in the appeal was dwindling. The Trubek case had not caught up to the other cases, so it could not be included in the request for review. In addition, Harper learned that Anne and Hector Kinloch, known as "Harold and Hanna Hoe," had left the state of Connecticut to take up employment elsewhere and therefore could not remain as plaintiffs. Thus, the clients of the League that remained as viable litigants for this action were Dr. Lee Buxton, Paul and Pauline Poe, and Mrs. Jane Doe (although the Does were married, "Mr. Doe" had never been listed on the court papers as a litigant). Thus the cases that Harper asked the Supreme Court to review became known as *Poe et al. v. Ullman* and *Buxton v. Ullman.*

Harper, on behalf of the PPLC, began to prepare legal briefs requesting that the Supreme Court take the case. For the first time in all the challenges to the 1879 Connecticut law, a lawyer laid his stress on a putative "right of privacy" of the litigants. Arguing that "when the long arm of the law reaches into the bedroom and attempts to regulate the most sacred relations between and man and his wife, it is going too far. There must be a limit to the extent to which the moral scruples of a minority, or for that matter a majority, can be enacted into laws which regulate the sex lives of all married people." Harper cited a handful of U.S. Supreme Court decisions from the 1920s through the 1950s in support of this proposition, but he was not clear whether he saw the right of privacy emerging from the Fourteenth Amendment's protection of liberty or from some other source. Harper also began to talk with three interest groups — the Planned Parenthood Federation of America (PPFA), the American Civil Liberties Union (ACLU), and a group of well-known physicians — who all wished to file amicus curiae briefs in support of his clients' position. The state of Connecticut chose not to make a submission contesting Harper's claims.

On May 23, 1960, the U.S. Supreme Court announced "probable jurisdiction" of Harper's appeal from the previous year's Connecticut Supreme Court ruling. The order noted cryptically that Justice Felix Frankfurter had recused himself from consideration of the two connected cases. What later became known is that Frankfurter had served as an unofficial legal adviser to the national Planned Parenthood organization many years before. But in 1960, most members of the PPFA were not aware of this relationship. Although it was not announced at the time, the confidential papers of the justices in conference would later reveal that the vote to hear the case had been five in favor (Earl Warren, William O. Douglas, John Marshall Harlan, William J. Brennan, and Potter Stewart) and three against (Hugo L. Black, Tom Clark, and Charles Whittaker).

The case was originally scheduled to be argued before the Supreme Court in the fall of 1960. But it was postponed until March 1961 as a favor to Fowler Harper, who was serving a four-month stint during the fall of 1960 for the U.S. State Department as a visiting legal consultant to several newly independent African nations. Before leaving for Africa, Harper completed his legal brief, emphasizing the privacy issues that he had raised in his argument petitioning the Court to take jurisdiction of the case. Harper's brief also noted that the Connecticut law prohibited the most effective methods of contraception (diaphragms, prescribed by licensed physicians) but permitted the least reliable (condoms, purchased and used without proper medical advice). The thrust of the League's brief was that hardships imposed by the nineteenth-century law and its deleterious social consequences outweighed any advantages. The longest section of Harper's brief addressed the social harms of the population explosion.

The amicus curiae brief of the ACLU developed in greater depth the privacy argument first broached by Harper. It argued that the Connecticut statutes forbidding the use and abetting of contraception violated the due process clause of the Fourteenth Amendment by invading the privacy of the Poes and Jane Doe and interfered with the right of Dr. Buxton to practice his profession responsibly. Ruth Emerson, the wife of Yale law professor Thomas Emerson, had a hand in writing the ACLU brief. The Planned Parenthood amicus brief was prepared mainly by Harriet Pilpel, with the assistance of Morris Ernst. It provided "a comprehensive documentation of the medical, legal, social and religious status of contraception in the United States" at the time. The final amicus brief, submitted by a group of nationally recognized physicians, addressed what it characterized as "the overwhelming consensus among doctors" that contraception is prudent when pregnancy poses medical risks. The brief for the appellee, the state of Connecticut, was prepared by Raymond Cannon, the state's assistant attorney general. It relied heavily on the Connecticut Supreme Court opinion, emphasizing that the anti–birth control statute constituted a proper exercise of the state's police power and in no way deprived Dr. Buxton or his patients of any protected rights without due process of law.

The oral argument in *Buxton* and *Poe* finally commenced before the full panel of nine justices at midafternoon and concluded the following afternoon. Harper spoke for the appellants and ceded part of his time to Harriet Pilpel of the PPFA. Raymond Cannon represented the interests of the state of Connecticut. Oral argument offers a final opportunity for appellate attorneys to make an impression on the Supreme Court. However, counsel hoping to emphasize a few key points in their cases are often thrown off stride by questions from the justices. Tradition holds that any justice may ask any question of a presenting attorney. The time taken to pose and respond to a question is counted against the attorney's allocated amount of minutes of argument.

In several exchanges with Chief Justice Earl Warren and Associate Justices Felix Frankfurter, John Marshall Harlan, and William Brennan, both Harper and Cannon were challenged as to the degree of enforcement of the Connecticut contraceptive use and abetting statutes and the ease with which birth control materials could be purchased in the state. Harper responded that the only prosecution of which he was aware was the one that launched the *Nelson* test case in 1940 and that contraceptives, particularly condoms, were currently widely available throughout the state. Cannon indicated that there had been only a handful of prosecutions for the sale of condoms, and then only in the state's minor police courts, over the last eighty years. Harper emphasized the point that the law served to intimidate doctors and others wishing to provide birth control counseling. Then Harper readily agreed with Justice William Brennan that one clear consequence of the law was that it prevented the operation of birth control clinics in the state.

An exchange between Chief Justice Warren and Raymond Cannon was particularly telling. The Chief Justice queried Connecticut's assistant attorney general: "If the diagnosis of Mrs. Doe is accurate and her life is to be endangered unless she receives the treatment prescribed, do you believe the state would prevent her getting such treatment?" Cannon responded: "It is up to the Legislature to determine what is for the greater good." The Chief Justice followed up: "Even if it is conceded the lady would die you still hold that the state has the right, for the reasons you give, to prevent her from getting needed care?" Cannon qualified his position only slightly: "Yes, plus the added factor that when seeking the advice she was not suffering diseases that affected her health. Pregnancy was not involved. He [the physician] may advise that if she became pregnant she might injure her health, but he can't tell her or advise her to use artificial contraceptives to prevent conception." Justice Potter Stewart then remarked wryly: "That's like telling a patient he has appendicitis and will die unless it is removed but not allowing its removal."

Cannon stressed in his presentation that the 1879 statute was constitutional because "a state has exclusive jurisdiction over the morals of its people." This prompted Justice Stewart to ask what was "the specific purpose of this statute with relation to uplifting the morals of the people." Cannon replied that "[i]t promotes the sanctity of marriage." To this answer, Stewart remarked sarcastically that he thought the statute might accomplish just the opposite result for a woman for whom pregnancy posed health risks: it would either mean death or abstinence from sexual relations, neither of which would promote the sanctity of marriage.

Under Article III of the U.S. Constitution, the Supreme Court is charged with rendering decisions only on live "cases" or "controversies." Many of those attending the oral argument in early March 1961 saw it unlikely that the justices would render a decision on the constitutionality of a quirky statute that had not been enforced for seventy-five years. Principally, this impression stemmed from Justice Felix Frankfurter's comment that the absence of enforcement of the anticontraception law meant that the dispute was "theoretical."

The justices held their confidential conference a few days later to discuss the disposition of the *Buxton* and *Poe* appeals. Notes kept by the justices reveal that the chief justice, as customary, began the discussion of the two cases. Warren indicated that he saw no live legal or constitutional issues concerning a statute that had almost never been enforced. To him this was contrived litigation, and he insisted that he did not want his Court to be made "guinea pigs for an abstract principle." Warren was also perturbed that there was not a "proper record here on which to decide the constitutional questions." For him, an act of a state legislature should only be found unconstitutional after a proper trial and clear findings. Hugo Black, the senior associate justice, agreed with Warren that there was not a live case involving the female appellants — "the ladies," as he referred to them. But he thought that Dr. Buxton might have a free speech claim since the abetting statute seemed to limit what a physician could render by way of advice to a patient.

Felix Frankfurter, the most voluble participant at the oral argument, spoke next. He stated his agreement with the chief justice that the appeal in both cases should be dismissed. As his comments in the oral argument had strongly hinted, he believed that the absence of prosecutions under the statute kept this action from rising to the status of a legitimate case or controversy. However, he stated, if birth control clinics were reopened in Connecticut, and thus if doctors and other medical personnel were arrested under the 1879 law, that would be another matter. In his words, "they should take the risk of going to jail and then bring the case of actual prosecution up here." For William O. Douglas, Frankfurter's frequent nemesis on the Court, the point was a simple one: the two actions, as they stood, presented appropriate opportunities for declaratory judgment and the old Connecticut law was unconstitutional on its face. Douglas, however, did not go into detail at this conference as to what he saw as a legal basis for holding the statute unconstitutional.

John Marshall Harlan, quiet in person but occasionally passionate in his written opinions, sided with Douglas. He maintained that the Court had "no business" not deciding these cases on the merits. Calling the Connecticut law "the most egregiously unconstitutional act that I have seen since being on the Court," he alerted his brethren that he intended to file a dissent if the Court majority voted to dismiss the appeal for failure to rise to a case or controversy. For Harlan, "[n]othing is more offensive to the concept of our right to be let alone than putting the criminal law into the privacy of the marriage relation."

The other members of the Court had little to say. Tom Clark, William Brennan, and Charles Whittaker indicated that they agreed with the chief justice and Felix Frankfurter that the fact situation presented in the skimpy state court record did not present a "justiciable" matter, namely, one involving a real, as opposed to hypothetical, dispute. Potter Stewart, without going into detail, suggested otherwise, expressing support for the likely dissenting position of his friend, John Harlan. Thus the preliminary lineup of the Court on the *Poe* and *Buxton* matters was 6–3 in favor of dismissing the actions for failure to rise to the level of a case or controversy. Chief Justice Warren, being in the majority, assigned the opinion of the Court to Felix Frankfurter, the man who had initially felt reluctant because of a possible conflict of interest, to sit on the panel to discuss the issues in *Poe* and *Buxton*.

Harmless, Empty Shadows

In the interim between a Supreme Court conference on a case and the official announcement of the disposition of the case in open court, the justice assigned to write the opinion of the Court and any justices who choose to compose dissents and concurrences are busy drafting their opinions and negotiating with justices in other chambers as to what language would be acceptable to those willing to join the opinions. Felix Frankfurter circulated the first draft of his majority opinion in early June. This sparked John Marshall Harlan to confirm what had been assumed since the conference: he was going to prepare a dissent. Actually, Harlan had charged one of his clerks, Charles Fried, to begin working on the draft of his dissent shortly after the conference on the *Poe* and *Buxton* cases. Fried produced a lengthy document that Harlan, with very little editing, would adopt as his own and circulate to the other chambers. Douglas, characteristically working with very little drafting assistance from his clerks, also produced a long dissent. Justice Black decided to dissent without preparing or joining another opinion. Thus, at its final conference of the 1960–61 term, the Supreme Court decided by a vote of 5 to 4 to dismiss the appeal from the PPLC for lack of justiciability. At the same conference, the justices dismissed by a vote of 6 to 3 the lagging Connecticut case, *Trubek v. Ullman.*

The decisions in the combined cases of *Poe et al. v. Ullman* and *Buxton v. Ullman* were announced in the term's final public session on June 19, 1961. Justice Frankfurter's opinion for the five-person majority noted that the anticontraception statute had been on the Connecticut statute books since 1879 but had not led to any prosecutions except in the case of *State v. Nelson.* Apparently Frankfurter had forgotten, as Ray Cannon had stated in oral argument, that several store owners had been picked up for selling condoms and prosecuted in the "minor police courts of Connecticut." In addition, the prosecution of a condom salesman took place and a fine was levied as recently as March 1961. However, Frankfurter's point was essentially, if not literally, accurate: the 1879 statute was not a practical deterrent to birth control in the state because "contraceptives are commonly and notoriously sold in Connecticut drug stores."

Then Frankfurter launched into the legal and constitutional rationale for avoiding consideration of actions that are not live cases or controversies. Frankfurter submitted that "within the framework of our adversary system, the adjudicatory process is most securely founded when it is exercised under the impact of a lively conflict between antagonistic demands, actively pressed, which make resolution of the controverted issue a practical necessity." After commenting that in the last eighty years of its history Connecticut had opted not to enforce the anticontraception law, he ruled that these actions thus lacked "the immediacy which is an indispensable condition of constitutional adjudication." In an oft-quoted phrase, he concluded that "[t]his Court cannot be umpire to debates concerning harmless, empty shadows."

Justice Brennan wrote a short opinion concurring in the Court's judgment because he saw no real and substantial controversy on the basis of what he termed a "skimpy record." He did, however, predict quite presciently that a "true controversy" would emerge when birth control advocates like the PPLC reopened birth control clinics. Only then, he emphasized, would he be willing to support a definitive ruling on the constitutionality of the 1879 law.

William Douglas saw controversy enough over the Connecticut anticontraception law in 1961 to dissent from the Court's judgment. In an opinion slightly longer than the one penned by Frankfurter, Douglas rejected the majority's view that the 1879 statute had little effect on those seeking birth control information and devices in Connecticut. The very fact that there had been no birth control clinics operating in the state in twenty years suggested to Douglas that *State v. Nelson* was more than a test case; he saw it as a continuing deterrent to couples seeking medical advice on family planning. He noted that at any moment Connecticut could began a rigorous enforcement of the anticontraception law. Referring to Ray Cannon's acknowledgment during oral argument that there had been a few prosecutions under the anticontraception law, Douglas stressed that no lawyer worth his salt would advise his clients to rely on some "tacit agreement" not to enforce the old law.

Because Douglas believed that the action filed by Dr. Buxton and his patients presented a real case, he was willing at that moment to consider whether the 1879 law met the constitutional challenges raised by Fowler Harper and the PPLC. In his view, the law clearly failed this analysis. Douglas based the reasoning in his dissent on a conviction that the old law violated the right of privacy that stemmed principally from the "undefined liberty" guaranteed to individuals by the due process clause of the Fourteenth Amendment. He cited several Supreme Court decisions, principally concerning an individual's right to be secure from "unreasonable searches and seizures," that

{ *Griswold v. Connecticut* }

suggested a concept of privacy. He also referred to a well-known 1890 law review article by Louis Brandeis and Samuel Warren that laid out a basis for a right of privacy. In 1963, Douglas delivered the James Madison Lecture at the New York University School of Law. The title he gave to his remarks was "The Bill of Rights Is Not Enough," and his reasoning in *Poe* and *Buxton* figured prominently in the points raised in this address.

In an opinion longer than all the other opinions in the case combined, John Marshall Harlan began with a detailed analysis of the justiciability of the legal actions involving Dr. Buxton and his patients. For Harlan, as for Douglas, the prosecution of Dr. Nelson and his contraception clinic staffers in the 1939 action of *State v. Nelson* was no friendly test case. It had been prompted by a citizen's complaint that resulted not only in terminating birth control services at the Waterbury clinic but also in closing all of the other contraceptive clinics in the state. A long-term consequence of this decision was that no clinics providing birth control services had the temerity to open their doors in the state in almost a quarter century. Harlan chided the Court majority for regarding the fear of prosecution under the 1879 law as "chimerical" and thus for "indulg[ing] in a bit of sleight of hand to be rid of this case." Harlan emphasized that he did not believe that individuals should hold their constitutional rights "at the whim and pleasure of the prosecutor."

If Douglas provided readers of his dissent with a taste of privacy, Harlan offered his readers a conceptual feast. Harlan grounded the right of privacy in unspecified liberties protected by the due process clause of the Fourteenth Amendment. He saw this liberty as a "rational continuum," that "includes . . . freedom from all substantial arbitrary impositions and purposeless restraints." To sustain this view of liberty, he cited scores of cases that touched on privacy. Among these cases were ones concerning academic freedom (the right to have one's private intellectual property secure from legislative censure) and compulsory sterilization (the right to preserve bodily privacy from the actions of the state). Drawing on analysis offered in the ACLU brief, Harlan endorsed the proposition that the moral priggishness behind the Comstock Act and its state progeny served as levers to tilt public policy away from contraception.

The privacy of the home seemed especially important to Harlan. A statute, such as the one at issue in the *Poe* and *Buxton* cases, purported to forbid the use of contraceptives. To Harlan this was an "obnoxiously intrusive" assault on the privacy of the home and the sanctity of marriage. Harlan may have supported an individual's right of privacy under the Fourteenth Amendment, but he was not a libertine. He believed that married couples had the right to use contraceptives in the privacy of their homes; he did not wish to extend the continuum of privacy to encompass adultery, homosexuality, fornication, or incest.

The opinion of the Court in the combined cases of *Poe et al. v. Ullman* and *Buxton v. Ullman* served to complete a judicial cycle that had begun with *State v. Nelson* and continued through *Tileston v. Ullman*. Frankfurter's majority opinion in *Poe* sent a clear message to the PPLC: the judiciary would not strike down the nineteenth-century statute unless all possible avenues of avoidance were closed. As disappointing as this ruling was to the PPLC and its lawyers, the privacy analysis in the dissents of Douglas and Harlan gave the Connecticut activists the intellectual battering ram that would ultimately enable them to succeed in overcoming the inertia that held the 1879 anticontraception statute in place.

CHAPTER 4

"To Be Let Alone":
The Emerging Right of Privacy

Mention of a putative constitutional right of privacy in the dissenting opinions of justices John Marshall Harlan and William O. Douglas in the 1961 U.S. Supreme Court decisions of *Poe v. Ullman* and *Buxton v. Ullman* was sparked only in part by the privacy discourse in the lawyers' briefs in the case. Well before these cases were argued there was a modest but largely unfocused history of privacy in American life. Legal treatise writers, philosophers, and even a few justices of the Supreme Court had entertained the idea of a right of privacy on several occasions before the 1960s. Therefore, to appreciate and understand the important next steps in the advocacy for birth control in Connecticut, it is necessary to digress in order to assay the status of privacy at the time, both as a historical concept and as a possible constitutional right.

Privacy by Implication?

Privacy as a value and an expectation grew very slowly in America. The first homes in the colonies lacked corridors, so access to one bedroom usually meant traipsing through another bedchamber. Floorboards had wide gaps that allowed heat to pass between floors, but sound traveled easily through the spaces between the boards as well. Many beds accommodated two or more persons. And some bedchambers were essentially small dormitories. Although toilet facilities were enclosed in outbuildings, individuals walking back and forth to them were visible from houses and the street.

Builders in the eighteenth century began to construct homes with corridors between bedrooms. Also beginning at about this time was the practice of insisting that visitors to a home "knocke att the dore, and after leave given, to come in." This injunction applied to neighbors as well as strangers. In addition, in the late eighteenth century, colonial courts began to step up the prosecution of Peeping Toms and eavesdroppers. In his famous 1761 argument against the offensive British writs of assistance, the Boston attorney James Otis stated that "now one of the most essential branches of English liberty is the freedom of one's house. A man's house is his castle; and while he is quiet he is as well guarded as a prince in his castle."

The American Revolution introduced a legion of legal issues that would simmer for years. In the 1776 Declaration of Independence, although Thomas Jefferson did not use the term *privacy*, he may have had the concept in mind when he expressed indignation at the British monarch "for quartering large Bodies of Armed Troops among us." Similarly, in the Pennsylvania Bill of Rights, adopted the same year as the Declaration, the signers argued in favor of a legal right to privacy by proposing "that the people have a right to hold themselves, their houses, papers and possessions from search and seizure" except when properly authorized by appropriate judicial officials for criminal investigations.

The first ten amendments to the U.S. Constitution — usually referred to as the Bill of Rights — was ratified in 1791 and furnished then, as they still do today, the textual underpinning for American civil liberties. Although the word *private* is enunciated in the U.S. Constitution as part of the phrase "private property," the term *privacy* is not specifically found in the Bill of Rights or in the body of the Constitution itself. Whether the men who wrote the Bill of Rights and the Constitution believed that a right of privacy should be derived by implication from other clearly expressed liberties has been a matter of contention almost since the words of the first ten amendments were penned well over two hundred years ago. This very issue would figure into the arguments of justices, lawyers, and scholars when the Connecticut statute banning birth control came before the courts in the 1950s and 1960s. All that needs to be noted at this juncture is that it *is conceivable* that privacy was on the minds of the writers of the Bill of Rights.

Those who see a right of privacy lurking between the lines or behind the words of the Bill of Rights point to the First, Third, Fourth, and Fifth Amendments. The right to freedom of speech and freedom of religion in the First Amendment promises that one's ideas are one's own and may not be dictated by governmental power or censured if expressed. Logically, this reading of the First Amendment may entail that one possesses the liberty not to share one's thoughts with others, especially with the government. The First Amendment also guarantees the right to assemble and to petition the government for redress of grievances. The necessary other side of these First Amendment rights, it is argued by those who see privacy covered by the First Amendment, are the rights not to associate with certain people and not to have the identity of one's affiliations or associates made public. Joseph Story, a U.S. Supreme Court justice and perhaps the leading legal scholar of the early national period, maintained in his 1833 *Commentaries on the Constitution of the United States* that the First Amendment freedoms were voiced by the framers in order to protect "private sentiment" and "private judgment." In the early years of the republic, it was generally believed, although never tested in court, that the First Amendment protected the privacy of individuals who wished to shield their identity by issuing anonymous statements or by using pseudonyms. In the first twenty years of American constitutional government, six men who were or later would be president wrote under pen names.

What about language in other sections of the Bill of Rights? The Third Amendment's prohibition of quartering of soldiers in private homes during times of peace stems directly from the fear of such violations of private space that concerned the writers of the Declaration of Independence and the Pennsylvania Bill of Rights. Similarly, the Fourth Amendment's prohibition of "unreasonable searches and seizures" safeguards the private papers and personal possessions of individuals, unless proper warrants are issued or probable cause is demonstrated; it too repeats phraseology in the Declaration and the Pennsylvania Bill of Rights. Finally, the Fifth Amendment may be said to offer some protection for personal privacy because it affords individuals the right not to be compelled to give evidence that might be used against them in criminal proceedings. Privacy is thus *implied* by language in selected portions of these several amendments.

Whether a constitutional right could be established by implied language was not a question many Americans thought to ask for the first hundred years of the nation's existence. Because the courts, especially the U.S. Supreme Court, seldom decided cases dealing with individual rights until well into the twentieth century, the issue of whether a right of privacy could be implied from selected portions of the Bill of Rights was essentially moot for most of the nation's history.

Returning to privacy in a nonconstitutional sense, there is ample evidence that state common law doctrine protected and promoted elements of privacy throughout the first century of U.S. history. The law of nuisance, for example, allowed those suffering from unreasonable noises and smells to pursue a cause of action against those responsible for interfering with the "quiet enjoyment" of property. The common law of trespass allowed an individual to sue a private party or the government if his house, papers, or possessions had been illegally intruded on. As in the colonial era, eavesdropping prosecutions continued into the nineteenth century. State courts in the nineteenth century were regularly called on to protect the core secrets of a business enterprise — what is now referred to as "intellectual property." This was accomplished through trademark litigation.

Certain types of communications between individuals have long been recognized as "privileged" in American law and thus not subject to a breach of privacy. Among such communications are those that take place between spouses, between lawyers and clients, and between clergy and parishioners. Confidentiality in doctor-patient relationships was relatively late in taking hold in America. In 1828, New York passed a statute that protected the confidentiality of doctor-patient communications; within a few years, most American states followed New York's lead.

The importance of maintaining the privacy of postal communications was recognized early in U.S. history. A 1792 act of Congress prohibited persons in the employ of the U.S. Post Office from opening a letter; an 1825 federal statute extended the proscription to nonpostal employees. Several states added their own sanctions to federal law, thus making it a state crime to tamper with the mails within the boundaries of their states. Historians do not report any examples of intercepted letters being used in American court proceedings in the nineteenth century. The most egregious violation of postal confidentiality in the nineteenth century was probably the destruction of abolitionist letters and pamphlets addressed to Southerners, which took place episodically from the 1820s through the end of the antebellum period. The law also sought to punish the unauthorized divulging of the contents of letters once delivered. This proscription extended even to newspapers claiming a First Amendment right to publish newsworthy information gleaned from private letters. According to Joseph Story, the confidentiality of personal communications needed to be preserved to ensure "the implied or necessary intention and duty of privacy and secrecy." If this were not the case, Story opined, letter writers would either face distress from the exposure of "inviolable secrets" or would compose letters to close friends with the same "cold and formal severity, with which he would write to his wariest opponents, or his most implacable enemies."

Commentators on the history of privacy in America before the Civil War have generally cast the American understanding of privacy as a personal one, related more to the circumstances of a person's immediate physical environment (essentially the home) than to an assertion of a generalized legal, moral, or natural right. Thomas Cooley, a Michigan judge and author of several influential legal treatises, submitted in a 1879 volume on tort law that "the right to one's person may be said to be a right of complete immunity" and then, in an inelegant but eminently quotable phrase, he defined privacy as the right "to be let alone." Cooley's memorable choice of words would be repeated countless times by lawyers, judges, and legal writers over the next 125 years. "To be let alone" became an aphorism for all seasons, just as apt in a post-1870 America in constant technological flux as it was for the more rural and slower-paced society of Abraham Lincoln, Andrew Jackson, and John Marshall.

An Apocryphal Wedding

The technological advances of the mid- to late nineteenth century posed significant challenges to the law of privacy. The spread of the telegraph in the 1850s caused several states to enact statutes criminalizing the tapping of telegraph lines or the interception of transcribed messages in telegraph offices. But the challenges posed to the emerging law of privacy by other technological developments would not be so easily accommodated. The telephone, the microphone, the recording dictograph, and — most of all — what was then called "instantaneous photography" all appeared on the American scene in the late nineteenth century. These inventions and their embrace by so many segments of society meant that personal privacy could no longer be shielded by protecting a site from a physical intrusion or by securing paper records from unreasonable seizure. Eavesdropping on telephone conversations by means of tapping the lines did not involve a physical taking of something, but it constituted, in the minds of many, an invasion of privacy. Nevertheless, as late as 1928, a majority of the U.S. Supreme Court ruled that wiretapping the phone conversations of suspected bookmakers did not constitute a taking of "material things." Documents could be photographed without permission, and in the view of many, this constituted another breach of privacy. But turn-of-the-century American courts were not consistently willing to rule that such an activity was a search or seizure.

When it came to legislative attempts in turn-of-the-century America to regulate business, courts frequently adhered to an outlook that some scholars have termed "propertied privacy." State and federal courts at this time were becoming increasingly hostile to statutory attempts to intrude on the bargains that businesses entered into with their workers. It was not the role of the state legislature, many appellate courts insisted — except in the most dangerous of working environments — to pass judgment on the proper conditions or terms of employment. These were matters to be hammered out between employers and employees. One classic instance of judicial enunciation of the propertied privacy doctrine took place in the 1905 Supreme Court decision of *Lochner v. New York*. In that case, a bare 5–4 majority of the justices determined that a state law limiting the number of hours that bakers could work each week was an unconstitutional intrusion on the "privity of contract" between a bakery owner and his employees. The fact that workers were at a distinct disadvantage to management at this point in American history when it came to negotiating the terms of employment was not relevant to the judges, lawyers, and legal writers who saw merit in decisions such as *Lochner*. The concept of propertied privacy was not consistently adhered to by American courts. There were certainly more instances in which appellate courts upheld state employment regulations in turn of the century America than found them to be constitutionally defective. However, a number of decisions like *Lochner* kept social reformers off stride until the mid-1930s, when the U.S. Supreme Court finally stopped issuing judicial fiats in economic regulation cases.

One of the lawyers who played a major role in challenging the concept of propertied privacy was Louis Brandeis, a well-known Boston attorney who would, in 1916, assume duties as a member of the U.S. Supreme Court. Brandeis was definitely opposed to the propertied privacy thrust of the courts of the late nineteenth and early twentieth centuries. He felt that decisions like *Lochner* exhibited a blindness to social reality and unjustly thwarted the intentions of the people's elected representatives. Brandeis did his part as an appellate attorney and later as a member of the Supreme Court to bury *Lochner* and decisions of that ilk. As important as Brandeis was as a social crusader on behalf of the working class, it is Brandeis, the defender of personal privacy, who is of special interest here.

Roscoe Pound, Harvard's law school dean in the first half of the twentieth century and one of the most thoughtful commentators on law and social issues in his time, once stated that a single law review article, "The Right to Privacy," written by Louis Brandeis and Samuel Warren in 1890, "did nothing less than add a chapter to our law." Pound, as was occasionally his wont, was indulging in hyperbole. Various understandings of privacy had been percolating in American history almost from the beginning of European settlement of the continent. But the Brandeis/Warren essay was instrumental in getting judges, lawyers, and other legal theorists to sit up and take notice that privacy was clamoring for status as a legal right. In order to appreciate the case that Brandeis and Warren made for this new right, it is instructive to take note of the situation that sparked the writing of the essay.

Samuel Warren, Brandeis's former law partner, was upset by the publication of intrusive articles in the society press. In the 1880s the Warrens were mainstays in Boston society and did a good deal of entertaining. The *Saturday Evening Gazette*, among other papers, loved to focus on the activities of the old-monied elites attending society parties. Warren suggested to Brandeis that the two of them collaborate in writing an article that would posit a right of privacy to protect good people, such as the Warrens, from the meddlesome attentions of the *Gazette* and publications of that type. What allegedly convinced Warren to approach his partner with the suggestion to write the essay was a lurid account in the *Gazette* of the wedding of Warren's daughter. More than one Brandeis biographer fastened on the wedding anecdote as the impetus for writing "The Right to Privacy." Years later, law professor and torts expert William Prosser observed that "one is tempted to surmise that she [the Warren daughter] must have been a very beautiful girl. . . . This was the face that launched a thousand lawsuits." Yes, it is a good story. But it is simply not true. Samuel Warren's daughter was only six years old in 1890. In addition, whatever the excesses of some New England papers, the *Gazette* was widely regarded as a respectable news organ for the upper class. The *Gazette* did indeed report on social events, but it contained only two mentions of Samuel Warren in the decade of the 1880s, both quite innocuous.

"The Right to Privacy" began with several bows to Thomas Cooley for his famous "the right to be let alone" statement. The authors then proceeded to spin out some of the legal precedents in the law of nuisance, the law of defamation, and the protection of private property. What seemed to concern Brandeis and Warren most was the press's intrusion into one's private life that could lead to loss of reputation or the divulgence of embarrassing personal facts. They also objected to the unauthorized publication of pictures of individuals. In their words, "[t]he press is overstepping in every direction the obvious bounds of propriety and of decency. Gossip is no longer the resource of the idle and of the vicious, but has become a trade, which is pursued with industry as well as effrontery." The authors wanted to find some legal way to leave it to an individual's own determination as "to what extent . . . thoughts, sentiments, and emotions shall be communicated to others." Publication of any of these expressions should be forbidden without the maker of the productions consent. The protection of personal writings and other forms of expression from unauthorized publication was not so much derived from the principle of private property but what the authors termed "an inviolate personality."

The essay concluded with a catalog of limitations to the right and suggestions of remedies to punish violations of the right. As believers in the First Amendment, the authors did not want the right to privacy to be construed as to prohibit publicity for matters that would be of general public interest. In addition, Brandeis and Warren were not willing to prohibit communications regarding matters that have already been "published" in a court of justice or legislative proceeding. The authors argued that the right to privacy should terminate if the individual published the facts himself or allowed them to be published with his consent. The truth of a matter published, the authors believed, should not, in itself, afford a defense for violation of the right of privacy. Nor should the "absence of malice" in the mind of the person engaging in the publishing be an automatic bar to a suit for violation of privacy. Damage to an individual's character from a publication was not the issue for Brandeis and Warren; the key principle to them was whether the publication, irrespective of its truth or intent to harm, injured a person's right of privacy. Finally, the authors were of the opinion that remedies for an injury to the right of privacy could be sought in an action for damages in tort law and, in some special cases, for an injunction against future publication of the offensive material.

The Brandies/Warren concept of privacy had mixed appeal in the period between 1890 and 1950. During this period courts in most American states adopted some form of a common-law right of privacy. Four states even legislated the right. Perhaps the first instance in state appellate court records recognizing a right of privacy was the New York case of *Schuyler v. Curtis* (1892). In this instance, the highest court of New York upheld the injunction granted by a lower court judge against an individual who wished to make a public exhibition of the statute of a deceased person. Relatives of the decedent successfully argued that the statute was of someone "not shown [to be] . . . a public character." One legal historian identified nearly three hundred other right-to-privacy decisions in state appellate courts in the sixty-year period after the publication of the Brandeis/Warren essay. No one knows how many lower state court privacy decisions were rendered during these years; probably the number is in the thousands. Most successful actions were filed by individuals against newspapers. Such a leading case was the Georgia decision of *Pavesich v. New England Life Insurance Co.* (1905). It marked the first time a state court, independent of a statute, recognized an individual's right of privacy. Paolo Pavesich was a well-known artist whose picture, without his authorization, appeared in an advertisement in the *Atlanta Constitution* touting the value of a life insurance policy with the defendant company. The image of Pavesich was that of a handsome, well-dressed man. He was not identified, but the company did not deny that the picture was one of him. Pavesich claimed an invasion of his privacy. The Georgia Supreme Court upheld Pavesich's claim, finding that the insurance's company's use of Pavesich's image without his permission constituted an intrusion into "matters private," even though Pavesich was considered a public figure.

It is one thing to have a theoretical legal right. But it is something else to see that right fully exercised. Perhaps surprisingly, experts on tort law have found no cases of common-law recovery for invasion of privacy between 1890 and 1950 against police for eavesdropping or wiretapping, even when the law enforcement agencies acted without warrants or other proper legal authorization. The absence of successful suits against police departments in the period for invasion of privacy was a consequence of several factors.

It most likely stemmed from the fact that private citizens were seldom aware of the eavesdropping that might have presented a possible transgression of their legal rights. An account of personal or intimate activities that appeared in a newspaper story alerted a person to a possible violation of privacy. But a police department's surveillance of an individual might never be revealed, especially if law enforcement agencies did not seek to file criminal charges in connection with the matter under scrutiny. In many cases, eavesdropping or telephone tapping was ordered by business owners or homeowners themselves. A company president might order a tap on the telephones in his plant in order to sniff out union activity, or a homeowner might install a tap to gather evidence against a spouse suspected of engaging in an extramarital affair. In such situations, courts were more willing to recognize the eavesdropping to be a legal right of businesses leaders and home owners than a violation of the rights of laborers or unsuspecting spouses. In addition, although courts or juries could understand the damage to a person's reputation by the publication of scandalous information in the press, they found it hard to see the harm in merely listening to conversations at work or in the home. Another reason that suits against the police for invasion of privacy were rarely successful in this period was that courts and juries did not feel comfortable finding in favor of unsavory or criminal elements. For these reasons, the common law right of privacy postulated by Brandeis and Warren in 1890 did not find much sympathy in the courts for many years. But the argument proffered by the two Boston lawyers lay dormant in the bound volumes of a prestigious law review, waiting for a more sympathetic era.

Some Early Quasi-Privacy Cases

Justice William O. Douglas, the author of the majority opinion in *Griswold v. Connecticut*, would "discover" in 1965 that a right of privacy inheres at the fringes of the Bill of Rights. Justice Douglas's explicit recognition of a right of privacy was not without foundation. As he noted in his "penumbra analysis" in *Griswold*, privacy loomed in the background of a number of important U.S. Supreme Court decisions in the late nineteenth and early twentieth centuries. Slowly, without directly saying so, members of the nation's highest court began to hint that privacy might have a *constitutional* as well as a legal basis. Many of these cases would serve as launching pads for Douglas's *Griswold* opinion.

In *Boyd v. U.S.* (1886), for example, the Court voided the seizure of an importer's papers relating to the allegedly owed duties on thirty-five cases of polished plate glass. In his majority opinion, Justice Joseph Bradley maintained that there is an "intimate relation" between the Fourth and Fifth Amendments because unreasonable searches and seizures prohibited by the Fourth Amendment "are almost always made for the purpose of compelling a man to give evidence against himself," a practice condemned by the Fifth Amendment. Bradley came very close to calling this seizure and the implicitly forced confession to be an invasion of privacy when he wrote the following: "The principles laid down in this opinion affect the very essence of constitutional liberty. . . . They apply to all invasions on the part of the government and its employees of the sanctity of a man's home and the privacies of life. . . . [I]t is the invasion of his indefeasible right of personal security, personal liberty and private property. . . . In this regard the Fourth and Fifth Amendments run almost into each other."

The well-known case of *Weeks v. U.S.* (1914) presents another early example of the justices of the Supreme Court stretching toward a right of privacy. This case involved the government seizure of tickets, coupons, and other evidence of lottery activity from a Kansas City,

Missouri, man named Weeks. The federal officers did not have a search warrant for obtaining this evidence. In overruling Weeks's conviction, the High Court's majority opinion, written by Justice William Day, held that illegally obtained evidence could not be used by federal prosecutors in an action in the federal courts. This is the first enunciation of the so-called exclusionary rule: the axiom that prosecutors cannot use illegally seized evidence against the accused person in a trial. It was extended to prosecutions under state law in the 1960s. The Court stated in *Weeks*: "If letters and private documents can thus be seized and held and used in evidence against a citizen accused of an offense, the protection of the Fourth Amendment declaring his right to be secure against such searches and seizures is of no value." Despite the ruling in *Weeks*, the federal officials did not always get the message. In *Silverthorne Lumber Company v. U.S.* (1920), representatives of the Department of Justice seized the records of the Silverthorne lumber business, operated by Frederick Silverthorne and his father. Copies were made of the records and the originals were returned to the Silverthornes. But the government proceeded to use information in the copies of the records to subpoena the originals and frame charges against the Silverthornes. Justice Oliver Wendell Holmes, writing for the Court majority, angrily argued that to permit federal officials to use information from copies of illegally seized documents to commandeer the returned originals would "[reduce] the Fourth Amendment to a form of words."

To explain some of the next key holdings of the Supreme Court, another digression is called for. Since its ratification in 1791 until the middle of the 1920s, the Bill of Rights had been read by the Court as protecting individual liberty only against *federal* restrictions. But the ratification of the Fourteenth Amendment in 1868 provided a potential mechanism to extend some of the guarantees of the Bill of Rights to individuals faced with alleged *state* interference with their liberties. In the first section of the Fourteenth Amendment, the so-called due process clause, reads as follows: "No State shall . . . deprive any person of life, liberty, or property, without due process of law." What the drafters of the amendment meant by the word *liberty* in this clause was not clear in 1868, and legal historians continue to this day to argue about what those nineteenth-century legislators' intentions might have been. Regardless, beginning in the mid-1920s the U.S. Supreme

Court began to read the word *liberty* in the amendment as embracing some of the protections of the Bill of Rights. In effect, the due process clause of the Fourteenth Amendment began to act as a lever to tilt some Bill of Rights protections to individuals when faced with state challenges to their rights as well as the long-standing protection against federal abuses. Which provisions of the first ten amendments were to be "incorporated" or "absorbed" as individual liberties vis-à-vis state as well as federal power became a matter of contention for the justices over the years. And Court watchers have followed the seemingly inexorable process of incorporation with great interest. Today, most of the key provisions of the Bill of Rights have been absorbed, but a majority of the Court has never been willing to say that all of the provisions of the first ten amendments apply to the states.

In the 1923 case of *Meyer v. Nebraska*, the Court was called on to review the constitutionality of a state law that prohibited instruction in foreign languages in a state's public and private elementary schools. In striking down the law, the opinion by Justice James McReynolds held that the liberty guaranteed by the Fourteenth Amendment included noninterference by the state of Nebraska with the vocation of modern language teachers such as Meyer. McReynolds framed his argument in terms of Meyer's property rights, but most of the other rights he later listed as examples of those protected by the due process clause of the Fourteenth Amendment were fundamentally private matters, such as "the right of the individual to contract, to engage in any of the common occupations of life, to acquire useful knowledge, to marry, establish a home and bring up children, [and] to worship God according to the dictates of his own conscience." In *Pierce v. Society of Sisters* (1925), in another opinion written by Justice McReynolds, the Court held that an Oregon law requiring that children attend public schools violated the rights of parents who wished to send their sons and daughters to private schools. For McReynolds, this was another example of a personal, essentially private, matter not explicitly noted in the text of the Constitution or its amendments that nevertheless warranted constitutional protection.

Another notable decision of the 1920s that saw the Supreme Court confront privacy issues was the well-known compulsory sterilization case, *Buck v. Bell* (1927). In contrast to the previous cases, however, the Supreme Court did not see the privacy issue as compelling enough to overrule government authority. Virginia, as many states at the time, had on its books a law permitting the sterilization of inmates of state hospitals afflicted with hereditary forms of insanity or mental retardation. The counsel for Carrie Buck, "a feeble-minded white woman" confined to the State Colony for Epileptics and Feeble Minded, argued that the Virginia law violated his client's right of bodily integrity which he saw as protected by the general language of the due process clause of the Fourteenth Amendment. In its majority opinion for the Court, Justice Oliver Wendell Holmes noted that Carrie Buck had already given birth to one retarded child and that she was herself the child of a retarded mother housed in the same institution. Holmes and the Court ignored the liberty and bodily privacy issues presented by Buck's case. Holmes's opinion included these harsh words: "[T]he public welfare may call upon the best citizens for their lives. It would be strange if it could not call upon those who already sap the strength of the State for these lesser sacrifices . . . in order to prevent our being swamped with incompetence. . . . Three generations of imbeciles are enough."

"Dirty Business"

The most important privacy case to come before the Supreme Court before 1960 was *Olmstead v. U.S.* (1928). Known especially for its stirring dissents by Brandeis and Holmes, *Olmstead* presents in stark relief the challenge of technology to constitutional interpretation. Roy "Big Boy" Olmstead was the general manager of an extremely profitable liquor-smuggling operation headquartered in Seattle, Washington. In defiance of Prohibition, Olmstead's business grossed an estimated $2 million a year. Olmstead and his several dozen cohorts imported liquor illegally from British Columbia on two ships that they owned. Besides the seagoing vessels, the smugglers maintained an office, several bookkeepers, a stable of delivery men, and their own attorney. They also had a central telephone switchboard and a bullpen of telephones, which became an attractive target for federal wiretapping. Although the wiretaps were installed in the basement of the building containing the telephone bullpen, there was no physical intrusion into the Olmstead group's offices. In addition, no warrants were procured to institute the wiretaps.

Over five months, federal agents listened to countless hours of phone conversations, ultimately transcribing 775 typed pages detailing the operation of the business. The evidence assembled demonstrated without question that the Olmstead group was involved in a big-time criminal operation. The leaders of the group were convicted in federal district court. However, partly because the state of Washington had a statute on its books prohibiting wiretaps, the defendants challenged the conviction on grounds that the federal agents had procured the evidence in a tainted fashion. On appeal, the U.S. Supreme Court agreed to review the convictions. But at the time it accepted the case, the Court decided to limit its scrutiny to the question of whether the actions of federal law enforcement officers violated the right of privacy of the defendants under the Fourth and Fifth Amendments to the U.S. Constitution.

The Court ultimately split 5–4 in favor of upholding the convictions. Chief Justice Howard Taft, a strong backer of Prohibition, was determined to use this case as a platform for his view that federal law enforcement should not be hamstrung by "bleeding heart" technicalities. Writing the majority opinion himself, Taft held that the wiretapping of the Olmstead operation did not constitute an unreasonable seizure of "something tangible" because all the federal agents had done was to transcribe "voluntary conversations secretly overheard." That action did not, in Taft's view, violate the defendants' liberties under the Fourth Amendment because no "material things" were expropriated.

Louis Brandeis, an associate justice of the Supreme Court since 1916, was incensed by the illegal and, in his view, unconstitutional behavior of the federal agents. As soon as the Court accepted the case, even before knowing how he and his judicial brethren would split on deciding the matter, he charged his law clerk, Henry Friendly, with preparing a memorandum on how the actions of the federal agents violated the defendants' rights. Ultimately the Friendly memo became the nub of Brandeis's dissent. Oliver Wendell Holmes was initially inclined to support the chief justice's majority opinion until Brandeis's entreaties persuaded him to switch his vote. Holmes ultimately took the further step of filing his own dissenting opinion. Chief Justice Taft was livid: he saw this as just another instance of Brandeis controlling the vote of his influential but aging colleague.

Both the dissents by Brandeis and Holmes saw the government's warrantless wiretapping of the Olmstead group as constituting a violation of the defendants' rights of privacy. Extracting exact phrases and sentences from the now almost forty-year-old article that he and Samuel Warren had written for the *Harvard Law Review*, Brandeis declared that "[t]he makers of our Constitution undertook . . . to protect Americans in their beliefs, their thoughts, their emotions, and their sensations. They conferred, as against the Government, the right to be let alone — the most comprehensive of rights and the right most valued by civilized men." To Brandeis it did not matter that the writers of the Fourth Amendment had not anticipated the invention of the telephone or the advent of wiretapping technology. The spirit of that amendment should not just protect individuals from unreasonable seizures of tangible things; it should also guard those same people from having their conversations "seized" by technological devices unknown to the George Masons and James Madisons of the eighteenth century.

In response to the contention of the government attorneys that the wiretapping had only violated the rights of the defendants in the interests of a greater good, Brandeis disdainfully observed: "Experience should teach us to be most on our guard to protect liberty when the Government's purposes are beneficent. . . . The greatest dangers to liberty lurk in insidious encroachment by men of zeal, well-meaning but without understanding." And then, in one of his most famous statements as a member of the Supreme Court, Brandeis wrote in his concluding paragraph:

> Our Government is the potent, the omnipresent teacher. For good or for ill, it teaches the whole people by its example. Crime is contagious. If the Government becomes a lawbreaker, it breeds contempt for the law; it invites every man to become a law unto himself; it invites anarchy. To declare that in the administration of the criminal law the end justifies the means — to declare that the Government may commit crimes in order to secure the conviction of a private criminal — would bring terrible retribution. Against that pernicious doctrine this Court should resolutely set its face.

In 1890 Brandeis and Warren had articulated a right to privacy essentially to shield the rich and famous from the intrusions of the press; now, in 1928, Brandeis rephrased the right slightly, hoping to benefit the poor and those accused of crimes.

Brandeis's dissent, as was his custom, was studded with hundreds of references to cases and statutes and ran to almost twenty pages in the *U.S. Reports.* By contrast, Holmes's dissent cited only three cases and totaled less than a page and a half. Holmes began by complimenting his "brother Brandeis" for his "exhaustive . . . examination" of the issues in the case but expressed the reservation that he was not convinced that "the penumbra of the Fourth and Fifth Amendments covers the defendant." Holmes said that he sympathized with the desire of federal officers to move aggressively to arrest and charge wrongdoers, but that he also wished to preserve the rights of the accused. If it is necessary to choose between the two goals of a criminal justice system, he declared that "for my part I think it a less[er] evil that some criminals should escape than that the Government should play an ignoble part." Regardless of the statutory legality of wiretapping by the government, Holmes characterizing it as a "dirty business." As to the Fourth and Fifth Amendment issues, Holmes submitted that "the reason for excluding evidence obtained by violating the Constitution seems to me logically to lead to excluding evidence by a crime of the officers of the law."

Comment in the nation's premier law reviews generally took the side of Brandeis and Holmes, praising them for their defense of an emerging right of privacy and their criticism of the offensive wiretapping by the federal officials. By contrast, Taft's majority opinion was generally found by law review writers and editors to be deficient for his literalistic view that the Fourth Amendment did not forbid the seizure, even if found to be "unreasonable," of "material things." Moreover, the majority opinion in *Olmstead* offended many legal commentators because it appeared to countenance illegal activity by the government. The dissenters' position was vindicated by a 1934 Act of Congress that prohibited the interception and divulgence of telephonic communications. Many years later — in *Katz v. U.S.* (1967) — the Supreme Court explicitly overruled its majority opinion in *Olmstead.*

The Demise of Propertied Privacy

In the middle 1930s, the U.S. Supreme Court finally laid to rest the "propertied privacy" era in American constitutional history. In the late nineteenth century and first third of the twentieth century, the Supreme Court frequently held that legislative regulation was unconstitutional if it intruded into the "privity of contract" between an employer and employee. Pursuant to this doctrine, maximum hour and minimum wage laws passed by various states were struck down. The Court, however, was willing to allow such regulations to survive constitutional attack if the industries targeted by legislation were perceived as particularly dangerous or, on occasion, if the regulations involved the labor of women.

President Franklin D. Roosevelt, reelected by a landslide vote in 1936, took it on himself shortly after the election to try to do something about the reluctance of the Supreme Court to support economic reform legislation that he proposed or endorsed. Arguing that the mid-1930s Supreme Court was dominated by old men who were not able to hold up their end of the Court's business, Roosevelt proposed a Judicial Reorganization Act that, if passed, would allow the President to appoint an additional justice to the Supreme Court for each justice over the age of seventy (this would apply to the lower federal courts as well). Roosevelt's announced reasoning was that the additional justices would be able to help their brethren keep up with the heavy load of cases. However, it was widely perceived that Roosevelt's motive was political — to pack the Court with pro–New Deal justices who could outvote the "four horsemen" (conservative justices Pierce Butler, James McReynolds, George Sutherland, and Willis VanDevanter).

Roosevelt's political threat to the Court, albeit very unpopular, was not without impact. In 1937, Associate Justice Owen Roberts, normally in the middle when it came to voting on economic regulation cases, inexplicably sided with the pro–New Deal justices (Brandeis, Harlan Fiske Stone, and Benjamin Cardozo) to uphold the constitutionality of a minimum wage law that was virtually identical to one struck down by the Court the previous year. The case was titled *West Coast Hotel v. Parrish* (1937), and it signaled a trend that would continue to the present day, namely, that the Supreme Court would not seek to act as a superlegislature when it came to economic regulation statutes; it would only strike down such laws if they had no reasonable relationship to the end sought by the legislative body. By the time the new alignment on the Supreme Court was made apparent in the

Parrish decision, the Court-Packing Bill had been returned to the Senate Judiciary Committee and was all but dead.

Stumbling Around in the Penumbra

After the dissent by Justice Brandeis in Olmstead, no Supreme Court opinion addressed the privacy issue with total focus until the Connecticut birth control cases of the 1950s and 1960s. Nevertheless, a handful of Supreme Court opinions from the 1930s through the early 1960s — both majority and dissenting — kept the idea of a constitutional right of privacy alive with tantalizing references to privacy emanations from the fringes of the Bill of Rights. Justice Holmes in *Olmstead* had spoken of the "penumbra" of the Bill of Rights, a surrounding or adjoining region in which rights exist to a lesser degree than in the central core of the first ten amendments. Holmes was partial to the term *penumbra* and used it a number of times in his opinions, decades before Justice William Douglas would appropriate the term and make it a bête noire of constitutional law.

In *On Lee v. U.S.* (1952), a federal undercover agent took incriminating testimony from On Lee by means of a concealed radio transmitter. The majority of the Court ruled that the government's procurement of evidence by this technique did not violate the Fourth Amendment liberty of the accused from unreasonable searches and seizures. *Olmstead* was cited as the principal precedent to uphold this government action. Justice William O. Douglas, in a brief dissent that quoted liberally from Brandeis's Olmstead dissent, wrote: "I joined in an opinion of the Court . . . (*Goldman v. U.S.* [1942]) which adhered to the *Olmstead* case, refusing to overrule it. . . . I now more fully appreciate the vice of the practices spawned by *Olmstead* and *Goldman.* . . . Mr. Justice Brandeis in his dissent in *Olmstead* espoused the cause of privacy. . . . What he wrote is an historic statement of that point of view. I cannot improve on it." Douglas concluded by declaring that the principle of the Fourth Amendment's protection against unreasonable searches and seizures should prevail regardless of "the nature of the instrument[s] that science or engineering develops."

In early 1952 Douglas filed dissenting opinions in two other cases that made clear that he supported a constitutional right of privacy.

Dissenting in *Beauharnais v. Illinois* (1952), Douglas accepted the view that the right of free expression guaranteed by the First Amendment has a preferred position in American constitutional law. But in passing, he noted that there are other rights, "for example, privacy" that are "equally sacred to some" and that "there is room for regulation of the ways and means of invading privacy."

Douglas commented at greater length on what he saw as the right to privacy in a dissenting opinion in *Public Utilities Commission v. Pollak* (1952). The case involved the playing of radio music, interspersed with commercials and announcements, through loudspeakers on streetcars in the District of Columbia. Some passengers contended that their constitutional rights were violated by being forced to listen to what they considered to be bothersome music while riding on the streetcars. The D.C. Public Utilities Commission investigated the complaints and found them to be without foundation. So a suit was filed in federal court. The Supreme Court would later support the commission finding by a vote of 7–1. The lone dissenter, the only member of the Court willing to detect a privacy issue in the case, was Douglas: "Liberty in the constitutional sense," he wrote, "must mean more than freedom from unlawful governmental restraint; it must include privacy as well, if it is to be a repository of freedom." Although Pollak and a cocomplainant were not forced to ride the District's streetcars, Douglas felt that in a practical sense, this form of conveyance was essential to many who worked and lived in the District. They were a captive audience. It did not matter to Douglas that the music was described at the utilities commission hearing as being pleasant or innocuous. For Douglas, the content of the forced communication was irrelevant: "Once privacy is invaded, privacy is gone. Once a man is forced to submit to one type of radio program, he can be forced to submit to another. It may be but a short step from a cultural program to a political program." At the end of the opinion, Douglas submitted: "The right of privacy should include the right to pick and choose from competing entertainments, competing propaganda, competing political philosophies. If people are let alone in those choices, the right of privacy will pay dividends in character and integrity." Legal scholars would later term Douglas's paeans to privacy in early 1952 as his "privacy spring."

Douglas had presaged his privacy spring a decade earlier when, in *Skinner v. Oklahoma* (1942), he wrote an opinion for the Court striking down a statute that permitted the sterilization of persons convicted three or more times for crimes involving moral turpitude. Douglas identified the privacy interest in *Skinner* in these words: "We are dealing here with legislation which involves one of the basic civil rights of man. Marriage and procreation are fundamental to the very existence and survival of the race."

Although no justice in the 1940s through the early 1960s appeared to feel as strongly about nailing down a right to privacy as Douglas, references or allusions to privacy can be found in the constitutional opinions of other justices in the period. Situations that involved the liberties guaranteed by the First Amendment seemed especially likely to shade into privacy. For example, in *West Virginia State Board of Education v. Barnette* (1943) Justice Robert Jackson ruled for the Court majority that Jehovah's Witness children in a state's public schools could not be compelled to salute the American flag. For Jackson, the objection of the Jehovah's Witness to participation in the patriotic expression of saluting the flag was permitted because the First Amendment protects silence just as it safeguards vocal or symbolic expression. It could be argued, as some commentators did, that the motivation that sparked the silence of the Jehovah's Witnesses was a private matter of conscience.

Other First Amendment cases reaching the Supreme Court in the period might be said to fall under the rubric of what has been called "political privacy." On a single Monday—June 17, 1957—the Court issued four decisions upholding the rights of members of the Community Party and others espousing controversial points of view during the so-called Red Scare of the 1950s. Dubbed "Red Monday," the 1957 decisions largely undercut the more stridently anticommunist decisions of the Court earlier in the decade. Two of the Red Monday decisions had particular privacy connections. In *Watkins v. U.S.* (1957), the Court held that a witness appearing before the House of Representatives' Un-American Activities Committee (HUAC) could not be compelled to expose his activities and those of his associates unless such testimony was found to be directly related to a function of Congress. The Court in *Watkins* spoke of a witness's "personal interest in privacy" and ruled that the courts have a duty "to insure that the Congress does not unjustifiably encroach upon an individual's right to privacy nor abridge his liberty of speech, press, religion, or assembly."

In a companion Red Monday case, *Sweezy v. New Hampshire* (1957), the political privacy doctrine was advanced even further. The question presented in this case pertained to the length that a state investigating committee could go in inquiring into the activities of a scholar. A concurring opinion issued by Felix Frankfurter and John Marshall Harlan in *Sweezy* argued for a balancing of a citizen's right to political privacy with the right of a state to protect itself. Justices Frankfurter and Harlan stated: "[T]he inviolability of privacy belonging to a citizen's political loyalties has so overwhelming an importance to the well-being of our kind of society that it cannot be constitutionally encroached upon on the basis of so meager a countervailing interest of the State . . . [as demonstrated here]."

The First Amendment is also the source of what has been called "associational privacy." The leading case here is *NAACP v. Alabama* (1958), in which the Supreme Court was asked to rule on the constitutionality of an order of a Southern state that the NAACP produce its membership roster and list of officers. The justices found that this order violated the First Amendment as made applicable to state action by the due process clause of the Fourteenth Amendment. The unanimous majority opinion, written by Justice Harlan, included this language: "The immunity from state scrutiny of membership lists which the Association claims on behalf of its members is here so related to the right of the members to pursue their lawful private interest privately and to associate freely with others in doing [so] as to come within the protection of the Fourteenth Amendment." At another point in the opinion, Justice Harlan indicated the rationale for keeping such lists confidential: "This Court has recognized the vital relationship between freedom to associate and privacy in one's associations. . . . Inviolability of privacy in group association may in many circumstances be indispensable to freedom of association, particularly where a group espouses dissident beliefs."

The most important "stretches" toward a constitutional right of privacy in this period were in the realm of Fourth Amendment search and seizure cases. In *Wolf v. Colorado* (1949), the Supreme Court confronted a potential unreasonable search and seizure. Wolf was convicted by a Colorado court of conspiracy to commit an abortion. He maintained, however, that evidence used against him had been illegally acquired and thus should have been banned from admission at his trial. The majority of the Court, as expressed in an opinion of Justice Felix Frankfurter, made explicit mention of a right of privacy: "The security of one's privacy against arbitrary intrusion by the police — which is at the core of the Fourth Amendment — is basic to a free society." However, the Supreme Court refused to throw out the conviction, arguing that the exclusionary rule adopted in *Weeks v. U.S.* (1914) was an arbitrarily created rule for use in the federal courts that did not need not to be accepted by all state courts. The dissenters in *Wolf* wished to order the defendant freed and have the *Weeks* principle extended to the state courts.

The principle in *Wolf* was finally taken to its logical legal conclusion in *Mapp v. Ohio* (1961). This case originated in June 1957 when Cleveland police offers demanded entrance to the home of Dollree (Dolly) Mapp in search of a person suspected in a local bombing. Dolly Mapp admitted the officers to her home but grabbed the purported search warrant and "placed . . . [it] in her bosom." A struggle followed, and Mapp was handcuffed. The officers proceeded to search her home, ultimately finding a cache of allegedly obscene materials. Mapp was prosecuted and convicted for the offense of possessing obscenity. Mapp argued through her attorney that the materials used against her at trial were obtained in violation of her rights and should have been suppressed. She was nevertheless convicted. On appeal to the U.S. Supreme Court, the question presented was whether the situation that arose in *Mapp* presented the proper occasion for making the federal exclusionary rule of *Weeks* binding on state courts in all fifty states. The Court agreed that it should and threw out Mapp's conviction.

Justice Tom Clark's landmark majority opinion in *Mapp v. Ohio* made explicit, albeit confusing, mention of a right of privacy: "The right to privacy, when conceded operatively enforceable against the States, was not susceptible of destruction by avulsion of the sanction upon which its protection and enjoyment had always been deemed dependent under the *Boyd, Weeks* and *Silverthorne* cases." A few sentences later, Clark stated that "privacy [is] no less important than any other right carefully and particularly reserved to the people."

After *Mapp* it appeared that privacy had crossed the constitutional threshold. Exactly how it got there and where it would henceforth reside was not clear. A definitive privacy ruling was needed. The Connecticut birth control cases presented that opportunity.

CHAPTER 5

Back in Connecticut

Clearing the Decks

The U.S. Supreme Court decision in *Poe v. Ullman* (1961), dismissing the challenge to the 1879 Connecticut anticontraception law for the failure to state a case or controversy, was a disappointment to the Planned Parenthood League of Connecticut (PPLC). The organization's leadership and its lawyers, however, did not allow much grass to grow under their feet before setting off in a new direction. On June 20, 1961, the day after the *Poe* decision was announced, Estelle Griswold, Fowler Harper, and PPLC president Lucia Parks met with the leaders of the Planned Parenthood Federation of America (PPFA) in New York City to discuss what strategy should henceforth be used in the attempt to overturn Connecticut's anticontraception law. One avenue of attack that was considered but then discarded without much serious discussion was to focus League attention and resources on the pending 1961 repeal bill in the Connecticut state legislature. However, forty years of failed repeal bills did not augur well for legislative reform at any time in the near future.

At the June 20 meeting of the PPLC and the PPFA, Fowler Harper reminded the attendees of Justice William Brennan's laconic remark in *Poe* that a "true controversy" over contraceptive services in Connecticut would present itself only when physicians or PPLC staffers were arrested for operating a birth control clinic. Harper urged those at the New York meeting to work with him to orchestrate exactly the situation envisioned by Brennan. He recommended that a Connecticut clinic be opened as soon as possible and that the PPLC should do everything in its power "to get Estelle Griswold arrested."

The PPFA and the PPLC agreed with Harper. They issued a joint press release that "welcome[d] the recognition of the [Supreme] Court that the law has in fact become a nullity." Then they made the following announcement: "[T]he Planned Parenthood League of Connecticut, with the full backing of the national birth control movement, will take steps as rapidly as possible to offer, under medical supervision, all contraceptive techniques." If the 1879 statute was indeed a "nullity," as Justice Felix Frankfurter had declared in his majority opinion in *Poe*, it would not be enforced against the operation of a clinic and married couples in Connecticut would henceforth be able to receive contraceptive services without legal opposition. But in the more likely alternative that the law would be enforced by prosecuting the operation of birth control clinics and arresting some PPLC personnel, a live controversy would finally present itself, and the U.S. Supreme Court could no longer avoid a decision on the merits of the old law's constitutionality.

The day after the joint PPFA/PPLC announcement that birth control clinics would soon open in Connecticut, the *New York Times* editorialized in support of this prospect: "The [1879 Connecticut anticontraception] law can now be tested only if courageous doctors, nurses and patients make known their violation of it and risk prosecution. . . . While we respect the moral and religious arguments of those who object to birth control devices, we do not believe that they have the right to impose their views by force of law in our pluralistic society on others who feel differently." In a more general quantitative sense, those favoring the availability of birth control information and devices had greater public support than those who favored strict enforcement of the 1879 Connecticut law. A 1962 national Gallup Poll found that 72 percent of Americans approved the easy availability of birth control materials and information. Even among Catholics, the proportion of the population favoring the ready availability of birth control information was 56 percent.

Despite the increasing public sentiment in favor of contraception and the press's positive view of Justice Harlan's dissenting opinion in *Poe*, the continuing prohibition of the distribution of birth control information in Connecticut meant that some women were not receiving this medical service. Lee Buxton was confident he knew who was being adversely affected by the 1879 law and the Supreme Court's nondecision in *Poe v. Ullman*. Shortly after the announcement of the *Poe* decision, Buxton offered the following sharp response to a reporter's question: "It all adds up to the rich getting contraceptives and the poor getting children."

The PPLC announced, in late June 1961, that it would be opening a birth control clinic for married couples in New Haven, Connecticut, about October 1, 1961. It would be called the Planned Parenthood Center of New Haven. Late that summer the PPLC moved its state offices and the Planned Parenthood Center of New Haven to a large nineteenth-century home at 79 Trumbull. The PPLC's administrative offices and Estelle Griswold's office were also on the second floor of this large converted home. Buxton estimated that there were about 40,000 indigent married women of childbearing age in Connecticut at the time. Of these women, the PPLC predicted that as many as 2,500 to 3,000 would seek contraceptive services yearly from the Planned Parenthood Center at New Haven. The budget for the Center's first year was set at $45,000. Renovations on the new PPLC offices and the Center took longer than expected, so the projected opening date for the clinic was pushed back to November 1.

A Friendly Bust

In anticipation of the launching of the Planned Parenthood Center in New Haven on November 1, 1961, local and regional newspapers carried stories on the confrontation that appeared to be taking shape. An Associated Press report presented this scenario: "By opening clinics, it [the PPLC] challenges the state to make arrests and force the closing of the clinics. It would then make a new appeal to the high tribunal." Perhaps as a result of the publicity, as well as the felt need for contraceptive services, dozens of married women in Connecticut called the PPLC to request appointments for birth control consultations and prescriptions.

The procedure the Center instituted to serve the birth control needs of its clients followed a standard pattern. Women telephoning or stopping by the Center to express an interest in receiving birth control services were asked to complete a brief questionnaire. Appointments were then made. During a woman's first appointment, a staff member of the Center took a medical and personal case history, which included confirmation that the woman was indeed married. Then the client attended a group orientation at which Center personnel explained the various methods of contraception offered by the clinic. After considering which form of contraception she would prefer, the client was given an examination by a staff doctor. Unless "contraindicated," the doctor prescribed the form of contraception preferred by the client. The doctor or a staff nurse advised the client on how to use the form of contraception selected. The client was furnished with the birth control device, drug, or contraceptive material prescribed by the doctor. Finally, the client made an appointment for a return visit and was charged a fee — ranging between nothing and $15, on the basis of family income.

On the advice of Fowler Harper, the PPLC did not schedule a news conference announcing the first round of contraception appointments until Thursday morning, November 2 — the day *after* the first ten birth control consultations had been conducted. Harper did not want to give local law enforcement officials the opportunity to close the clinic before the 1879 law had actually been violated. He wanted no more delays in mounting a constitutional test of the old law. Ten contraceptive examinations and consultations took place on the evening of November 1 at the PPLC facility. They occurred without any unusual or disruptive incidents.

At the press conference on November 2, Estelle Griswold and PPLC president Lucia Parks informed the several dozen reporters in attendance that the New Haven clinic had in fact begun providing contraceptive services to married women, in violation of Connecticut state law. The gauntlet had been dropped. Fowler Harper told a reporter: "I think it would be a state and community service if a criminal action were brought. I think citizens and doctors alike are entitled to know if they are violating the law."

The occasion for enforcing the 1879 law was provided by a complaint filed by James G. Morris, the night manager of a New Haven rental car agency and Catholic father of five. Morris was incensed after reading about the clinic's opening in the New Haven papers. He felt that contraception was a sin and wanted to see the 1879 law enforced to the letter. Morris filed a complaint on Friday, November 3, with the circuit court prosecutor, Julius Maretz. Morris's complaint alleged that the facility at 79 Trumbull was "passing out immoral literature and breaking the law." He also compared the clinic to a house of prostitution. The next morning, Morris was quoted in the *New York Herald Tribune* as asserting that "every moment the clinic stays open another child is not born." He vowed that "[e]very time they try to open a birth-control clinic, I will force its closing, as long as the [Connecticut anticontraceptive] law is on the books." Morris's over-the-top rhetoric made him a perfect foil for the staid Connecticut birth control movement. One PPLC officer mentioned almost gleefully, "[h]e fell right into our laps."

Like state's attorney Bill Fitzgerald many years before, Maretz did not have much sympathy for the 1879 law. But he felt duty-bound to enforce it. Shortly after speaking with James Morris and agreeing to act on his complaint, Maretz met with the New Haven captain of detectives to request a police investigation of the PPLC clinic at 79 Trumbull. The captain complied with Maretz's request, assigning detectives John Blazi and Harold Berg to the case. That same afternoon the two detectives walked to the nearby PPLC clinic to commence their investigation.

Detectives Blazi and Berg arrived at the clinic while another round of contraceptive consultations was taking place. They were greeted by Estelle Griswold. She appeared to the two detectives to be positively delighted by their visit. Griswold had, in fact, been preparing for this confrontation ever since she assumed the executive directorship of the PPLC in 1953; it was to become one of the high points of her life. For almost two hours, she answered all the detectives' questions, explained clinic procedures, and cheerfully provided copies of the clinic's recently prepared literature. She acknowledged to the detectives that she was aware that she and other clinic personnel were violating the Connecticut anticontraception law. She indicated that her purpose in doing so was to test the law's constitutionality, if possible before the U.S. Supreme Court. While the "investigation" was taking place, Lee Buxton arrived at 79 Trumbull. He joined the discussion and proceeded to corroborate the statements about the clinic's operation that had been proffered by Griswold. He also indicated to the police detectives that although the clinic was staffed by a number of volunteer medical personnel and social workers, only Mrs. Griswold and he, as directors, were responsible for the clinic's operation.

No action was taken for a few days to arrest Griswold or to institute proceedings against the PPLC clinic. The physicians at the clinic were even able to conduct two more consultative sessions with married clients the next week. On November 9, after completing his review of the report of the November 3 visits by the two New Haven detectives, prosecutor Maretz instructed Berg and Blazi to return to 79 Trumbull and request the names of two or more women who had received contraceptive advice and materials from the clinic. He hoped that some of the clinic's clients would voluntarily allow their medical records to be used to test the 1879 law's constitutionality. This co-operation would make unnecessary any legal struggle over patient confidentiality. When presented with this suggestion, Griswold readily agreed to attempt to identify women who would cooperate with the police, provided that the women would not be singled out for personal prosecution under the old statute.

Griswold was successful in finding two clients of the Center willing to allow release of their medical records to state prosecutors. One was Joan Bates Forsberg, a Yale Divinity School graduate in her early thirties and the mother of three children. The other was Rosemary Stevens, a graduate student in Yale's Public Health School and the wife of a Yale Law School professor, Robert Stevens. Forsberg had visited the clinic and had been prescribed a supply of sixty of the recently government-approved antiovulation pills. Stevens, who had also had a consultation with the PPLC medical staff, had been prescribed a tube of Ortho-Gynol contraceptive jelly. Both women gave statements to the detectives regarding their reasons for wishing to practice birth control and as to their experiences at the New Haven clinic. They also indicated that they had both begun using the contraceptive materials prescribed by Dr. Buxton and his staff. Finally, for evidence to be used by the prosecution, Forsberg and Stevens provided to Maretz some of the unused birth control materials that had been prescribed to them at the clinic. A third woman, Marie Wilson Tindall, was also asked by the PPLC to cooperate with the prosecutors. Mrs. Tindall, a thirty-seven-year-old married African American woman, agreed to do so. She too gave a statement to the detectives and relinquished for evidence her diaphragm and a partially used tube of contraceptive jelly.

On Friday, November 10, Julius Maretz issued arrest warrants for Estelle Griswold and Lee Buxton that had been signed by state circuit court Judge J. Robert Lacey. The warrants alleged that Griswold and

Buxton, in defiance of Sections 53–32 and 54–196 of the Connecticut statutes (the recently codified sections of the 1879 anticontraception statute), "did assist, abet, counsel, cause and command certain married women to use a drug, medicinal article and instrument, for the purpose of preventing conception." No warrants were issued for any other PPLC personnel or for any clients of the clinic. Maretz asked Griswold and Buxton, through their attorney, to essentially write their own script for the arrest: Did they want to be apprehended by a large contingent of police and taken to police headquarters in a patrol wagon, with newspaper photographers in attendance to record their "perp walk"? Or did they just prefer to turn themselves in quietly that afternoon? On the advice of Roraback, Griswold and Buxton opted for the latter scenario. Joking that they had blown their one chance to ride in a patrol wagon, Griswold and Buxton appeared at police headquarters at the agreed-on time and were booked for the crimes specified in the warrants. Continuing the congenial spirit of the earlier questioning, during the arrest and booking, neither of the accused was required to sit for mug shots or be fingerprinted. Griswold had dressed for her arrest as she would have accoutered herself for church or a wedding. After paying a $100 bond each, Griswold and Buxton were released on their own recognizance pending an initial court appearance near the end of the month.

After the arrest of Griswold and Buxton, Harper advised the PPLC to discontinue birth control services and close the New Haven clinic. Harper did not want the clinic to face harassment from the public or intimidation from the state until the constitutional issue in the case had been settled. This meant that scores of women who had wanted to obtain birth control through the low-cost Connecticut clinic were disappointed. About two hundred clients — including those who had already visited the clinic and those whose appointments had been canceled — were mailed a letter from the PPLC listing seven contraception products and where these products could be found, mainly in local drug stores and supermarkets. The letter also provided the addresses and phone numbers of Planned Parenthood clinics in the neighboring states of New York and Rhode Island.

The original complainant, James Morris, angry that only two PPLC personnel had been arrested, told reporters: "I think that a Planned Parenthood Center is like a house of prostitution. It is against the natural law, which says marital relations are for procreation and not entertainment." By contrast, Cass Canfield, chairman of the PPFA, labeled the closing of the clinic as an "absurdity." Canfield informed the press that Connecticut "has apparently decided to ignore the clear implication of the Supreme Court decision when it stated that the law has . . . become a nullity." Canfield called on those who supported the right of couples to be able to practice family planning to offer public support to Griswold and Buxton "so that this ignominious law can be given the final interment it has so long deserved."

Connecticut Circuit Judge J. Robert Lacey set November 24 as the date for an initial hearing of Griswold and Buxton for violating the anticontraception statute. That proceeding lasted only a few minutes. Both Griswold and Buxton pled not guilty. Catherine Roraback filed what had become the PPLC's customary demurrer, arguing that the 1879 anticontraception law denied Griswold and Buxton their constitutional rights of liberty under the Fourteenth Amendment. Judge Lacey accorded both sides until December 8 to prepare trial briefs and ready their cases for adjudication in open court. Thus, after a hiatus of more than twenty years, another Connecticut contraception clinic was going to have a chance to argue in a court of law for its right to exist.

———

Going Through the Motions

The central argument in the trial brief prepared by Catherine Roraback was the familiar contention that the 1879 anticontraception law violated her clients' right to privacy as protected by the due process clause of the Fourteenth Amendment to the U.S. Constitution. After the analysis of Justice Harlan's dissent in *Poe v. Ullman*, Roraback declared that the contested Connecticut law breached "the most sacred area of family" and resulted in an "extreme invasion of the privacy of the marital relation." In addition, as recommended to her by lawyers of the PPFA, Roraback presented a First Amendment argument. The gist of this claim was that the language of the abetting portion of the statute violated the First Amendment freedom of expression of Mrs. Griswold and Dr. Buxton. Whereas the trial brief submitted by Roraback ran to over twenty pages, the responding trial brief filed by Julius Maretz was only three pages in length. Maretz's document simply directed Judge Lacey's attention to the previous Connecticut state supreme court decisions upholding the statutory ban on birth control in the state. Then, of course, he cited the U.S. Supreme Court rulings in *Nelson, Tileston,* and *Poe* that failed to disturb the Connecticut Supreme Court's birth control decisions.

On December 8, 1961, the two attorneys appeared before Judge Lacey and made their arguments on the defense's demurrer. Roraback delivered her presentation first, stressing the familiar privacy argument. Then she asserted that the courts of Connecticut should not be tied to the letter of a nineteenth-century law that was no longer relevant "to current circumstances and situations." For the first time in open court, Roraback raised the argument that the 1879 law violated the freedom of speech of Dr. Buxton by criminalizing any medical advice that he might render to patients on the practice of birth control.

Maretz, in response, argued that state officials were duty bound to enforce the anticontraception law as written, regardless of when or under what conditions it was enacted. He noted that the 1959 Connecticut Supreme Court decision in *Poe v. Ullman* was unanimous in upholding the law's constitutionality. Maretz posed the rhetorical question: What better evidence of "current circumstances and situations" is there for Judge Lacey to take note than a two-year-old unanimous opinion of Connecticut's highest court?

On December 20, Judge Lacey filed a brief written opinion denying the Roraback's demurrer. The judge ruled that the statute under which Mrs. Griswold and Dr. Buxton were prosecuted was a "proper exercise of the police power of the state and did not invade rights guaranteed by the Fourteenth Amendment to the Constitution of the United States." He noted that Connecticut's highest court had rejected the Fourteenth Amendment challenge to the 1879 statute on four prior occasions and that he felt bound by the rule of stare decisis (the doctrine of adhering to legal precedents) not to depart from the Connecticut rulings in *State v. Nelson* (1940) *Tileston v. Ullman* (1942), *Poe v. Ullman* (1959), and *Trubek v. Ullman* (1960). In addition, Judge Lacey submitted that the birth control counseling of Dr. Buxton and the medical staff at the New Haven clinic did not warrant the protection of the First Amendment to the U.S. Constitution or parallel guarantees of the Connecticut constitution. His argument here was that free expression protected by the federal and state constitutions is not an absolute right; it must be balanced with the interests of the state. By contrast, the Connecticut statute that prohibits the aiding or abetting in the procurement of contraceptives is, according to Judge Lacey, "one of complete suppression and absolute prohibition. It admits of no exception." Having disposed of the defense's constitutional objections, Judge Lacey scheduled a bench trial of Griswold and Buxton for January 2, 1962, to see if they had in fact violated the 1879 anticontraception law.

Their Day in Court

On the appointed morning, about a hundred spectators joined the litigants and court personnel for the trial of "State of Connecticut v. Estelle T. Griswold and C. Lee Buxton." For the most part, the trial, which lasted about six hours, unfolded with few surprises or moments of tension. Maretz called John Blazi and Harold Berg as the state's first two witnesses to testify regarding the November 3 "raid" on the PPLC birth control clinic. The two detectives described their conversations with Mrs. Griswold concerning the operation of the clinic, and Maretz entered into evidence the family planning literature that Griswold had voluntarily provided.

Blazi and Berg were followed to the stand by the three married women — Joan Forsberg, Marie Tindall, and Rosemary Stevens — who had been willing to waive their rights of medical confidentiality in order to test the constitutionality of the 1879 anticontraception law. Along with the testimony of the three cooperative clients, some of the three women's unused birth control pills and other contraceptive materials were entered into evidence. Roraback made little attempt in her brief cross-examinations to bring into question any of the testimony offered by the prosecution witnesses. After Rosemary Stevens was excused from the stand, the state rested.

The first defense witness was Estelle Griswold. The opportunity to appear in open court in defense of birth control was something that she had been waiting to do for years. Led in her testimony by Roraback's sympathetic questions, Griswold offered a lengthy description of the operation of the clinic at 79 Trumbull. She also testified that she believed strongly that medically prescribed methods of birth control should be made available in facilities such as the Planned Parenthood Center of New Haven to married women "in order that they might protect their health as mothers, the emotional and economic stability of their families, and promote responsible motherhood." Despite Maretz's objections to many of Roraback's questions, most of Griswold's testimony was allowed into evidence. Griswold's arrest and prosecution presented the government with a bit of a dilemma: if the 1879 law was a "harmless empty shadow" — as Justice Frankfurter had maintained in his *Poe* opinion in 1961— how could Griswold face punishment under such a law?

Dr. Buxton was the next defense witness. In his capacity as medical director of the Center, Buxton testified that he had indeed counseled married women on birth control and made contraceptive prescriptions in line with this advice. He stated that, in his judgment as an expert on obstetrics and gynecology, the practice of birth control was occasionally necessary to preserve the lives and health of women with certain medical conditions, for example, hypertensive cardiovascular heart disease. He also testified as to the degree of acceptance of birth control in America at that time, noting that advice to married couples on the use of contraception had become a commonplace of medical practice in the country.

Roraback also called two New Haven physicians not attached to the PPCL clinic to reinforce Buxton's testimony. They were both asked the following questions: (1) Is it accepted medical practice in the state of Connecticut for a physician to recommend the practice of birth control to a married woman suffering from certain medical conditions? and (2) is it accepted medical practice in the state of Connecticut for a physician to recommend the practice of birth control to a married woman for the purpose of planning her family or spacing her children? Maretz objected to these questions on the grounds that the answers were not relevant or material to the factual issue of whether the sections of the statute in question were violated by Estelle Griswold and Lee Buxton. These objections were sustained.

The only bizarre moment in the trial occurred when James Morris, the man who had first complained to the prosecutor about the New Haven clinic, stood up, waved his arms and began to speak in a loud voice. Judge Lacey admonished him to be still and not interrupt the trial. When Morris refused to comply, Lacey had him removed from the courtroom.

In her closing remarks, Roraback stressed that a physician's adherence to the nineteenth-century Connecticut anticontraception statute flew in the face of the best current medical advice to married women. She hinted that her constitutional arguments would be the basis of an appeal, should Judge Lacey rule against her clients. Maretz, by contrast, maintained that, in charging Griswold and Buxton, he was only performing his duty under the law to prosecute lawbreakers. In his view, if the defendants' arguments in support of birth control had any merit, they should be addressed to the state assembly rather than to the courts of the state.

To no one's surprise, Judge Lacey found Griswold and Buxton guilty of the charges under Sections 53–32 and 54–196 of the General Statutes of the State of Connecticut "in that they did assist, abet, counsel, cause and command certain married women to use a drug, medical article and instrument for the purpose of preventing conception." He imposed a fine of $100 on each defendant.

Spinning the Wheels of Justice

Less than two weeks after Judge Lacey's ruling, the PPLC filed an official appeal with the Appellate Division of the Sixth Connecticut Circuit Court. The judge's speed in passing judgment in the New Haven contraception case was more than offset by the time it took him to dispatch a routine posttrial matter. In Connecticut law, before a party can appeal a judge's ruling in a bench trial to a state appellate court, the trial judge must issue written findings. These include the judge's determination of the facts as gleaned from the evidence presented at the trial, his conclusions from those facts, and his rulings on the testimony and evidence. Normally a simple matter, Lacey failed to publish his findings for over five months. Finally, in a statement dated June 12, 1962, Lacey published the necessary findings.

Judge Lacey listed twenty-four separate factual findings. Drawn mainly from statements made by witnesses at the trial and exhibits presented to reinforce or clarify the testimony, these findings were unremarkable. The judge followed with ten conclusions. Among these was his determination that the three married clients of the Center who had cooperated with prosecutors were found to have been in violation of Section 53–32, the contraceptive "use" section of the General Statutes of Connecticut. Although the state did not elect to prosecute the married women who provided testimony, for the judge to name them officially as lawbreakers must have been disconcerting to the three of them. The next section of the findings concerned three rulings that Judge Lacey made at the trial, sustaining objections by the prosecution to questions put by the defense attorney to Detective Harold Berg and the two non-PPLC physicians.

The final section of the findings consisted of Judge Lacey's decisions on various points of law — fourteen in number — raised by Catherine Roraback. The most important of these was his conclusion that the Section 53–32 does not exempt married women from coverage. Roraback had argued on behalf of Griswold and Buxton that neither of her clients could be convicted under the abetting statute if no crime had been committed by the three married women who testified at the trial that they had used contraceptives. But Lacey concluded that the use statute did not exclude married women, thus denying the defense's argument that married women possessed a right of privacy under the Fourteenth Amendment to the U.S. Constitution. Consequently, the Judge ruled, Griswold and Buxton could be prosecuted under Section 54–196 for helping these married women to procure illegal materials and devices — namely, contraceptives — because their actions did not constitute protected free expression under the First Amendment to the U.S. Constitution or Sections 5 and 6 of the Connecticut Constitution, or protected private behavior under the language of the Fourteenth Amendment to the U.S. Constitution.

Roraback and the PPLC quickly sought a hearing before the appellate division of the state circuit court. Building on the research of Fowler Harper, Roraback's appellate brief once again tracked the constitutional privacy arguments of Justice Harlan in *Poe* and contended that Judge Lacey had erred in overruling the demurrers that she and her associate counsel had raised. Disagreeing with Lacey's conclusions, she stressed at several places in her brief that a right of marital privacy should exempt married women from the Connecticut statute's absolute bar on contraceptive use. As a consequence, again in opposition to the conclusions of Lacey, she maintained that those counseling and prescribing contraceptives to married women, such as Mrs. Griswold or Dr. Buxton, should also be protected by a right to privacy as well as the right to freedom of expression.

Oral argument before a three-judge appellate panel took place on October 19. One of the arguments that Roraback presented before the assembled justices was that, whatever the purpose of the old anti-contraception statute at the time it was passed, it was difficult to find a contemporary purpose for the law. Joseph Clark, who replaced Julius Maretz in making the case for the state of Connecticut, claimed that it was up to the legislature, not the courts, to change a law such as this if it no longer served a purpose. By contrast, Clark pointed out that the Connecticut assembly had many times in the last forty years considered repeal or modification of the 1879 law, and, for whatever reason, it had decided to keep the law as written on its books. The state supreme court, he concluded, should defer to the assembly's continuously expressed preference not to change the nineteenth-century law.

In the interim between the oral argument and the decision by the Appellate Division of the state circuit court, a lengthy essay on birth control — marking the fiftieth anniversary of the opening of Margaret Sanger's first birth control clinic in New York City — appeared in the *New York Times*. One finding reported in the article was that at this time (late 1962) more than 75 percent of all married couples had practiced or would practice one form or another of birth control at some point in their married lives. After pointing out some of the vagaries of state law (for example, in Maryland in 1960 it was illegal to sell contraceptives in slot machines — except in places "where alcoholic beverages are sold for consumption on the premises"), the article concluded that only in Massachusetts and Connecticut "is there serious interference with birth control or family-planning activities." The *Times* article attributed the resistance to birth control in Massachusetts and Connecticut to the continuing strong influence of the Catholic Church in those states. The article found it ironic that it was Protestant crusaders and Protestant legislative majorities that were successful in restricting, even banning, birth control in the nineteenth century but that by 1960 it was Roman Catholics who were most resistant to the repeal of such old laws.

In mid-December 1962, Lee Buxton had grown tired of waiting for the decision of the Appellate Division. He expressed his frustration to a reporter: "If the medical profession were as desultory as lawyers, most of our cases would be dead by this time." At last, on January 7, 1963, the Appellate Division panel released a unanimous opinion upholding the convictions of Estelle Griswold and Lee Buxton. The three-member court, in an opinion written by Judge Bernard Kosicki, refused to depart from the early Connecticut Supreme Court contraception decisions dating back to *State v. Nelson*. The appellate court then ruled that it was not necessary for the three married women testifying at the trial to be convicted or even prosecuted under the use statute for defendants Estelle Griswold and Lee Buxton to be convicted themselves of abetting illegal behavior. The court concluded that the test for determining guilt in such a circumstance is "whether one charged as an accessory shared in the unlawful purpose and knowingly and willfully assisted the perpetrator in the acts which prepared for, facilitated or consummated the offense." The necessary proof of the violation of the use statute, the appeals court emphasized, was not coerced but voluntarily provided to the prosecution by Forsberg, Stevens, and Tindall. Regarding the free expression argument raised by Roraback, Judge Kosicki maintained that "there can be no practical separation of facts to divide the acts of prescribing and furnishing the contraceptive materials and the words and speech accompanying such acts, both were part of the practice of medicine which, to the extent inhibited by the statute in question, must yield to the police power of the state."

After declaring that a court should not argue with the "wisdom or unwisdom" in legislation unless it is "plainly violative of some constitutional mandate and admit of no other reasonable construction," the appellate panel identified the promotion of population growth as a reasonable motivation for the 1879 legislative enactment. The court stated that a society possesses a "primordial right to its continued existence" and may responsibly act by statute to deter "practices that tend to negate its survival." Whether this was a correct assessment of the legislative intent behind a now eighty-five-year-old statute was one thing, but that sentiment seemed decidedly out of step with responsible medical and scientific opinion in 1963. A report of the National Institutes of Health had just recommended a substantial increase in government support for birth control research in order to address the looming threat of world overpopulation that, at that time, was adding about 50 million people to the planet yearly. Clearly, times had changed since Anthony Comstock was patrolling the slums and red light districts of New York City in the early 1870s.

As displeasing as this opinion was to the PPLC, at least the appeals panel did not follow Judge Lacey's dilatory tactics: it promptly certified the PPLC's constitutional claims to the Connecticut Supreme Court of Errors. Within a few weeks, Roraback had filed the necessary papers for an appeal to the state's highest court. On February 19, 1963, the justices of the state Supreme Court granted the PPLC petition for certification on all the constitutional questions raised in the appeal.

While waiting for oral argument before the state Supreme Court, the attention of those interested in contraceptive policy turned briefly to the state legislature's handling of yet another repeal bill. The 1963 version received committee endorsement and passed the state house of representatives by vote of 149–66. However, the legislature's Public Health and Safety Committee recommended no action on the bill until a ruling on the PPLC's New Haven appeal was issued by the state supreme court. One observer of the legislative scene in Connecticut had this to say about the battle over birth control: "They go through this pattern every two years. The . . . [repeal] bill is approved in the House, but it is returned by the Senate to committee, from which it never emerges." This prediction once again held true. The 1963 repeal bill never reached the floor of the state senate. The Catholic-dominated legislature succeeded in once again standing in the way of the wishes of a majority of Connecticut's adult voters. In the backwash of the legislative defeat of the repeal bill, the *New York Times* editorialized: "The people of Connecticut — all of them — deserve to have their natural and civil rights respected by removing the 1879 [anticontraception] law from the books."

Another Predictable State Supreme Court Decision

Connecticut state legislators were not the only group tiring of defending the nineteenth-century anticontraception statute. In the face of the PPLC challenge to the 1879 law about to come before the state Supreme Court, the Roman Catholic Church seemed to be losing its passion for attacking birth control. In the spring of 1963, Boston Archbishop Richard Cardinal Cushing commented in the course of a radio interview that the Catholic Church was no longer willing to argue in favor of anticontraception statutes such as those still on the books in Connecticut and Massachusetts. If another legislative effort or referendum on birth control were to be mounted in Massachusetts, Cardinal Cushing declared, the church would explain its position "but not . . . go out campaigning." This perspective was shared by former Connecticut state senator and diocesan lobbyist Joseph R. Cooney, who attended some of the legislative hearings on the 1963 repeal bill. When given the opportunity to speak in opposition to the bill, he was conspicuously silent. He later told reporters that the matter was now in the hands of the courts.

Just as the PPLC prepared for its appearance before the state supreme court, Estelle Griswold's leadership as League executive director came under fire. During the previous year the PPLC had purchased and begun expensive renovations for its administrative offices at a property at 406 Orange Street in New Haven, close to the 79 Trumbull Street property and near the Griswold home. Already upset at the remodeling expenses on the Orange Street property, some board members were further disturbed by Griswold's suggestion that she and her husband be given the opportunity to purchase the un-attached carriage house at the rear of the Orange Street lot and use that as their principal residence. Estelle's husband, Dick, had an advanced case of emphysema and found it difficult to climb the stairs in their large home on Trumbull Street. So the idea of a smaller house close to the new PPLC offices appealed to both Griswolds. Some members of the board, however, were not comfortable with the prospect of a sweetheart property deal to benefit the League's highest-paid employee. In addition, personal feelings about Estelle Griswold's "aggressive" and "stubborn" leadership style, never far below the surface, bubbled forth during this tiff. Hurt by the criticism and what she perceived as lack of support from the League's board, Griswold tendered her resignation in a formal letter to League president Lucia Parks. Griswold's letter triggered a fervent defense of her abilities, if not her style, from many members of the League. Griswold was eventually talked into withdrawing her resignation, and she and her husband prudently abandoned the notion of the carriage house purchase. The figurative scars, however, that Griswold felt she incurred from this controversy would never quite fade.

While this contretemps within the PPLC leadership was evolving, the work of the lawyers in the test of the constitutionality of the 1879 anticontraception statute continued without apparent interruption. Besides stressing the Fourteenth Amendment privacy arguments that had been advanced by Justice Harlan in his *Poe* dissent, Roraback took note of the points raised by Justice Douglas, also dissenting in *Poe*, and the views presented by law professor Norman Redlich, on the Ninth Amendment as a possible source for the right of privacy. By the end of the summer of 1963, Roraback had produced a more than sixty-page document. She submitted a draft of her brief to the PPFA attorneys. In the past, the PPFA had been critical of Roraback's ability to marshal the proper constitutional arguments to challenge the old anticontraception statute. On this occasion, however, they were complimentary of her work.

The brief of the state of Connecticut was prepared by Joseph Clark. In a document only one-third the size of Roraback's, Clark once again rested his argument on Connecticut precedent. The legislature of the state had considered and rejected dozens of bills to repeal the ban on contraception or install a doctors' exception to the 1879 anti–birth control law. In addition, in *Nelson*, *Tileston*, and *Poe* the state's highest court had affirmed the law's constitutionality. Citing judicial deference to clear legislative intention as an honorable principle of jurisprudence, Clark saw no reason for the Supreme Court of Errors to reverse the consistent line of its birth control decisions and thus urged them to stay the course in the current appeal.

Oral argument was held before the Connecticut Supreme Court of Errors for a little over two hours on November 12, 1963. The most important new member of the state court since the PPLC's last time in its chambers was the new chief justice, John W. King, who had taken the center seat a few months earlier. In making her presentation to the court, Roraback pointed to several recent U.S. Supreme Court decisions that had begun to recognize an emerging right of privacy. However, as she begun emphasizing the importance of privacy in the marital relationship as necessary to allow couples to plan the birth of their children, Chief Justice King asked her whether she believed the 1879 law "swept too broadly" by failing to distinguish between married and unmarried individuals. Roraback readily agreed with the Chief Justice on this point.

King prodded Joe Clark even more insistently on the overbreadth issue. The chief justice said that he could understand a legislature, interested in promoting population growth, wanting to discourage the practice of birth control. He also maintained that he could understand a legislature intent on discouraging fornication and adultery banning the use of contraceptives among unmarried individuals. But, he challenged Clark, what moral benefit accrues from keeping contraceptives out of the possession of married couples? Then he raised the touchy issue of enforcement: Would the state engage (or had it already engaged) in policing the sexual habits of married couples under the statute? Clark tried to avoid this question by declaring that the state had not and would not be conducting raids on marital bedrooms. King also challenged Clark on the overbreadth matter. Clark's response to this concern was that the statute did not sweep in a broad, indiscriminate fashion: married couples, just as unmarried individuals, could abstain from sexual activity.

Shortly after the oral argument before the state Supreme Court, the PPLC opened a "birth control information center" at their new offices at 406 Orange Street. The center only handed out pro–birth control literature; it did not function as a clinic. Nevertheless, it attracted the attention of James Morris. Mounting a one-man protest, Morris picketed in front of the PPLC center long enough to have his picture taken by a newspaper photographer. In the Associated Press photograph that appeared in many papers on December 10, 1963, Morris held a picket sign in one hand that read "The Law is the Law, or is it? Morality is in danger!" In the other hand he held a rosary.

The written decision of the Connecticut Supreme Court in the matter of *Connecticut v. Griswold and Buxton* was finally announced on April 28, 1964, almost six months after the oral argument in the case. Given the short and uncomplicated unanimous opinion that the state supreme court issued, the principals and their attorneys found it hard to explain why it took the justices so long to put their words down on paper. The opinion, written by Justice John M. Comley, made clear that both sides acknowledged that Mrs. Griswold and Dr. Buxton violated the use and abetting subsections of the 1879 statute. Then the court declared that "every attack now made on the statute . . . has been made and rejected" in one or more of the previous Connecticut birth control decisions: *State v. Nelson* (1940), *Tileston v. Ullman* (1942), *Buxton v. Ullman* (1959), or *Trubek v. Ullman* (1960). One issue considered by the Connecticut Supreme Court in its 1964 opinion was "whether or not in the light of the facts in this case, the current developments in medical, social and religious thought . . . and the present conditions of American and Connecticut life, modification of the prior opinions of this Court might not 'serve justice better.' " The court answered this query in the negative. Thus the highest court of the Nutmeg State found that the old anticontraception law had survived all of the legal challenges raised by the litigants, including the constitutional claim of the right of privacy.

The Connecticut high court decision in April 1964 was, of course, yet another disappointment to the forces in the country that favored the emerging right to privacy and an expansion of the opportunities for birth control. But the Connecticut activists, as well as the national PPFA, realized that the Connecticut state supreme court was very unlikely to disrupt its own clear line of cases. Hope for the PPLC had always rested with the U.S. Supreme Court. Now that all the preliminary possibilities of redress had been exhausted, Roraback and her associates could finally take their case to where it stood a real chance of success.

The excitement that accompanied an appeal to the nation's highest court was tempered in 1964 by serious health crises of two important players in the drama. Richard Griswold's long-standing emphysema was getting worse. In March 1964, he had undergone major surgery that, it turned out, would only buy him a few more months of life. In addition, Fowler Harper, who had been advising Roraback for months in the preparation of the challenge to the 1879 anticontraception law, began treatment for prostate cancer. On these somber notes, the PPLC commenced the laborious preparations of an appeal to the U.S. Supreme Court.

CHAPTER 6

Attracting the Attention of the Supreme Court

Appealing for Jurisdiction

Despite his deteriorating health, Fowler Harper was more experienced in constructing appellate arguments than Catherine Roraback. Hence, he took the principal role in seeking to persuade the U.S. Supreme Court to hear the appeal from Estelle Griswold and Lee Buxton. The task before him was to convince the nation's highest court to take "probable jurisdiction" of his clients' appeal, which sought to overturn the decision of the Connecticut Supreme Court of Errors that had found them guilty of violating the 1879 anticontraception law. Under federal law — Title 28 U.S. Code, Section 1257 — a party to a dispute may seek U.S. Supreme Court review of a final judgment rendered by the highest court of state "where the validity of a statute of any State is drawn in question on the ground of its being repugnant to the Constitution . . . of the United States, or where any . . . right, privilege, or immunity . . . is specially set up or claimed under the Constitution . . . of . . . the United States."

On the face of things, it seemed clear to Harper and the Planned Parenthood League of Connecticut (PPLC) that Griswold and Buxton had just been involved in exactly the kind of dispute that fell under the terms of Section 1257 and that their appeal should be accepted for a full hearing by the U.S. Supreme Court. On July 22, 1964, he filed a Notice of Appeal to the U.S. Supreme Court under Section 1257. In his short statement he indicated which Connecticut statutes were at issue (Sections 53–32 and 54–196) and which provisions of the U.S. Constitution (Amendments One, Four, Nine, and Fourteen) that his clients had invoked in the Connecticut courts. Then he set to work on yet another legal brief. After toiling a good part of the summer, Harper filed a nineteen-page document with the clerk of the Supreme Court on September 14.

Harper's brief began with the assertion that there are "substantial federal questions involved" and thus the appeal was authorized under Section 1257. The questions presented pertained to whether Section 54–196 of the General Statutes of Connecticut (the "abetting" statute) deprived his clients — now referred to as "the appellants" — of their liberty without due process of law contrary to the Fourteenth Amendment of the U.S. Constitution and also denied their right of free expression on the subject of birth control in violation of the First and Fourteenth Amendments of the federal Constitution. In addition, he maintained that the case also presented the question of whether 53–32 (the "use" statute) denied the appellants and the married clients of the Planned Parenthood Center of New Haven of their right to privacy as protected by the Fourth, Ninth, and Fourteenth Amendments to the Constitution. Later in the brief, Harper would maintain that these "fundamental questions of personal liberty and property rights . . . [had] never been passed upon by this Court."

Harper then proceeded to summarize the facts of the case. After noting that his clients had been arrested for violating the stipulated sections of the Connecticut statutes, he adroitly pointed out that the married women served by the Planned Parenthood Center were exactly the women of lower socioeconomic status whom Justice William Brennan had suggested in his concurring opinion in *Poe v. Ullman* (1961) as most in need of low-cost birth control services.

In support of these contentions, Harper's jurisdictional brief raised several major points. First of all, he argued that the two Connecticut statutes deprived Dr. Buxton of his right to free expression to dispense appropriate medical advice to his patients. He cited a number of First Amendment cases to bolster this point, and he made reference to the presumption of constitutionality that the Supreme Court normally accords to speech, even controversial speech, in the American system of constitutional government. Harper noted that medical experts currently see contraception as necessary for the health of married women with some diseases or conditions, and, in a more general sense, most primary care physicians routinely include information on birth control when counseling healthy married women of childbearing age. He completed this point by stressing the social benefit of birth control in the face of rapidly increasing world population.

Harper also argued in his brief that the Connecticut anticontraception law prevented both Dr. Buxton and Mrs. Griswold from exercising their right to make a living and thus took their "property" without due process of law. What he meant by this is that their advocacy of birth control was restricted unduly (and unconstitutionally) by the Connecticut statutes. Dr. Buxton was prevented by Section 54–196 from advising patients consistent with his scientific and medical training, and Mrs. Griswold, as a paid officer of the PPLC, was unreasonably (and unconstitutionally) restricted in the range of advice that she could render to married women.

Then Harper launched into a complicated constitutional and logical argument linking Griswold and Buxton to the three married women who testified at the January 1962 trial. Although technically guilty of violating Section 53–32 as noted by the intermediate appellate court of Connecticut, Joan Forsberg, Rosemary Stevens, and Marie Tindall were not prosecuted for using contraceptives. But they could have been under Connecticut law. However, if Section 53–32 were held to be unconstitutional as a violation of the right to privacy of the three women, then Griswold and Buxton could not be found guilty of violating the abetting statute, Section 54–196, because they could not be found guilty of being accessories to activities that were not judged to be criminal. One way to establish the innocence of Griswold and Buxton under 54–196 would be for the U.S. Supreme Court to hold that the "use" statute, Section 53–32, was unconstitutional as applied to the women who were prescribed and had used contraceptives. Thus it became necessary for Griswold and Buxton to "assert the constitutional liberties of individuals not party to the litigation," namely, Mrs. Forsberg, Mrs. Stevens, and Mrs. Tindall. This would accomplish two purposes: it would allow the accessory statute to be fully tested for the benefit of Griswold and Buxton, and it would serve as an entree to protect the constitutional rights of Connecticut married women using or wishing to use contraceptive services. In support of the principle that a party to a litigation may assert the constitutional rights of unidentified individuals who are not parties, Harper cited the 1953 U.S. Supreme Court case of *Barrows v. Jackson*, in which a majority of the justices held that the rights of nonwhites in a racially restrictive covenant case could be raised to help establish that injuries were sustained by African Americans who were denied the right to purchase certain properties.

About two-thirds of the way through his brief, Harper finally reached the critical privacy argument. He argued that forbidding the use of contraceptive devices to married women in Connecticut denied these women their liberty and privacy as protected by several amendments to the federal Constitution. He referred to *Meyer v. Nebraska* (1923), which he argued established the freedom "to marry, establish a home, and bring up children." He cited the recent Fourth Amendment Supreme Court decision of *Mapp v. Ohio* (1961) that safeguards the home from unreasonable searches and seizures. He mentioned, without specific reference, Fifth Amendment "privilege against self-incrimination cases" and Third Amendment injunctions against quartering soldiers in private homes during time of peace as part of the right of privacy. And, of course, he cited language about the right to privacy from the dissenting opinions of John Marshall Harlan and William Douglas in *Poe v. Ullman* (1961).

Harper concluded this section of his jurisdictional brief with a discussion of privacy as constituting one of the "rights retained by the people" in the Ninth Amendment, drawing on the analysis of Norman Redlich's 1962 law review article, "Are There Certain Rights . . . Retained by the People?" He quoted with approval Redlich's statement that "[t]he original Constitution and its amendments project through the ages the image of a free and open society" and that the "textual standard" of the open-ended Ninth and Tenth Amendments should be "the entire Constitution." For Harper, then, "the aspects of privacy protected by the First, Third, Fourth and Fifth [Amendments] . . . are comparable to the rights of the married women who sought medical instruction from these appellants."

The brief of the State of Connecticut challenging U.S. Supreme Court jurisdiction in the matter involving Estelle Griswold and Lee Buxton was filed with the Supreme Court on October 1, 1964. It was compiled mainly by Joseph Clark and was much more procedurally grounded than Harper's jurisdictional statement. For example, Clark argued that several of the constitutional arguments advanced by Fowler Harper were not presented in a timely or legally appropriate fashion. According to Clark, some of the arguments were not raised in the initial demurrers and thus could not now, under federal rules, be raised on appeal to the U.S. Supreme Court. Clark was hoping that the Supreme Court would use putative procedural defects to once again avoid a decision on the merits of Connecticut's anticontraception statutes.

Clark's brief also maintained that the regulation, even banning, of birth control was fully within the province of a state legislature's police power. In support of this proposition, he cited state supreme court decisions from Massachusetts, Michigan, New York, Wisconsin, Virginia, Illinois, and New Jersey. Furthermore, if Connecticut legislators, like those in Massachusetts, had wished to write a "physicians' exception" into the state's anticontraception law, they had numerous occasions to do so over the previous half century. The fact that no such exception had yet found its way into Connecticut law was, he submitted, a telling indication of the wishes of the people of that state.

Clark also maintained that there was no important question of federal law presented in the case. The leading precedent he cited was the Massachusetts case of *Commonwealth v. Gardner* (1938). In that decision, the Supreme Judicial Court of Massachusetts held that a nineteenth-century state law banning the use of contraceptives could not be interpreted to include an implicit "health exception" for birth control devices prescribed by physicians. The U.S. Supreme Court's dismissal of the appeal in *Gardner* for "want of a substantial question," Clark argued, should be adhered to by the Court in the Connecticut appeal. In response to Fowler Harper's argument that Griswold and Buxton were denied their right of free expression under the First Amendment, Clark simply responded that it was not speech that led to the appellants' convictions; it was their actions in helping to furnish contraceptive materials to the three women who testified at the trial that occasioned Judge Lacey finding them guilty of violating the 1879 Connecticut law.

Two weeks after the submission of Clark's written motion to dismiss the appeal to the U.S. Supreme Court, Harper filed a very short reply brief. He contested Clark's assertion that critical constitutional claims were not presented in a timely or appropriate fashion. He did this by identifying relevant pages in past PPLC arguments and pleadings before the Connecticut courts.

Taking Jurisdiction

Both the PPLC and the state of Connecticut were fairly certain the U.S. Supreme Court would accept jurisdiction of the appeal. Justices William Brennan, John Marshall Harlan, and William Douglas, in their separate opinions in *Poe v. Ullman*, almost seemed to be begging for a live case or controversy to strike down the Connecticut anti-contraception law. In addition, Justices Felix Frankfurter and Charles E. Whittaker, two members of the majority when *Poe* was decided in 1961, were no longer on the Court. In their place were two appointees of President John F. Kennedy, Byron White and Arthur Goldberg. Tom Emerson, for one, believed that White and Goldberg possessed the sort of judicial flexibility that would be needed to craft, or at least support, a constitutional right of privacy.

In October and November of 1964, the law clerks of the Supreme Court justices culled through thousands of requests for reviewing cases that arrive at the Court each year. Among them was the motion for probable jurisdiction in the Connecticut birth control case from Fowler Harper and the accompanying motion to dismiss from Joseph Clark. One of Chief Justice Warren's law clerks, John Hart Ely, prepared a short memorandum, dated November 23, 1964, for his boss that began with the ominous phrase "Dr. Buxton is back." After tersely summarizing the facts in the case and the arguments of the two parties, Ely concluded: "For me, this is not an easy case on the merits. However, it seems clear that the issues are significant and that probable jurisdiction should be noted." Michael Maney, a clerk for John Marshall Harlan, referred to *Griswold v. Connecticut* as "*Poe* round two" and saw it as the perfect vehicle for writing Harlan's views on privacy into the Constitution. Justice William Douglas's clerk compiled a memorandum on the case for his justice. Regarding the important jurisdictional issue of whether Griswold and Buxton had asserted their constitutional rights in a timely fashion, Douglas's clerk wrote: "It is to be noted that none of the Conn cts [courts] suggest any procedural deficiencies" that would prevent the Court from accepting the appeal in the Connecticut birth control case and reaching a decision on the merits.

On December 3 the nine justices met in a regularly scheduled confidential conference. Among the cases reviewed for full hearing at this time was *Griswold v. Connecticut*. Written tallies kept by several of the justices indicate that the vote in favor of hearing the case was nine to zero. On December 7, the Supreme Court issued the laconic announcement "probable jurisdiction noted" in the case of *Griswold et al. v. Connecticut*. The unanimous vote was not revealed at this time and would only be known years later when the papers of several of the justices serving on the Court in 1964–65 were made available to scholars. The Supreme Court's acceptance of probable jurisdiction meant that the lawyers for the state of Connecticut and the PPLC would need to prepare another series of briefs and, eventually, present themselves for a public oral argument before all nine members of the Court.

At about the time the jurisdictional briefs of Fowler Harper and Joseph Clark were being considered by the Supreme Court, the PPLC was going through a rough patch. Estelle Griswold was once again on the outs with some League board members and individuals in the New Haven branch of the PPLC. Griswold's critics accused her of being stubborn and not being able to work with those who disagreed with her. Griswold, as was her wont, took the criticisms personally and once again composed a formal letter of resignation as executive director. Lee Buxton, believing that the national organization, the Planned Parenthood Federation of America (PPFA), did not offer sufficient support to Griswold at this critical moment in the history of the birth control movement, tendered his own resignation as chair of the PPLC Medical Advisory Committee. After much hand-wringing and low-level negotiations, peace was restored in the organization and Griswold and Buxton withdrew their letters of resignation.

Then there was the declining health of Fowler Harper. In appreciation for his preparation of the jurisdictional brief and out of compassion for the advance of his cancer, the PPLC in late 1964 voted Harper a gift of several thousand dollars. A proud man, Harper initially contemplated declining the money. But the heap of medical bills piling up on his desk led him eventually to accept what he called a "fee." The effort that Harper devoted to the PPLC jurisdictional brief in the Connecticut birth control case would prove to be the last legal work in his turbulent life. He entered the Grace–New Haven hospital around December 1. During this stay in the hospital, Harper convinced his friend and Yale colleague, Thomas I. Emerson, to share responsibility with Catherine Roraback in carrying the Connecticut birth control case through to conclusion. At Harper's urging, Estelle Griswold wrote an official letter on behalf of the PPLC inviting Emerson to take a leading role in the Supreme Court action. Griswold still held out hope that her old friend would recover, but that was not in the cards. On January 8, 1965, the day after the PPLC executive committee had voted another $2,500 gift to Harper, the League's longtime attorney died of the cancer that had ravaged his system for so many years. He was sixty-seven. The next day's obituaries in the Connecticut and New York papers, besides carrying warm comments about Harper from colleagues and referring to his political radicalism, made prominent mention of his role as a counsel for the PPLC in challenging Connecticut's nineteenth-century anticontraception statute.

Thomas Emerson had received his baccalaureate degree and Phi Beta Kappa key from Yale's undergraduate college; he later graduated from the Yale Law School where he served as the editor in chief of the *Yale Law Journal;* and at the time he took over the *Griswold* appeal, he was Yale's Lines Professor of Law. Emerson had had a varied legal career before 1965. Like Fowler Harper, he had defended communists and other unpopular clients and had worked for many years as a government attorney. Fresh out of law school in 1931, Emerson was a member of the defense team that won a retrial in the historic race relations case of the so-called Scottsboro boys, nine black Alabama teenagers accused of raping two white women. Emerson went to Washington during the New Deal, where he worked as a lawyer for the National Recovery Administration, the National Labor Relations Board, the Social Security Board, and the Office of the Attorney General. During World War II, he was the deputy administrator for enforcement of the Office of Price Administration and general counsel for both the Office of Economic Stabilization and the Office of Mobilization and Reconversion. Emerson had long been an active member of the leftist National Lawyer's Guild, serving as its national president in 1950 and 1951. He had been a member of the law faculty at Yale since the mid-1940s and was the author of a popular law school casebook on civil rights. He was fifty-seven years old at the time that he inherited chief responsibility for the appeal to the Supreme Court of the case of Estelle Griswold and Lee Buxton. Emerson shared Harper's passion for social justice; his argumentative style, however, was much less intense than his predecessor as the lead PPLC attorney. In contrast to Harper, Emerson was better versed in constitutional law, and his personality was better suited to the rarefied atmosphere of appellate argumentation.

Asserting the Rights of Parties Not Present

The Supreme Court brief that Tom Emerson produced on behalf of Estelle Griswold and Lee Buxton was filed with the clerk of the Supreme Court on February 11, 1965. In light of the limited time that Emerson had to get himself up to speed, his brief was remarkably thorough and copiously documented. It began, quite appropriately, with a footnote on its first page to the memory of Fowler Harper: "The authors of this brief wish to record their great and obvious debt to Professor Fowler V. Harper, who worked on this matter up to the time of his death on January 8, 1965." It also benefited from the assistance of Catherine Roraback and received some input from the Planned Parenthood Federation of America and various civil liberties organizations to which it was circulated in draft form. In the main, however, the brief for the appellants bore Emerson's personal stamp as a facile academic legal writer.

In the course of summarizing the previous litigation on the Connecticut anticontraception law, Emerson adroitly pointed out that the two sections of the statute under review did not ban the sale or use of contraceptives if used for the prevention of disease, as opposed to birth control. This would become an important point in Emerson's later analysis of the "reasonableness" of the law. In his preliminary comments, he also indicated that in *Poe v. Ullman* (1961), the Connecticut Supreme Court of Errors and the U.S. Supreme Court had taken "judicial notice" of the fact that "contraceptives are commonly and notoriously sold in Connecticut drug stores." This fact also would figure into Emerson's argumentation. It took the PPLC attorney thirteen pages to dispense with all of the preliminaries. The remaining eighty-three pages consisted of a detailed four-part argument.

Emerson's first major point was that Estelle Griswold and Lee Buxton possessed the legal standing to raise constitutional issues and related questions bearing on the validity of the contested Connecticut

statutes. This had been covered, of course, in Fowler Harper's jurisdictional brief, but Emerson believed — correctly, it turned out — that
his adversary, Joseph Clark, would raise standing issues again in his
Supreme Court brief. It was not only important for the PPLC attorney to argue for the rights of Griswold and Buxton; it was also necessary for him to be able to assert the rights of individuals who were not
direct parties in the litigation but still intimately affected by the operation of the statutes. He had in mind the three married women who
had testified in Judge Lacey's courtroom — Joan Forsberg, Rosemary
Stevens, and Marie Tindall — who had been prescribed contraceptives
by the Planned Parenthood Center of New Haven and had begun to
put them to use. To convincingly demonstrate the arbitrariness of the
old Connecticut statute and how it impinged on the right to privacy,
Emerson believed that he should be permitted to argue that Sections
53–32 and 54–196 had deleterious effects on many married persons in
Connecticut, the three who testified at the trial serving only as a small
sample of such individuals. The brief argued that Connecticut women,
in the normal course of their lives, were faced with the untenable decision of whether to choose artificial forms of birth control and risk prosecution under state law, take their chances with a pregnancy that might
pose grave health risks or be extremely inconvenient, or practice abstinence from sexual intercourse.

One line of reasoning that Emerson used to justify asserting the
rights of unnamed individuals in his defense of Griswold and Buxton
was to argue that the property rights of his clients — a medical director of a birth control clinic and the executive of a center dispensing
contraceptive advice — to give professional advice on birth control
would be infringed it they were not permitted to give that advice to
clients of the Center. Under the due process clause of the Fourteenth
Amendment, Emerson argued that Griswold and Buxton would be
denied property without due process of law if they were kept from
rendering their best professional advice on birth control and, where
dictated, prescribing contraceptives. To make this claim, the counsel
for the appellants thus needed to assert the rights of those who might
wish to receive the advice or the contraceptive materials. Emerson
cited as justification for this point the case of *Pierce v. Society of Sisters*
(1925), in which owners of a private school were permitted to claim
the rights of potential students and their parents.

Emerson cited another education case from the 1920s, *Meyer v. Nebraska* (1923), in support of the proposition that "[w]ithout doubt, [liberty protected by the Fourteenth Amendment] denotes not merely freedom from bodily restraint but also the right of the individual . . . to engage in any of the common occupations of life, . . . to marry, establish a home and bring up children . . . and generally to enjoy those privileges long recognized at common law as essential to the orderly pursuit of happiness by free men." To claim that due process protection, Griswold and Buxton needed also to assert the rights of clients of the center. In a parallel fashion, the counsel for the appellants argued that to test whether the First Amendment freedom of expression of Griswold and Buxton to voice their professional opinions on birth control was violated by the Connecticut anticontraception law required that there must be individuals standing ready to hear and perhaps act on their opinions. In Emerson's words: "appellants . . . may assert the rights of others which affect enjoyment of their own rights." On this point, the appellants' brief also referred to *Barrows v. Jackson* (1953), the racial restrictive covenant case cited in Harper's jurisdictional brief.

Emerson argued further that the close linkage of the two Connecticut statutes being challenged required an assertion of the rights of unnamed parties. The appellants could not have been legally charged with violating the "abetting" statute, Section 54–194, unless some persons were found to have received the advice offered by Griswold and Buxton at the Center and thus were seen to have violated the "use" statute, Section 32–32. This point, the appellants' brief noted, was virtually conceded by the appellees.

Finally, for purposes of standing, Emerson sought to distinguish one of the earlier Connecticut birth control cases, *Tileston v. Ullman* (1943), from the case under consideration. As opposed to Dr. Tileston in the early 1940s, Dr. Buxton in 1965 was not asking for a declaratory judgment on behalf of his patients. Unlike Tileston, Buxton's own liberty was placed at risk by the state's prosecution of him for dispensing birth control advice and prescribing contraceptive articles at an operating clinic. However, to be able to claim his rights, it was necessary to assert the rights of unnamed married women. Emerson sought to walk a fine, even contradictory, line: he acknowledged that the Supreme Court was justified in refusing to take jurisdiction of Dr. Tileston's case twenty-two years earlier because the "real parties" were not before the courts in that litigation. But in the case of Dr. Buxton and Mrs. Griswold, he argued that it was proper to assert the rights of individuals not named in the indictment because it was necessary to do so to permit a full test of the rights of the named appellants.

An "Irrational" Law?

The second major point advanced by Emerson was that the two linked anticontraception statutes denied Griswold and Buxton their rights to liberty and property without due process of law, as guaranteed by the first section of the Fourteenth Amendment. To attempt to establish this position, Emerson presented a long and detailed analysis of why he felt the Connecticut statutes were arbitrary and capricious, and bore no reasonable relationship to a proper legislative purpose, thus denying the litigants due process of law. This proved to be the heart of his brief, running all the way from page 21 through page 78.

The analysis commenced with Emerson's statement of what he believed to be the appropriate standard for establishing due process for laws that concern individual rights. He took it from the majority opinion in *Meyer v. Nebraska* (1923): "[L]iberty may not be interfered with . . . by legislative action which is arbitrary or without reasonable relation to some purpose with the competency of the state to effect." Emerson was quick to emphasize that he was not asking the Court to apply this standard to all cases; he felt it should hold only for cases that concerned fundamental personal liberties. He was, in short, not asking the Court to return to the infamous line of economic regulation cases from the late nineteenth and early twentieth centuries that saw the Supreme Court striking down countless state laws that regulated or restrained commercial enterprises. For a legislative enactment to meet this standard of due process, the intention or purpose of the lawmakers needed to be clearly understood. Emerson contended that the original purpose of those who drafted and voted in favor of the Connecticut anticontraception statute was "shrouded in obscurity." The very vagueness of purpose, Emerson argued, should be itself a good reason for the current Supreme Court to pay minimal attention to the initial legislative judgment. However, Emerson examined in turn each of the possible legislative purposes that had been mentioned by judges in past cases. Not surprisingly, he found none of the alleged legislative purposes so compelling as to overcome the rights of his clients and the thousands of unnamed married couples in Connecticut.

In contemplating any of the possible legislative purposes, Emerson argued, the Court should look to "current circumstances, not those existing in 1879 or earlier in this century." Thus, the argument that the 1879 law was intended as a health measure, to protect men and women against diseases or injuries caused by contraceptives, was no longer relevant — if it ever had been. Practicing birth control in the 1960s was safer than being pregnant or bearing children. What possible medical problems that might occur could be met by government licensing and medical supervision. Likewise, the occasionally heard argument in the late nineteenth and early twentieth centuries that contraception was bad public policy because it retarded population growth no longer had relevance in a world that was reeling from the hardships and social costs of overpopulation. Finally, Emerson addressed the view that the 1879 law served the purpose of restricting sexual intercourse to the propagation of children. Although this was in fact an articulated legislative purpose for Section 53–32 at the time of the statute's enactment, Emerson did not believe it to be compelling even eighty years ago: it is "contrary to the basic drives of man" and a "far-reaching invasion of individual liberty."

It is true that the Connecticut anticontraception law that was enacted in 1879 was part of a general statute banning the distribution of obscene materials. But, just as standards for defining and identifying obscenity had changed in the previous eighty-five years, so had attitudes toward birth control. Few residents of Connecticut in 1965 would consider the use or abetting of contraception to be obscene. In fact, Emerson's brief devoted several pages to the current public support for birth control in the writings of physicians, the attitudes of clergy and religious organizations, and the views of individuals as determined by public opinion polls. Most of the statements quoted by Emerson expressed the view that birth control, besides the obvious consequence of impeding conception, had positive social benefits. He quoted physicians and psychologists to the effect that sexual abstinence in a married person was not physically or psychologically healthy; artificial contraceptive was almost as effective as abstinence and served better in promoting marital happiness. He noted that general public opinion was then strongly supportive of the right and wisdom of marital couples to practice contraception: 81 percent of Americans in a recent Gallup poll agreed with the statement "birth control information should be available to anyone who wants it."

The PPLC brief presented numerous quotations supportive of contraception from all points of the Judeo-Christian religious compass. For all Protestant denominations and Judaism, contraception was permitted, even encouraged. For example, the PPLC brief included this statement on the morality of birth control from the Council for Christian Social Action of the United Church of Christ in 1960: "Responsible family planning is today a clear moral duty. We believe that public law and public institutions should sanction the distribution through authorized channels of reliable information and contraceptive devices. Laws which forbid doctors, social workers and ministers to provide such information and service are infringements of the rights of free citizens and should be removed from the statute books." The "official" Catholic position, Emerson acknowledged, was still that the use of extrinsic aids to prevent conception was morally wrong, but he pointed out that the Catholic Church no longer supported the government prohibition of use of contraceptive devices for those outside the Catholic faith. Emerson's brief quoted Vernon J. Bourke, a Catholic philosopher, to this effect: "a Catholic can justifiably favor repeal of the Connecticut and Massachusetts anti-contraception laws, or breathe happily if they are declared unconstitutional." To further assess the current public opinion on birth control, Emerson surveyed federal, state, and local policy on birth control. He found that various federal programs provided birth control services and that forty-eight of the fifty states had made birth control legal under at least some circumstances.

The final analytical point that Emerson raised under his due process argument was that the 1879 statute failed the "arbitrary and capriciousness" test. This standard amounts to a weighing of benefits against drawbacks. Given the PPLC's belief that the law "cut[s] so deeply into so many facets of individual liberty" and is "so totally irrational in . . . [its] social impact, . . . the burden of proving . . . [the 1879 statute] arbitrary and capricious, even by the most exacting standard,

{ *Griswold v. Connecticut* }

is fully met." Some of the irrational consequences and concomitants of the anticontraception law identified by the PPLC brief included the following: the choice between ill health, even death, and abstinence in a state in which contraception is proscribed; the emotional fears and stress for parents stemming from an unwarranted pregnancy; the denial of the right of married couples to make their own decisions on the most intimate and important aspects of their lives together; the burden of an unwanted child; and the abridgment of the right to practice medicine in conformity with best scientific practices. To Emerson, it was incumbent on the Supreme Court to "weigh Connecticut's invasion of the right to practice medicine according to scientific principles by the strictest of standards, similar to those applied in free speech cases."

The Connecticut statute also appeared irrational to the appellants in relationship to other state laws. For instance, Connecticut was one of many states that permitted the abortion of a fetus to preserve the life of a mother. Abortion, an invasive and socially unpopular course of action, was thus favored by Connecticut state law over that of contraception, a practice that had wide public and religious support. Similarly, compulsory sterilization for some inmates of state asylums was legal and thus also favored over contraception in Connecticut law. In terms of the operation of the anticontraception law, there were additional "irrationalities." Those most susceptible to punishment if the Connecticut "use" statute was actually enforced would be poor women who would need to depend on the public clinics that charged low fees or provided free services; middle- and upper-class women would be able to receive contraceptive advice and prescriptions from their more discreet private physicians. An even more irrational consequence was that the 1879 law operated to keep married women from receiving birth control advice and prescriptions, whereas unmarried men were generally permitted to use condoms for the purpose of preventing disease. In fact, many packages of condoms were readily available in grocery stores and drug stores and clearly marked "for the prevention of disease." In addition, another irrational consequence of Section 53–32 was that by forbidding contraception, the law served to encourage abortion: some women obeying the anticontraception injunction became pregnant and chose the dangerous and morally questionable lure of abortion over bearing an unwanted child.

A putative purpose advanced as a constitutional basis for the nine-teenth-century Connecticut anticontraception law was that the law discouraged sexual intercourse outside of marriage. The logic of this position was that the risk of an unprotected pregnancy served as a deterrent to sexual activity among unmarried individuals. In actuality, the operation of the law, as just noted, supported the use of condoms for the prevention of disease. In addition the widespread availability of condoms in retail stores and the absence of a ban on their adver-tising almost encouraged their use by unmarried individuals. If the 1879 law was intended to discourage sexual activity among unmarried individuals, Emerson argued that it "swept too broadly." Laws then on the Connecticut statute books proscribing adultery, fornication, and "lascivious carriage" were better and more narrowly targeted to enforce morality among unmarried individuals. Emerson concluded his due process analysis with this strong statement: "Seldom has the Court had before it legislation for which the purposes were so obscure or the alleged benefits so ill-founded. And probably never has the Court had before it legislation which touched so drastically and so arbitrarily upon so many fundamental rights of the citizen. Fortu-nately, the law is aberrational."

———

A Template for the Right of Privacy

As powerful and as detailed as was Emerson's due process argument, it would be his third point—that the 1879 anticontraception law vio-lated the right to privacy—that would prove to be the most conse-quential for the Supreme Court and most talked about in the academic legal community. Emerson began his discussion of privacy by announcing what would be the thesis of his argument: "The Con-stitution nowhere refers to a right of privacy in express terms. But var-ious provisions of the Constitution embody separate aspects of it. And the demands of modern life require that the composite of these specific protections be accorded the status of a recognized constitu-tional right."

For Emerson, crafting a constitutional right of privacy began, ap-propriately, with the First Amendment: "Freedom of religion is a key element in any system for maintaining the independence and the dignity of the individual. So also is the right to hold beliefs and opinions without coercion from the state." To illustrate this statement he referred to Justice Robert Jackson's majority opinion in *West Virginia State Board of Education v. Barnette* (1943), in which the Supreme Court struck down a statute requiring that children in the public schools salute the American flag because that law intruded on individual conscience by attempting to dictate orthodoxy in religion and politics. Later in the brief Emerson noted that "associational privacy" under the umbrella of the First Amendment was recently deemed worthy of protection in the race relations case of *NAACP v. Button* (1963). Then Emerson jumped to the Third Amendment, which holds that "No soldier shall, in time of peace be quartered in any house, without the consent of the Owner, nor in time of war, but in a manner to be prescribed by law." According to Emerson's brief, at the time this amendment was drafted, the quartering of soldiers in private homes constituted an "invasion of privacy [that] was one of the chief dangers threatening the personal life of the citizen."

The Fourth Amendment, Emerson then argued, "[u]ndoubtedly [establishes] the most significant constitutional provision directed toward protection of privacy." This amendment was couched in terms of search, seizure, and arrest because those were the "chief manifestations of invasion of privacy under conditions existing when the Bill of Rights was adopted." But for Emerson, the context of threatened personal space was much broader in 1965 than in 1791. To document this point he quoted language from an 1886 Supreme Court decision, *Boyd v. United States*, excoriating law enforcement officials for entering and searching a man's home without legal authorization: "It is not the breaking of his doors, and the rummaging of his drawers that constitutes the essence of the offence; but it is the invasion of his indefeasible right of personal security, personal liberty and private property." Then, not surprisingly, the appellants' brief quoted a passage from Justice Brandeis's famous dissent in *Olmstead v. United States* (1928): "The protection guaranteed by the [Fourth and Fifth] Amendments is much broader in scope. . . . [The Founders] sought to protect Americans in their beliefs, their thoughts, their emotions and their sensations. They conferred, as against the Government, the right to be let alone — the most comprehensive of rights and the right most valued by civilized men." The brief also alluded to the recent search and seizure case of *Mapp v. Ohio* (1961) in which the Court identified the right of privacy as being "no less important than any other right carefully and particularly reserved to the people." In addition, the brief characterized the Fifth Amendment's privilege against self-incrimination as "protect[ing] the conscience and dignity of the individual from all outside forces."

The right of privacy, Emerson continued, is also subsumed within the "certain rights . . . retained by the people" language of the Ninth Amendment. Emerson acknowledged Norman Redlich's contribution to the dialogue on privacy by referring explicitly to his 1962 essay. For Emerson and the PPLC, the "sanctity and privacy" of marriage "involves precisely the kind of right which the Ninth Amendment was intended to secure." Another general privacy argument advanced by the attorneys for Griswold and Buxton involved the incorporation doctrine. As noted by Emerson, the Supreme Court has held since the 1930s that certain key portions of the Bill of Rights were "incorporated" by the due process clause of the Fourteenth Amendment and thus served as protections for the individual vis-à-vis state action as well as against the actions of federal officers. Moreover, Emerson emphasized, the Supreme Court has not limited incorporated rights to specific guarantees of the Bill of Rights: "[T]he due process clause of the Fourteenth Amendment embraces certain additional aspects of liberty not necessarily included in one of the specific provisions of the Bill of Rights." The case that Emerson identified to support this contention was *Rochin v. California* (1952), a decision in which state law enforcement officials broke into a defendant's bedroom and extracted evidence of drug possession by pumping his stomach without his consent. Rather than finding the actions of the police in this case to constitute a violation of the Fourth or Fifth Amendment, the Court held that this law enforcement behavior was incompatible with the "respect for those personal immunities which . . . are 'so rooted in the traditions and conscience of our people as to be ranked as fundamental.'"

Emerson argued further that the emerging constitutional right of privacy was paralleled over the last generation by a growth in the right of privacy in tort law. He noted that legal experts have found hundreds of instances where state courts had ruled in favor of the protection of privacy in tort law. The appellants' brief also cited a 1956 legal treatise on tort law, coedited by Fowler Harper, which highlighted the growth of the tort of privacy in cases involving the sanctity of the home and the preservation of sexual activity within marriage from outside intrusion. Near the end of this section of the appellants' brief, Emerson paid his respects to the dissenting opinions of Douglas and Harlan in *Poe*.

To those who would maintain that it is alarmism to believe that Connecticut authorities would ever enforce the anticontraceptive statutes against married couples, Emerson had this response: "It is no answer to say that the statutes have not been enforced in this way. The vice is that they can be. As long as the statutes are on the books, the fundamental rights of privacy of married couples in Connecticut are threatened." Emerson also addressed the claim that if the anticontraception law should be struck down by the Supreme Court on the ground that it violates a right of privacy, so too should Connecticut statutes that proscribe such private behavior as fornication, adultery, and homosexuality. To this challenge, his response was simple and accurate: "We are not concerned with those statutes here." Emerson, of course, could not predict the future, nor would he live long enough to see the doctrine that would emerge in *Griswold* stretched to protect the privacy of activities that were still scorned in 1965.

The fourth and final point in the appellants' brief was that the Connecticut statutes, *on their face*, violated the freedom of speech of Estelle Griswold and Lee Buxton. Not only would a physician or the executive director of a birth control clinic who renders advice on contraceptives run afoul of Section 54–196. So too, according to Emerson, would a minister counseling a parishioner on family planning or a mother who speaks to her newly married daughter about birth control. The "very breadth and ambiguity" of the "abetting" statute, Emerson argued, served to abridge freedom of expression because it likely inhibited the discussion of family planning that would normally take place in an open society. Furthermore, it was not just speech tied to conduct (for example, a doctor prescribing birth control pills) that could fall under the sweep of the abetting statute. Pure speech such as the handing out of Planned Parenthood literature or the conducting of group orientation sessions at the New Haven Center were also proscribed by the terms of the law. The failure to separate speech cleanly from action, the brief emphasized, placed the abetting statute in constitutional jeopardy on First Amendment grounds.

Supplying Burglar Tools?

Drafts of Tom Emerson's brief in *Griswold* benefited from the careful scrutiny of experienced appellate lawyers from civil liberties groups and the PPFA who were preparing their own amicus curiae briefs in support of the PPLC position in *Griswold*. In addition, Emerson was permitted to review the draft amicus briefs from the four groups who were given permission by the Supreme Court to submit their arguments in support of the PPLC appeal. From these briefs he could and did extract some useful statistics and quotations. In addition, he also had the willing assistance of Catherine Roraback, the young lawyer who, along with Fowler Harper, had been responsible for the PPLC case in the Connecticut courts. By contrast, Joseph Clark, the assistant prosecuting attorney for the appellee (that is, the state of Connecticut), received only occasional advice on procedural matters from an attorney friend, Irwin P. Harrison. Clark's superior, Philip Mancini, Jr., and the now retired former prosecutor, Julius Maretz, were both named on the appellee's brief, but neither offered Clark much help. Clark's final brief was filed with the clerk of the U.S. Supreme Court on March 9, 1965.

At about one-third the length of the Griswold/Buxton brief, Clark's brief for the appellees was heavily procedural in orientation. Clark's brief furnished a useful history of Sections 53–32 and 54–196 from the time of their initial passage to their current incarnation in the General Statutes of Connecticut. This summary revealed that the original 1879 statute had passed virtually unchanged through five major revisions of the statutory code of Connecticut. The summary also noted all the attempts at repeal or modification that had been mounted but failed between 1917 and 1963 (a 1965 repeal bill was pending but would be delayed while the Supreme Court was considering the *Griswold* appeal). In this section of his brief, Clark also asserted that thirty states then had laws regulating contraception. Moreover, it was his assessment that the facts of the Griswold/Buxton case would violate the laws on the books in Massachusetts,

Minnesota, Mississippi, Missouri, Nebraska, and New York, as well as those of Connecticut.

Clark divided the text of the appellee's brief into four sections. The first dealt with the issue of standing. Clark commenced this portion of his argument by citing a number of cases from other states that supported the principle that a litigant cannot attack a statute on the grounds that it violates the rights of third parties. Included in this catalog of decisions was the 1943 Connecticut case of *Tileston v. Ullman*, in which the highest court of Connecticut upheld the constitutionality of the 1879 statute on the ground that Dr. Tileston did not possess the right to raise the rights of patients not named in this complaint. For Clark, this case was controlling. He wrote somewhat sarcastically: "One wonders if the appellants in making . . . [the] distinction between *Tileston* and the instant case have just cynically thrown in a few constitutional issues on behalf of the physician in the hopes of coming out from under the umbrella of *Tileston*." Clark then returned to a procedural argument advanced in his jurisdictional brief, contending once again that the attorneys for the appellants did not file a timely claim that the two sections of the Connecticut general statutes were void on their face or invaded the privacy of Griswold, Buxton, or the married women of the state.

The second and longest section of the state's brief defended the position that Connecticut state attorneys had taken in all the previous birth control cases, namely, that the 1879 law was a proper exercise of the police power of the state. Clark provided case citations to appellate decisions from several states that had concluded that regulation of contraceptives is a "legitimate exercise of the state's police power to regulate public morals." On the two previous occasions in which the U.S. Supreme Court had considered appeals of criminal convictions stemming from the operation of birth control clinics — *Sanger v. People of the State of New York* (1919) and *Gardner v. Commonwealth of Massachusetts* (1938) — the Court had dismissed the cases for "want of a substantial federal question." Clark simply asked the Supreme Court to follow those past decisions.

The third major section of the appellee's brief addressed the question of whether the constitutional rights of the appellants were violated by the Connecticut anticontraception laws. In regard to Dr. Buxton, the PPLC brief had claimed that his right to practice medicine was impaired by Section 54–196, which prohibited him from prescribing contraceptives to married women. By using a rather limited definition of terms, Clark argued that the practice of medicine "is directed to the treatment, cure, and/or prevention of disease." Because none of the women testifying in court were in ill health, issuing prescriptions to them for contraceptives had nothing to do with the practice of medicine. Clark characterized the advice Buxton provided on contraception as "social philosophy [that] must fall before the police power of the state." Clark was even more cavalier in his characterization of the advice offered by Mrs. Griswold. Because she was not a medical doctor, her claim of a right to earn a living by providing information on contraceptive options to married women visiting the New Haven Center was akin to a "claim made by one charged with being a supplier of burglar tools." In response to the argument offered by the appellants' brief that the right of free expression of Griswold and Buxton was violated by the anticontraception law, Clark's response was simple: "It was not the speech of the appellants that caused their conviction. It was their action." He described their action in recommending contraceptives to married women as no more deserving of First Amendment protection than that of a person screaming "fire" in a crowded theater or of someone placing a wager over the telephone.

The fourth and final section of Clark's brief was essentially a potpourri of responses to selected claims made by the appellants in their brief. For example, in reply to the argument of the PPLC that the privacy of married women was invaded by the Connecticut anticontraceptive statute's broad sweep, Clark submitted that the three women who testified had provided evidence voluntarily; they had not had evidence wrested from them illegally or surreptitiously. The brief also devoted a couple of pages in response to the appellants' and the amici's contention that there is a recognized role for contraception in the practice of modern medicine. Clark's response would not have pleased the women visiting the New Haven Center in November 1961: he said that there are no medical benefits of contraception and that unplanned pregnancies pose no bodily risks to normally healthy women.

For a few paragraphs Clark then returned to a parsing of the Connecticut birth control case precedents. He noted that the appellants had stressed the factual difference in their current appeal from those in *Tileston v. Ullman* (1943) and *Poe v. Ullman* (1961). They had, however, conveniently ignored the case that was closest in point to their current appeal, *Trubek v. Ullman* (1961). According to Clark, in both *Trubek* and *Griswold*, the right to prescribe contraceptives to healthy married women was the central legal issue. And in both cases, he argued, the doctor's decision to issue a prescription for contraceptives was not a medical necessity but was merely "in accord with . . . [the PPLC's] social philosophy." Because the Connecticut Supreme Court of Errors had rejected the *Trubek* challenge to the constitutionality of the state anticontraception law and the U.S. Supreme Court had elected not to review *Trubek*, Clark argued that the Supreme Court in *Griswold* should adhere to that precedent.

The final substantive point raised in the appellee's brief concerned Emerson's contention that widespread use of birth control would be necessary to combat the world population explosion. Clark presented statistics from a Connecticut newspaper that indicated that the birth rate in Connecticut had declined for seven consecutive years. Without further argumentation or transition, Clark submitted that questions on the "desirability" of the anticontraception statutes should be left to "a responsive legislature," and therefore the nation's highest court should affirm the judgment of the Supreme Court of Errors of Connecticut.

Friends of the Court or Friends of the PPLC?

The Latin term *amicus curiae* translates literally as "friend of the court." A brief of amicus curiae is usually submitted by a professional group, organization, or institution of government not involved as an actual party to the litigation but still having a stake in the outcome of the case. Hence, amici generally mount an argument consistent with their own organizational policy views. The participation of interest groups in a major constitutional case such as *Griswold v. Connecticut* is fairly typical. On rare occasions, an individual may submit an amicus brief. Beginning with the Warren Court years and continuing to the present, many Court cases feature a greater bulk in pages of argumentation from the briefs of amici than from the briefs of the parties to an appeal. The privilege of filing amicus briefs at the U.S. Supreme Court level is governed by the Rules of the United States

Supreme Court. Rule 42, for example, permits interested organizations or persons to file as amici if they have consent of all parties to the action. Normally, obtaining consent to file is a formality. However, if one of the official parties refuses to honor a request from a potential amicus, the group or individual can petition directly to the Court to be heard.

Amici, in soliciting permission to file, usually allege that they possess information or a perspective that may be useful to the Court in deciding the case. In reality, most amici wish to be heard because they support the position of one of the parties to the dispute; thus, they are more often friends of one side than friends of the court. Sometimes amici perform a useful service by bringing unusual or creative arguments to the attention of the justices that the official parties to a litigation might be hesitant to espouse — but may be pleased to have sympathetic interest groups take the heat for them. Legal scholars disagree as to how much attention the justices actually pay to amici.

Four groups expressed a desire to be heard by the Supreme Court as amici in *Griswold v. Connecticut:* the PPFA, the American Civil Liberties Union (ACLU) jointly with the Connecticut Civil Liberties Union, the Catholic Council on Civil Liberties (CCCL), and a group of nationally prominent physicians. All of these amici argued against the constitutionality of the Connecticut anticontraception law. Raymond Cannon, the attorney for Connecticut in the appeal to the Supreme Court a few years earlier in *Poe v. Ullman,* had refused to give the customary consent to file to a similar array of associations and groups interested in being heard as amici. Joseph Clark, in *Griswold,* followed this less than gracious precedent. As a result, the groups wishing to file as amici were forced to seek permission directly from the justices.

In March 1965, the Court announced that all four groups would be granted the privilege of submitting amicus briefs in the case. However, the PPFA's request to be granted its own block of time to participate in the oral argument was denied. Because amici — with the exception of the Solicitor General of the United States — are seldom afforded independent status in oral argument, no one was surprised that the justices refused the PPFA petition. In contrast to Harper's position in the *Poe* case four years earlier, Tom Emerson was not willing to relinquish any of the PPLC's time at the oral argument to the national Planned Parenthood organization. The interests of the four amici caught the attention of the nation's press. Stories appeared after the submission of the amicus briefs, likely prompted by press conferences held by the groups announcing their participation in what promised to be an important Supreme Court decision on individual rights and public policy.

The longest and most substantive of the amicus briefs was the one filed by the PPFA. The text of the brief was forty pages in length (ten pages longer than the appellee's brief); it was followed by over a hundred pages of appendices. Longtime Planned Parenthood attorneys Morris Ernst and Harriet Pilpel were responsible for preparing the PPFA argument and attachments. The PPFA stated its interest in the case in emotion-laden language: "The Planned Parenthood Federation ... has a profound interest in freeing its Connecticut affiliate and the residents of the State of Connecticut from the shackles of these laws [Sections 53–32 and 54–196 of the General Statutes of Connecticut] and in establishing the freedom of all Americans to access medical services for family planning."

The first point raised by the PPFA was that the Connecticut anti-contraception statutes forced married couples in the state to relinquish either their right to sexual relations or their right to plan their families. For several pages, the PPFA brief detailed the physical and psychological harms to married couples of sexual abstinence and the affront to their privacy presented by the Connecticut statutes. In this connection, the brief also emphasized the health dangers posed to some married women by pregnancy that, in most other states, could be legally obviated by contraception. Modern birth control devices, the brief argued, are safe and effective. Furthermore, Connecticut physicians who adhere to this law, and thus refuse to advise married couples of the benefits of contraception, defy medical ethics as well as the laws of negligence.

Referring to the Connecticut laws as "draconian," the Ernst/Pilpel brief stated that Section 53–32 "reaches into the marriage bed of every Connecticut couple. Its presence on the books threatens and authorizes search, seizure, and arrest, all of which would involve inquisitorial and physical invasion by the police and the courts into marital intimacies." The Connecticut laws, the brief later argued, do not serve one interest for which they were intended: the prevention of sexual immorality. Condoms are readily available in Connecticut and can be sold to all adults, whether married or single. Similarly, the rhythm method is available to married and unmarried individuals and is advertised in lay publications that are obtainable by all readers. In addition, the most effective contraceptives — diaphragms and antiovulation pills — require physician prescriptions, which Connecticut doctors are forbidden to issue by Section 54–196. Furthermore, the brief argued, there is something irrational in a statutory scheme that forbids the prescription of safe and reliable contraceptives to married women but permits abortion and compulsory sterilization in certain circumstances.

For the PPFA, probably the most deleterious consequence of Sections 53–32 and 54–196 was that they made criminal the provision of contraceptive services to those most in need of them: women of lower socioeconomic status who were being denied birth control prescriptions because of the absence in the state of public birth control clinics. The two laws also subjected medical personnel to criminal prosecution if they exercised their rights to counsel their clients on various birth control options. This, Ernst and Pilpel argued, violated their freedom of speech as protected by the First Amendment to the U.S. Constitution.

All of the arguments presented in the first half of the PPFA brief were advanced, in one form or another, in the appellants' brief filed by Tom Emerson, so that section of the Planned Parenthood brief was likely not very useful to the justices. However, the second half of the PPFA brief and the accompanying appendices provided a trove of information on the status of contraceptive services in the nation at the time. It noted that the federal government, most states, and many localities provide birth control services. In a subsection on the "medical place of contraception today" and in a related appendix, the PPFA provided excerpts of comments voiced by experts on birth control and statements of positions on the subject promulgated by major medical associations.

The second section of the brief and one of the appendices also summarized the positions on contraception held by various churches and religious experts. The overwhelming position on birth control in Judeo-Christian religion at that time, according to the PPFA brief, was that expressed by the Conference of Anglican Bishops: "[T]he means of family planning are in large measure matters of clinical and aesthetic choice." Included in this section was a statement of Boston's Richard Cardinal Cushing that the Catholic Church was presently engaged in a "process of reconsideration" of church policy regarding "artificial" methods of contraception. In assessing the place of birth control in "contemporary community mores," the Planned Parenthood brief pointed to the overwhelming support for contraception expressed in public opinion polls and in the statements of American opinion leaders.

The conclusion of the PPFA brief continued the hyperbolic tone expressed in the body of the argument. In criticizing the birth control opinions of the Connecticut Supreme Court of Errors, Ernst and Pilpel declared: "Perhaps the reason why these opinions read as if the Fourteenth Amendment does not apply to the state of Connecticut is because if any statute were ever tried and held wanting under relevant constitutional tests, this is it. . . . No alchemy of language . . . can erase the due process clause in several of its more important aspects from the United States Constitution. The Connecticut laws here under attack are not compatible with a free society."

A second amicus, the so-called physicians' brief, was written by attorney Whitney North Seymour. The PPFA helped to sponsor this brief as well as its own. The physicians' brief strongly endorsed doctor-prescribed contraceptives for married women interested in planning or spacing the birth of their children. It contained statements in support of contraception by individual physicians and medical organizations. Of the country's then eighty-five medical schools, the physicians' brief carried the imprimatur of seventy-four chairs of departments of obstetrics and gynecology and sixty-four chairs of departments of pediatrics. A similar brief representing the views of prominent doctors had been prepared and submitted by Seymour, also with PPFA support, in *Poe v. Ullman*. The 1965 physicians' brief repeated many of the same defenses of modern contraception that were advanced by doctors and medical organizations and cited in the fifty-page appendix B, "The Medical Consensus on Contraception," of the PPFA amicus brief.

Another amicus brief, only seventeen pages in length, was a joint submission of the ACLU and the Connecticut Civil Liberties Union. The ACLU had been on record for years as being opposed to the Connecticut anticontraception statutes and had submitted a similar amicus brief in *Poe*. The first two sections of the civil liberties brief offered short restatements of the arguments of the PPLC, the first in defense of the right of privacy and the second critical of Section 53–32 for bearing no reasonable relationship to its supposed legislative purpose. There were no novel legal arguments advanced in these sections, but the passion of the civil liberties community was powerfully expressed: the brief referred to the Connecticut anticontraception statute as being a product of the "religious-moral zealotry generated by . . . [a] Comstockian rampage" and that the current status of the law in the state of Connecticut "requires married couples either to abstain from sexual intercourse or to play Russian roulette with less effective contraceptive methods."

The third and final section of the civil liberties amicus brief presented a heretofore novel constitutional argument challenging the Connecticut anticontraception law. It contended that Section 53–32 violated the equal protection clause of the Fourteenth Amendment, which holds that "No State shall . . . deny any person within its jurisdiction the equal protection of the laws." One of the Supreme Court cases cited in support of this proposition was *Yick Wo v. Hopkins* (1885), a nineteenth-century decision that had almost been forgotten by twentieth-century courts. *Yick Wo* involved a San Francisco, California, ordinance requiring licenses to operate laundries in the city. The ordinance, however, did not apply to those operating laundries housed in brick buildings. Recent Chinese immigrants to San Francisco ran hundreds of laundries in San Francisco, but they were almost exclusively situated in wooden buildings. The ordinance thus served as a potent vehicle to close down Chinese laundries. Yick Wo and other Chinese laundry owners felt unfairly targeted by a law that they considered to be inspired by racism and nativist zeal, so they challenged the ordinance on constitutional grounds. The U.S. Supreme Court found that the San Francisco law might have seemed "fair on its face and impartial in appearance," yet it was "applied and administered by public authority with an evil eye and an unequal hand." The brief also cited in support of their equal protection claim the case of *Skinner v. Oklahoma* (1942), in which the Supreme Court had struck down a state law that had mandated the sterilization of some criminals who had three times been convicted of grand larceny but did not apply the same punishment to serial embezzlers.

Perceiving a comparable "unequal hand" at work in the Connecticut anticontraceptive legislation, the civil liberties bodies argued in their amicus brief that Section 53–32 singled out for prosecution the class of women who wished to plan or space their children through the use of contraceptives while effectively granting immunity from criminal sanction to those who sold or advertised the proscribed articles. This, according to the two civil liberties bodies, constituted "invidious" or "class" discrimination against women and was therefore prohibited by the equal protection language of the Fourteenth Amendment. The equal protection claim suggested a creative gender-based avenue to challenge Section 53–32.

The final amicus brief was fashioned by Robert B. Fleming on behalf of the CCCL. Formed in 1958, the CCCL represented the views of a group of liberal Catholic clergymen, professors, and editors. This body sought to present its brief to the Supreme Court in *Griswold* because it believed "that an argument presented from a Catholic perspective may truly be of aid to the Court in its adjudication of the sensitive issues raised by this case." The CCCL did not claim to speak for the Catholic church as an official body, but it did seek to present to the Court "an informed Catholic point of view."

Fleming, himself a father of six children, maintained that the CCCL's opposition to the Connecticut anticontraception statutes was grounded in respect for the "necessity of conjugal privacy." Since just the middle of the 1950s, the CCCL brief declared, there has been a "revolution" in the Catholic family. The brief contended that the ideal of large families among many Catholics, just as for most Protestants, had gone out of fashion. The income of a single wage earner could no longer provide the financial support for six to ten children; fifteen-room Victorian houses are in short supply; the emotional needs of married couples are being given more credence than ever before; and the emphasis on education for women has led to more Catholic wives who wish to work outside the home. Changes such as these in the Catholic community have persuaded Catholic clergy and theologians to recognize the increasing importance of what Fleming termed the "non-procreative ends of marriage." Along with this new view of marriage has come a recognition that contraceptive use for married couples, Catholics included, is a reasonable and private choice that should no longer be threatened by a law like Section 53–32—what the CCCL characterized as "the state's profane interference."

At the time that the briefs of the appellants, the appellees, and the amici were being prepared, yet another bill to repeal Sections 53–32 and 54–196 was before the Connecticut General Assembly. Introduced on February 10, 1965, the pending repeal bill was almost identical to the one proposed in the previous session of the legislature that had been passed by the House but never reported out of Senate committee. A hearing on the 1965 bill was held on March 23. The most notable thing about that hearing is what did not happen: the Hartford Archdiocese did not dispatch any speakers to oppose the bill. In March it was anticipated that the repeal bill would once again receive the endorsement of the legislature's Public Health and Safety Committee, but no formal votes were anticipated in either house of the legislature. Just as in 1961, all the interested parties seemed to be waiting for a definitive ruling by the U.S. Supreme Court on the fate of the 1879 law. This time the legal and constitutional issues were properly before the Supreme Court, so it appeared likely that a conclusive judicial decision would finally be forthcoming.

If the U.S. Supreme Court, however, once again found a way to avoid ruling on the constitutional merits of the anticontraceptive law, the state General Assembly was not poised to repeal Sections 53–32 and 54–196. State legislative reapportionment, recently mandated by 1962–64 Supreme Court decisions would eventually bring more urban, Catholic Democrats into the lower house of the Connecticut legislature. That would mean more votes against this and future PPLC campaigns to legalize the use of contraceptives in Connecticut. So legislative repeal of the 1879 statute, never a likely prospect, seemed even more of a long shot in 1965 than in past legislative sessions. The *Griswold* case before the U.S. Supreme Court was thus not just the best chance for removing the Connecticut ban on contraceptives; it now appeared to be the only chance.

CHAPTER 7

The Supreme Court Hears the Birth Control Case

The Brethren

The oral argument before the U.S. Supreme Court in the case of *Griswold and Buxton v. Connecticut* was scheduled for Monday, March 29, 1965. Tom Emerson was slated to make the presentation for the appellants, Griswold and Buxton, and Joseph Clark was ready to represent the appellee, the State of Connecticut. Before discussing what transpired in these long-awaited appearances before the High Court, a few words are in order about the nine robed men who would sit in judgment of the 1879 Connecticut anticontraception statute and be asked to extend formal constitutional protection to the right of privacy. The justices are profiled in order of their seniority on the Court.

The so-called center seat on the Supreme Court bench belongs to the chief justice. In 1965 that position was occupied by Earl Warren, one of the most heralded and beloved justices in American history. Because of the many controversial decisions of the Warren Court, however, Warren himself was also one of the most vilified figures in American life. "Impeach Earl Warren" billboards cropped up in the South in the 1950s; a few were still standing when the *Griswold* case was before the Court. Warren was a big man with an impressive head of white hair. He had been nominated as chief justice by President Dwight Eisenhower in 1953. Just a few months after assuming his seat on the Court, Warren wrote the unanimous opinion in *Brown v. Board of Education* (1954), striking down racial segregation in the nation's public schools and initiating a judicial assault on racial injustice. Warren had been a three-term California governor and a former state attorney general. As chief justice, Warren became both a leader and a symbol of a liberal constitutional revolution that could not have been predicted given his preappointment partisan Republican background. The famous decisions of the Warren Court years included not only civil rights, but also judicially mandated legislative reapportionment, a respect for the rights of individuals accused of crimes, and support for the civil liberties of people having the temerity to criticize their government. As chief justice, Warren was able to write or broker majority decisions on most of the great issues coming before the American judiciary during his sixteen-year tenure on the Court. Although not regarded as a seminal legal thinker or powerful writer, Warren's leadership skills and his political acumen enabled him to hold together a brilliant but contentious group of associate justices. At the time of the oral argument in *Griswold*, Warren had just turned seventy-four. He had voted with the Court majority in *Poe v. Ullman* (1961). But given the likelihood that the Court would see this challenge mounted by the Planned Parenthood League of Connecticut (PPLC) to the Connecticut anticontraception law as ripe for decision, and given Warren's vote in other civil liberties cases, he was likely to side with Griswold and Buxton.

The senior associate justice was Hugo L. Black. Nominated to the Court in 1937 by President Franklin Roosevelt, Black would serve until a few days before his death in 1971 at the age of eighty-five. He was one of the longest-serving justices in the nation's history. Nominated because he was a strong advocate of FDR's New Deal while a member of the U.S. Senate, Black made himself into one of the Court's greatest legal scholars. He sought to read the U.S. Constitution literally and, whenever possible, to seek out the views of the framers of the core document and its amendments. Belying his youthful membership in the Ku Klux Klan and a 1944 Supreme court opinion supporting the internment of Japanese Americans (*Korematsu v. U.S.*), Black had been a strong proponent of racial justice and individual liberties for most of his more than three decades on the Court. He had generally sided with the chief justice on the great decisions of the Warren Court. However, late in his career on the bench, he became hostile to the interests of student protesters and antiwar radicals. In siding against the demonstrators in the black armband case of *Tinker v. Des Moines* (1969), for example, Black expressed support for the adage that "children should be seen and not heard." Black had dissented from the Supreme Court's dismissal of the appeal in *Poe v. Ullman* on the grounds that he believed the constitutional questions raised should have been reached and decided. But in that opinion he had not revealed his sympathies on the merits of the birth control dispute. Given Black's literal constitutional jurisprudence, however, he was unlikely to join, much less write, an opinion supporting the rather creative constitutional interpretation of the Fourteenth Amendment and the Bill of Rights being urged on the Court by Tom Emerson and his clients.

The other Roosevelt appointee still sitting on the Court in 1965 was William O. Douglas, born a poor boy from a small town in Washington state. Because Douglas would end up writing the opinion of the Court in the *Griswold* case, his background and proclivities deserve a bit more commentary than that expended on the other justices. Rauol Berger, a well-known expert on the U.S. Constitution and someone who knew Douglas personally, termed him "the oddest duck to ever serve on the United States Supreme Court." Douglas had been a law professor at Yale in the 1920s and early 1930s. He went to Washington in the Depression to serve as a commissioner, and later chair, of the Securities and Exchange Commission. Douglas took his seat on the Supreme Court bench in 1939 and did not retire until 1975. Douglas's thirty-six-year tenure is a Supreme Court record for longevity. In the early 1940s, Douglas was seriously considered as the Democratic nominee for the vice presidency; later in the 1940s he ran a stealthy, blundering campaign for the presidency from his seat on the Court. Douglas was a vigorous outdoorsman, a conservationist, and a world traveler. As an advocate of the "work hard, play hard" philosophy of life, Douglas would regularly rush from a session of the Court to a fishing expedition or an international vacation.

Even more than Black, Douglas was a champion of the underdog: his judicial record defending civil liberties is perhaps unsurpassed in the history of the Supreme Court. His dissent in *Dennis v. U.S.* (1951), voting to uphold the free speech rights of leaders of the American Communist Party, was not popular at the time but is now regarded as one of the greatest defenses of free expression in American history. In the 1960s, Douglas made no secret of his opposition to the Vietnam War. More than any other justice, he sought, albeit unsuccessfully, to have the Supreme Court confront the constitutionality of the Southeast Asian conflict. Douglas was less concerned about adhering to precedent than in doing what he felt to be right from a public policy standpoint. A quick and facile legal writer, he was not particularly careful or nuanced in constructing his arguments. Some legal commentators have even referred to him as sloppy or careless in his craft. Douglas seldom took advantage of the skills of his law clerks to help compose or edit opinions; in fact, he treated his staff shabbily. Douglas found it difficult to compromise or negotiate with colleagues over language, so he ended up writing more stirring dissents than commanding majority opinions.

Douglas was a great defender of the rights of man but not particularly comfortable with individual human beings. Even given his long service on the Court and in other capacities in the federal government before his appointment, Douglas failed to develop many close friendships in Washington. His best friends were probably his fishing buddies back in Washington state. He was voted "Father of the Year" in 1950 by the National Father's Day Committee, but he was estranged at several times in his life from his own children.

But it was Douglas's relationships with women that most often drew critical comment from contemporaries, journalists, and historians. Perhaps surprisingly, Douglas was the first justice in the long history of the Supreme Court to have a marriage end in divorce. He was divorced from his first wife in 1953; he followed it up with two more marriages (1954 and 1963) and two more divorces (1963 and 1966). He married his fourth wife in 1966: he was then sixty-seven, and she was twenty-three. To say that Douglas had an eye for the ladies would be an understatement. His sexual indiscretions were well known during his life to friends and family; in recent years, they have been juicy topics for biographers.

Douglas was a clear vote in favor of striking down the Connecticut anticontraception laws. He had written judicial opinions on several previous occasions about the importance of privacy in American law. With the possible exception of Louis Brandeis, the justice whose seat Douglas had assumed when he joined the Court in the late 1930s, no justice was as fervent an advocate of privacy as the man some called "Wild Bill." Douglas had also written one of the dissents in *Poe v. Ullman* almost four years earlier.

The only appointee of former President Harry S. Truman who remained on the Supreme Court in 1965 was Tom C. Clark. A former attorney general, Clark would serve on the Supreme Court from 1949 until resigning in 1967 so as not to present a conflict of interest with his son, Ramsey Clark, who was about to be appointed as attorney general under President Lyndon Johnson. Clark was probably more important in judicial history for his advocacy of improved judicial administration — before, during, and after his tenure on the Supreme Court — than he was as a justice participating in some of the great cases of his day. As a former prosecutor, Justice Clark was particularly tough on political radicals. He sided with the Supreme Court majority to uphold the convictions of the leaders of the American Communist Party in *Dennis v. U.S.* (1951), and he was in dissent in the controversial "Red Monday" cases of 1957 in which the Court saw fit to afford communists some of the protections of the Bill of Rights. Clark was not totally out of step, however, with the pro–civil liberties opinions of the Warren Court. He wrote the majority opinion in *Mapp v. Ohio* (1961), which extended the "exclusionary rule" to defendants facing criminal charges in state courts. In fact, Clark's opinion in *Mapp* was one of the decisions relied on by those who saw an emerging constitutional right of privacy stemming from key provisions of the Bill of Rights. Clark also wrote the majority opinions in *Heart of Atlanta Motel v. U.S.* (1964) and *Katzenbach v. McClung* (1964), upholding the constitutionality of the Civil Rights Act of 1964 as being justified by the commerce clause of Article One of the U.S. Constitution. Clark had been a silent member of the five-person majority in *Poe* to avoid a decision on the Connecticut birth control law, so how he would vote on *Griswold* was uncertain.

The next in seniority on the Supreme Court in 1965 was John Marshall Harlan, the justice who had written the longest and most celebrated dissent in *Poe*. Justice Harlan was the grandson of a previous justice, the first John Marshall Harlan, who served on the Court from 1877 to 1911. The current Justice Harlan was nominated by President Eisenhower in 1955. Before his appointment, Harlan had been a Rhodes Scholar, a brilliant lawyer for a prestigious Wall Street law firm, and, for a short time, a U.S. court of appeals judge. Harlan was a principled conservative and a skilled legal craftsman. He generally found himself at odds with the liberal, activist jurisprudence of the Warren Court. For instance, he expressed strong dissents in the Court's several legislative reapportionment decisions in the 1960s. Although he generally sided with the instrumentalities of government in suits filed by individuals, he felt strongly about the need to nail down a constitutional right of privacy, as his long and passionate dissent in *Poe* indicated. So he, like Douglas, was a solid vote in favor of finding the Connecticut anticontraception law unconstitutional. Sadly, Harlan's eyesight was deteriorating badly; he was nearly blind by the time of the *Griswold* appeal.

The third Eisenhower appointee on the Court in 1965 was William Joseph Brennan Jr. Brennan had served as a New Jersey Supreme Court judge before his nomination to the High Court in 1956. Because Brennan, like Earl Warren, was decidedly more liberal once on the Supreme Court than in his previous public life, President Eisenhower regarded his nomination as one of his mistakes. Although Brennan had a hand in many of the great decisions of the Warren era, recognition of his critical role in constitutional law would not emerge until after Warren and most of the other liberal justices of the 1960s had died or retired. Overshadowed by the more strident Black and Douglas, Brennan was a safe vote in defense of the freedom of expression, the protection of the rights of the accused, and the civil rights of minorities. Brennan wrote the majority opinion in *Baker v. Carr* (1962), one of the leading legislative reapportionment decisions. He was a consistent opponent of capital punishment and a defender of women's rights, including the right to an abortion. In his final decade on the Court, 1980 to 1990, Brennan because an articulate voice in opposition to the Republican-appointed justices of the 1970s and 1980s. He believed that the U.S. Constitution should be interpreted broadly and that the intentions of the framers of the document, if such intentions could ever be deciphered, should not bind courts of a later century. Brennan had written a brief concurring opinion in *Poe*, arguing that the constitutionality of the Connecticut anticontraception statute was not "ripe" for decision in 1961 but could be properly tested under the U.S. Constitution if a case ever presented itself in which a birth control clinic was effectively shut down by Sections 53–32 and 54–196. Brennan would have his wish with the pending appeal in the Connecticut birth control case. He was thus a sure vote in favor of Griswold and Buxton, and perhaps in the creation of a constitutional right of privacy.

The fourth and final Eisenhower appointee still serving on the Court at the time of the *Griswold* appeal was Potter Stewart. Nominated in 1959, Stewart would serve on the Court until 1981. Stewart may be best known for one of the great throwaway lines in American legal history: he wrote in a 1964 opinion that he might not be able to define obscenity, "but I know it when I see it." Stewart, like many members of the Warren Court, hailed from a family of judges. He was active in the moderate wing of the Cincinnati Republican Party in the 1940s and 1950s before his nomination to the U.S. court of appeals. Stewart boasted that he adhered to no overriding legal philosophy, that he simply decided the cases before him as he thought best. Scholars who have studied Stewart's decisions agree that he was a truly "nondoctrinal" jurist. If there was a key to his constitutional leanings, it was Stewart's general support for the autonomy of state governments. He was a defender of states' rights without falling prey to racism. He dissented in the leading rights-of-the-accused case, *Miranda v. Arizona* (1966), and the landmark children's rights case, *In Re Gault* (1967). Stewart had voiced a curious dissent in *Poe v. Ullman.* After saying that he agreed with Douglas's and Harlan's reasons for dissenting from the dismissal of the appeals in *Poe,* Stewart added cryptically: "[I]n refraining from a discussion of the constitutional issues, I in no way imply that the ultimate result I would reach on the merits of these controversies would differ from the conclusions of my dissenting Brothers." Thus, if the Supreme Court felt that a challenge to the 1879 Connecticut anticontraception law was ripe for decision, the appellate attorneys on both sides in *Griswold* would find Stewart's vote tough to call.

President John F. Kennedy was responsible for placing two justices on the Supreme Court during his brief time in office. The first was Byron R. White, nominated in 1962. In college, White had been a fine student and a star athlete; he followed his baccalaureate degree with a Rhodes Scholarship to Oxford. Immediately before his appointment to the Court, White had served in the Kennedy administration as a deputy attorney general. In this capacity he took a leading role in civil rights enforcement in the South. He was initially perceived as a Kennedy liberal, but legal scholars disagree as to whether White remained true to his liberal pedigree during his three decades on the Court. The first former Supreme Court law clerk to be appointed to the Court himself, White did not base his decisions on abstract principles or technical doctrine but on a "pragmatic estimate as to how effective his choice would be." For example, White voted with the majority in the legislative reapportionment cases of *Wesberry v. Sanders* (1964) and *Reynolds v. Simms* (1964), dissented in the landmark criminal justice case of *Miranda v. Arizona* (1966), remained on the side of school integration in *Swann v. Charlotte-Mecklenburg Board of Education* (1971), but disagreed strongly with the majority in the 1973 abortion case of *Roe v. Wade.* Just as White had once gloried in competition on the gridiron, he threw himself into pickup basketball games with the much younger law clerks and took pleasure in the give and take of oral argument. White had ascended to the Court seat previously occupied by Charles E. Whittaker, who had been one of the justices who had joined the majority opinion in *Poe.* Given White's background and Kennedy-like politics, it was probable — although by no means certain — that White would vote against the constitutionality of Sections 53–32 and 54–96.

The newest appointee on the Court at the time *Griswold v. Connecticut* was argued and decided was Arthur J. Goldberg. Nominated by President Kennedy in 1962, Goldberg assumed the Supreme Court seat vacated by the resigning Felix Frankfurter. Before his appointment to the Court, Goldberg had been Kennedy's Secretary of Labor. Before that, he had been the general counsel of the United Steelworkers and the Congress of Industrial Organizations. Goldberg was generally credited with orchestrating the AFL-CIO merger in 1955. As a justice, Goldberg was the author of the majority opinion in *Ecobedo v. Illinois* (1964), a decision mandating the right of an accused person to a lawyer during a police interrogation. He also wrote the opinion for the Court in *Aptheker v. Secretary of State* (1964), which held that the right of a left-wing historian to travel abroad was a liberty protected by the Fifth Amendment to the Constitution. More than a political liberal, in contrast to the man he replaced on the Court, Goldberg subscribed to the practice of judicial activism. Shortly after the *Griswold* case, Goldberg would resign from the Court at the insistence of President Lyndon B. Johnson in order to accept an appointment to become ambassador to the United Nations. Goldberg appeared to both sets of lawyers in the Connecticut birth control case to be a clear vote in favor of finding Sections 32–53 and 54–196 unconstitutional. The opinion that Goldberg would ultimately write in *Griswold v. Connecticut* would turn out to be his final opinion as a member of the Supreme Court.

"Dangerous Implications"

In the scholarly literature on decision making in the U.S. Supreme Court, it is generally recognized that law clerks do not dictate the decisions of their masters; nor are the clerks merely gophers for identifying cases or checking citations. The actual role of the clerks depends almost entirely on what their particular justices permit them to do. So the degree of influence of the clerks varies from justice to justice and case to case. In the papers of the justices serving on the Supreme Court in 1965 are various memoranda prepared by the law clerks for their justices. The vast majority recount the facts and issues presented in cases being considered for certiorari (discretionary review of lower court decisions under Rule 10 of the Rules of the Supreme Court) or probable jurisdiction motions from federal or state courts (as in *Griswold*). A smaller number deal with recommendations for action on cases being considered by the Court. The most interesting of such memos dealing with *Griswold v. Connecticut* was a thirty-page document prepared by John Hart Ely, one of Chief Justice Earl Warren's clerks. It was dated February 26, 1965. Copies reside in the papers of several of the justices, so a fair assumption is that Ely's "bench memorandum" made the rounds of the different Supreme Court chambers in the month before the oral argument. Some of the points raised by Ely may have triggered particular questions at the oral argument or figured into the discussion on the disposition of *Griswold*.

Ely began his memorandum with an informal summary of the facts, procedural path, and the arguments presented by the various lawyers in the *Griswold* appeal. More than was common with most memoranda written by clerks and addressed to their justices, Ely was not adverse to making his own views known. For example, he encouraged Chief Justice Warren to take special notice of Emerson's argument that the anticontraception law has only been enforced against clinics and not against private physicians or individual married women. To Ely, as to Emerson, this indicated that the law, as it operated, discriminated against women in low-income groups. "Although this argument takes up little space in appellants' brief," Ely noted in a parenthetical comment, "it is one which to me seems very important." Later in the memo, in the context of his view of the briefs of amicus curiae, Ely addressed a similar point regarding what he saw as the discriminatory nature of the Connecticut statute. Although he was not impressed for the most part with the amici, Ely did see in the joint brief of the American Civil Liberties Union (ACLU) and the Connecticut Civil Liberties Union (CCLU) a useful point. That brief had presented an equal protection argument under the Fourteenth Amendment to the effect that the 1879 law denied women the equal protection of the laws by preventing them from using contraceptives to space and plan their children, while at the same time the law did not prevent the class of those individuals engaged in the manufacture and sale of contraceptives from making money on artificial birth control devices.

Ely did not hide his disappointment with the brief of the State of Connecticut as appellee. He wrote: "The appellee's brief unfortunately does not put forth as good a defense of the [anticontraception] law as can be made, nor are there *amicus* briefs in support thereof." He was particularly disdainful of Joseph Clark's contention that the 1879 law did not impair Dr. Buxton's rights as a physician. Clark had argued that Dr. Buxton was engaging in social policy, not in the practice of medicine, when he prescribed birth control devices to healthy women. At that point in his memorandum Ely added this caustic footnote: "One would hope that the case for the State would be argued by someone other than the man responsible for the brief, but it appears that you will not be so lucky."

In urging the chief justice to vote to reverse the Connecticut Supreme Court of Errors, however, Ely cautioned that "the Court should carefully choose its ground of decision, for some of those urged by appellants have dangerous implications." Ely was particularly loathe to hang a major constitutional ruling on the ephemeral thread of privacy. He wrote:

> Just as I think the Court should vigorously enforce every clause in the Constitution, I do not think the Court should enforce clauses which are not there. No matter how strong a dislike for a piece of legislation may be, it is dangerous precedent to read into the Con-

stitution guarantees which are not there. Despite Justice Brandeis's lifelong crusade for a right of privacy, and despite the desirability of having such a right for the basis of a tort action, the Constitution says nothing about such a right.

Ely acknowledged that some of the first ten Amendments offer protection for certain forms of privacy. But, he argued, "it by no means follows that because several parts of the Constitution protect aspects of what might be called privacy, the Constitution therefore contains a general right of privacy, with a content over and above the content of the various specific provisions." Furthermore, he advised, it would not be legitimate to claim that the Ninth Amendment protects privacy without a strong historical showing that privacy was on the minds of the men who drafted that amendment.

Even if the Supreme Court should hold that there is such a thing as a right of privacy, Ely was unconvinced that the facts in the Griswold case would qualify. There was no demonstration by the appellants, he wrote, that the sanctity of sexual relations within the marriage unit was disrupted by the Connecticut law. Sex within marriage may be an intimate activity, but a law proscribing the use of contraceptives by married couples, particularly a law that was never enforced, was not analogous to such offensive governmental practices as "eavesdropping, spying, midnight raids and searches." In other words, the hypothetical enforcement of the "use" statute did not bother him. Justice Harlan, in dissent in *Poe v. Ullman*, had called the Connecticut anticontraceptive law an "outrage." But, for Ely "[t]his vague 'outrage' approach to the 14th Amendment comprises, in my opinion, the most dangerous sort of 'activism.'"

Near the end of his memorandum, Ely returned to the inequitable enforcement argument. For him, the most serious adverse consequence of the 1879 law was that the "poor and ill-informed who most need contraceptive advice and family planning" were denied those services. When the law was enforced by the Supreme Court of Connecticut—both in *State v. Nelson* (1940) and in *Connecticut v. Griswold* (1964)—it served the purpose of effectively closing down birth control clinics. Because the Connecticut anticontraceptive law was being selectively enforced, Ely saw a clear parallel to the eighty-year-old case of *Yick Wo v. Hopkins* (1885). Ely quoted with approval the passage in *Yick Wo* that found an equal protection problem with a law that might "be fair on its face and impartial in appearance" but was applied "with an evil eye and an unequal hand."

Ely also saw merit in the First Amendment argument of the appellants. He agreed with Tom Emerson that the state of Connecticut did not clearly "sort out" the difference between the arguably permissible speech of a physician such as Dr. Buxton advising a married woman on birth control with conduct that the state might have the right to proscribe. However, because it was clear to most observers after *Poe v. Ullman* that the Connecticut statute prohibiting the "use" of contraceptives was a "dead letter," how can it be said that a licensed physician counseling a married woman to use contraceptives was advising her to commit a crime?

The decision of the Connecticut Supreme Court should be reversed, Ely concluded, "on either 1st Amendment ground[s], or on the ground that the law is administered so as to hurt only the ill-informed or poor." He had the audacity to suggest to the Chief Justice, and by implication other members of the Supreme Court, that to reverse on other grounds (that is, the right of privacy, or the view that legislation should not have been predicated upon the moral judgment of the Roman Catholic church) "would, in my opinion, have very dangerous implications." Ely's memorandum was on the mind of Chief Justice Warren and, perhaps, other justices when the oral argument in *Griswold v. Connecticut* took place a few weeks later.

———

May It Please the Court

The oral argument is an obligatory and dramatic penultimate act in a major Supreme Court case. The stage is the elegant public courtroom in the Supreme Court Building on First Street Northeast and Maryland Avenue in the nation's capital. The Court conducts oral arguments in only one or two hundred cases a year. Most oral arguments are an hour in length — thirty minutes for each side. The "Notice to Counsel" sent to the attorneys preparing for an oral argument advises them to pay strict heed to the time limits. When a lawyer has five minutes left in his or her allotted time, a white light flashes on the attorney's podium. When the time expires, he or she is confronted by a red light. Attorneys are admonished to conclude their arguments immediately when the red light appears unless they are responding to a question put by a justice.

Because the justices can and do hurl questions at the attorneys at any time during their presentations, even the best-planned argument can be sidetracked or cut short by a query from the bench. The questions come fast, and justices often do not give an advocate a chance to answer. Justices often interrupt the lawyers — and each other. The discourse in oral argument is often disjointed and messy. A justice's questions may suggest interest or support for an advocate's position, or they may appear contrary or even malicious. Counsel appearing before the Supreme Court are advised by experienced appellate advocates to respond to justices' questions simply and directly. Because the justices expect attorneys to be able to depart from their prepared remarks when challenged, lawyers able to speak extemporaneously under pressure have a decided advantage over lawyers who prefer pat presentations. The justices are also accustomed to respect and deference. Therefore, attorneys appearing before the Supreme Court are cautioned never to exhibit arrogance or impatience. "The Brethren," as the justices are sometimes called, are also not adverse to a little humor at the expense of attorneys arguing appeals before them. Appearing before the Supreme Court tends to be a harrowing experience for even the most experienced appellate advocates. Almost no one walks away from the podium feeling good about his or her performance.

One consolation to a lawyer who has just been battered by scores of unrelated, often hostile questions is that how well or poorly he or she performed in the oral argument may not matter much to the case being litigated. Justices and their clerks generally pay more attention to the record of the case and the appellate briefs than what is said in a few minutes of hasty responses to often strange question. Some justices rarely speak at oral argument, so it is almost impossible to know their views at that time. Others enjoy the give and take of the courtroom in a sporting sense, but do not have particularly strong views on the positions being argued. They, too, are hard to read. It is unlikely that a brilliant oral argument has ever won a bad case. But in a close case, the performance of an attorney might turn a vote or two.

Some of the tension of an attorney's appearance before the Supreme Court in oral argument is mitigated by a few informal features of the setting. The tables of attorneys are positioned so close to the Court's bench that counsel can occasionally overhear whispered comments from the justices. A few of the Brethren have been known to maintain running colloquies throughout an oral argument that have nothing to do with the case at bar. In addition, from the bench during open sessions, some justices summon clerks or aides to run errands. William O. Douglas was notorious during oral argument for sending out for books and other research materials to assist him in writing his tracts on conservation and travel. Occasionally, a few justices take it on themselves to reassure nervous advocates. In the 1960s, one attorney arguing a case before the Supreme Court for the first time tried to keep this thought in his mind: "If anything really went bad, Earl Warren would come down off the bench and put his arm around [me]."

The pageantry of an oral argument is enhanced by the audience. Sometimes several hundred people attend an open session of the Supreme Court. The courtroom was, in fact, filled close to capacity when case 496 in the October Term 1964 (the 1964–65 Supreme Court year), *Estelle T. Griswold and C. Lee Buxton, Appellants v. State of Connecticut, Appellee,* was called late in the afternoon of March 29, 1965. In the audience were Estelle Griswold and Lee Buxton, several PPLC board members and officers, Miriam Harper, the widow of Fowler Harper, and Ruth Emerson, who had helped her husband write the brief for the appellants. Catherine Roraback sat at the appellants' table with Tom Emerson. Joseph Clark, who would argue the case for the State of Connecticut, was accompanied to Washington by the retired former state prosecutor, Julius Maretz, and Irwin Harrison, the friend who had assisted Clark in preparing his Supreme Court brief. Also in attendance were the wives of two prominent U.S. senators, Mrs. Robert F. Kennedy and Mrs. Edward Kennedy, as well as Secretary of the Treasury Henry Fowler.

Tom Emerson, for the appellants, rose when the case was called and began to address the justices with the proper protocol, "Mr. Chief Justice, may it please the Court." He commenced his presentation with a statement of the facts in the case, highlighting the wording of the "use" and "abetting" statutes and introducing the appellants and the Planned Parenthood Center in New Haven. Justice Arthur Goldberg, the newest member of the Court, was the first to break in with a question. He wanted to know if the women who received services at the Center were, in fact, all married women. Emerson responded that the Center was committed to providing birth control services only to married women; if an unmarried woman received any counseling at the Center, it would have been through misrepresentation or a mistake. Justice Hugo Black, the senior associate justice then raised an interesting question: Was an equal protection issue presented by the clinic's failure to serve unmarried women? Emerson responded by saying that the appellants were not raising an "equal protection question as such." Although the attorney for Griswold and Buxton did not say so, he or any members of Planned Parenthood in Connecticut could have informed the justices that in the early 1960s, establishing the right for married women to receive contraceptive services was about as far as the advocates of birth control in the state dared to go. Establishing a right for unmarried women to achieve that right would have to wait for another day in court.

Justice William Brennan then shifted the discussion by asking if the sale of contraceptives was a crime in Connecticut. Emerson indicated that it was in fact a crime under the "abetting statute," Section 54–196, but as far as he knew, there had never been any prosecutions of vendors of contraceptives. This led to a discussion among Emerson, Justice Brennan, and other justices as to the question of whether contraceptives could legally be sold in Connecticut for the purpose of preventing disease, as opposed to the purpose of preventing conception. Emerson pointed out that disease prevention was in fact the purpose of contraceptives, mainly condoms, as cited by vendors of these goods in Connecticut.

Justice Brennan asked Emerson if there had been any court decisions in Connecticut that had held permissible the sale of contraceptives for the purpose of preventing disease. Emerson answered that Connecticut courts had not rendered any such decisions but that courts in Massachusetts, with a similar law banning the use of contraceptives, had held that the sale of these articles was not against the law if the purpose of the sale was disease prevention. Brennan, perhaps trying to be helpful to Emerson, suggested that the prosecution of a clinic's staff for prescribing contraceptives for the purpose of family planning but not prosecuting vendors for marketing contraceptives for the purpose of disease prevention might present another equal protection issue.

The questions of both Black and Brennan indicated that they were disappointed that the appellants had not presented equal protection arguments. It is possible that the equal protection queries from Black, Brennan, and — later in the oral argument — from other justices had been sparked by John Hart Ely's bench memorandum. Emerson stuck to his guns, however, trying to focus on arguments that he had, in fact, stressed in his brief: "We have never made any argument on equal protection as such, Your Honor. . . . We pitch it [our argument] on due process in the basic sense . . . that it [the 1879 law] is arbitrary and unreasonable, and in the special sense that it constitutes a deprivation of right against invasion of privacy." He noted that the appellants also raise First Amendment and Ninth Amendment arguments.

Then, perhaps unwisely, Emerson indicated that his due process argument was not the same as the economic due process issue that figured so prominently in the first third of the twentieth century in cases like *Lochner v. New York* (1905), *Nebbia v. New York* (1934), and *West Coast Hotel v. Parrish* (1937). Justice Black was not so sure: "It sounds to me like you're asking us to follow the constitutional philosophy of that case [*Lochner*]." This led to a sharp exchange between Black and Emerson over whether the ghost of *Lochner* was being raised from the dead by the appellants. Emerson endeavored to get back to civil liberties cases he had cited in his brief such as *Meyer v. Nebraska* (1923), *Pierce v. Society of Sisters* (1925), and the recent decision in *Aptheker v. Secretary of State* (1964).

Emerson emphasized that the Connecticut law on contraception is "totally unique": it is the only remaining statute in the country that makes it a criminal offense to use contraceptive devices. He was challenged on this point by a justice who referred to statements in the appellee's brief indicating that the facts in the current litigation would have violated the contraceptive statutes in six other states. Emerson was ready for this argument. He precisely pointed out how the statutes of the other states had been interpreted by their courts to permit the use of contraceptives by married women or had simply been ignored. When a member of the Court suggested that these other statutes might be "dead letters," Emerson readily agreed.

Justice Black asked Emerson if the appellants were to prevail on the overbreadth argument, would that settle the constitutionality of contraceptive statutes in states other than Connecticut? Emerson cleverly responded that it would depend on why the Court might say the law was overbroad. If the Court said it was overbroad because it violated the right of privacy, that ruling would, in his view, imperil the laws of Massachusetts and other states that put significant restrictions on contraceptive practice among married couples.

Emerson referred at this juncture to an argument that he had raised in his brief, namely, that the appellants believed that privacy was an emerging constitutional right, embodied in the First, Third, Fourth, Fifth, and Ninth Amendments. He perhaps hoped that his comment about privacy as guaranteed by selected provisions of the Bill of Rights might prompt some questions on that matter, or at least allow him to return to his prepared comments. Emerson was then asked how the people of Connecticut might have suffered given the law proscribing the use of contraceptives in the state. He answered that the most serious harm was to poor and uneducated women who did not have private physicians to seek out for birth control counseling and contraceptive prescriptions. He once again indicated that the 1879 law had never been enforced against private physicians, only against birth control clinics.

At this juncture, Justice John Marshall Harlan, the author of the long and thoughtful dissent in *Poe v. Ullman* (1961), spoke up for the first time in the oral argument. Harlan wanted to know whether the attorney for the appellants was ever going to be coming back to his First Amendment argument. Emerson responded: "Well, I'm not getting far on any of my arguments. . . ." This led to general laughter in the courtroom. Emerson continued: " . . . but I can't guarantee that I'll get back to the First Amendment, no." Justice Harlan, ever the gentleman, replied: "Well, I'll withdraw the question."

What Emerson did choose to talk about at that point were what he characterized as his two lines of argument on due process. First, he submitted that a state cannot enact into law a principle of morality unless it has an objective relationship to the welfare of the people or conforms to current community standards. He declared that there is no objective information that contraceptives are harmful to married couples; in fact, regarding the case of women for whom pregnancy is a dangerous health risk, the evidence is to the contrary. As to community standards, Emerson reminded the justices that government programs at all levels permit and endorse the use of contraceptives.

Moreover, the overwhelming support for birth control as documented by public opinion polls is another index of the conformance of contraceptive use to current community standards. Emerson was then asked whether he had in mind national or local standards. He responded — perhaps with a jaundiced eye toward the Court's struggle with the issue of local versus national standards in obscenity cases — "I hope I don't get involved in that at the moment." This led to more laughter in the courtroom.

Emerson then mentioned his second due process point, that the Connecticut anticontraception law is arbitrary and capricious. Emerson was prepared to launch into a summary of some of what he felt to be the unreasonable consequences of the 1879 law that he had outlined in his brief. But at that point he must have noticed or been prompted that his time was running short. So he wisely requested permission to reserve the rest of his oral argument time — about ten minutes — for rebuttal. The Chief Justice acceded to this wish. After twenty minutes in the nation's hottest judicial spotlight, Emerson had barely begun his due process analysis, and he had not yet had the opportunity to raise the appellant's crucial First Amendment or privacy arguments.

It All Comes Down to the Police Power

Although Tom Emerson was not a smooth speaker, he was an experienced appellate advocate. Also, as his brief for the appellants demonstrated, he was a brilliant constitutional scholar. Emerson's adversary in oral argument was neither. Joseph B. Clark had four years of experience in New Haven private practice before becoming an assistant prosecutor in 1961. He had inherited the Griswold/Buxton case from Julius Maretz. Clark no doubt knew he was overmatched. The Connecticut anticontraception law had been under intense judicial scrutiny for twenty-five years. It had survived various challenges, most notably falling one vote shy of being struck down in *Poe v. Ullman* the year that Clark came to the prosecutor's office. Now those contesting the law had the advantage of excellent legal talent and the support of powerful national and state interest groups. They also appeared now to have avoided or knocked aside the procedural defenses that had preserved the law in the past. Finally, with two new members since the *Poe* decision, the Supreme Court seemed more sympathetic than ever before to the position of litigants like Griswold and Buxton. So it fell to Clark to defend to the last gasp what he later privately termed a "foolish" law. Given all the impediments he faced, Clark acquitted himself well in the oral argument. If the performances of Clark and Emerson had been rated on debating points, most in attendance at the oral argument would have awarded the decision to the young assistant prosecutor. But litigation before the U.S. Supreme Court does not work that way.

Clark commenced his presentation by attempting to cast the Connecticut anticontraception law in the same mold as the New York and Massachusetts laws that had been upheld by the Supreme Court in the cases of *Sanger v. People of New York* (1918) and *Gardner v. Commonwealth of Massachusetts* (1938). In those cases, Clark maintained, the Court wisely held that how contraceptives were regulated was a matter best left to the states. He was quickly challenged, however, by a justice who asked if those state laws proscribed the mere use of contraceptives as Connecticut did. Clark acknowledged that only Connecticut of all the fifty states still prohibited the use of contraceptives. Clark was asked if there had been convictions for selling contraceptives in Connecticut. He responded that there have likely been a handful of convictions for selling condoms over the years, but the local records are not clear and, to the best of his knowledge, none of those convictions was ever appealed to the Supreme Court of Errors. Clark did attest that the only times doctors in Connecticut have been prosecuted under Section 54–196 were in *State v. Nelson* (1940) and the current case. Clark was also asked whether selling contraceptives under the cover of "prevention of disease" would be deemed criminal under either Section 53–32 or 54–196. Clark replied that this question was premised on an "irrelevant" or "ludicrous" basis. When he was finally compelled to answer, however, he acknowledged that a sale for the purpose of preventing disease would not violate the relevant Connecticut statutes. When one of the justices joked that he would not ask Clark to describe the type of contraceptive that would protect against disease, there was general laughter among members of the audience. On this light note, the Court adjourned for the day.

The nine justices convened in open court the next morning at 10 AM, and Clark was recalled to the lawyers' podium. He opened his remarks by alluding to the issue of population growth in Connecticut that had been raised in the questions put the previous day to Tom Emerson. Contrary to what his adversary had indicated, Clark pointed out that the birth rate had declined in Connecticut for seven straight years, and the birth rate nationally had also been dropping. The implication he drew from these statistics was that the fears that many twentieth-century demographic experts entertained about a "population explosion" had not been realized.

Justice Potter Stewart then inquired as to whether the Connecticut anticontraception statute was passed with an eye toward maintaining or increasing the population of the state. Clark said he would not make either claim. Rather, he declared that the original purpose of the old law was "to reduce the chances of immorality" by deterring sexual intercourse outside marriage. Justice Stewart questioned the relevance of this purpose to the current litigation because the appellants were seeking to provide contraceptive services only to married women. How, Clark was asked, could he defend the statute as it applied to married couples? Clark's response was simply that the law is a valid exercise of the state police power. When pushed harder on this point by Stewart, Clark repeated the distinction between birth control and contraception in his brief: a married man and woman can legally practice birth control in Connecticut without the use of contraceptives. They can use the rhythm method or practice abstinence. For Clark, such choices might reasonably be preferred by Connecticut under the police power doctrine. Stewart was not persuaded. He posed two additional questions: First, could a state pass a law banning all marriages? Second, by contrast, could a state pass a law compelling all married couples to use contraceptives? A question was then posed by another justice as to whether a state could ban the rhythm method of birth control. Perhaps sensing the weakness of the police power argument in the face of such hypothetical questions, Clark attempted to shift the focus of the discussion. He stated that the Connecticut law performed the useful moral purpose of discouraging married people from extramarital temptations. Yet another justice interjected that such a moral purpose could hardly be realized for those Connecticut residents — married or unmarried — who "ha[d] the price of a ticket to New York," where the use of contraceptives was not prohibited.

Sticking with the thread spun by Stewart, Goldberg asked Clark how he would answer the argument that, if the moral purpose of the Connecticut statute was to discourage immoral behavior, then how does banning the use of contraceptives meet a standard of due process that is "carefully tailored to meet the evil"? The young prosecutor responded that Connecticut had other laws on its books, such as those criminalizing adultery and fornication, that could encourage moral behavior. The law banning contraceptives could reinforce such laws. Returning to what had become his mantra before the Court, Clark once again declared that the statute was definitely within the scope of the police power of Connecticut to enact.

The justices next began to pepper Clark with questions about whether he felt the appellants had standing to challenge the constitutionality of the anticontraception law. Clark responded that he did indeed see a "great standing problem." First of all he pointed to some logical inconsistencies in the appellants' claim of standing. He pointed out that Griswold and Buxton were "holding themselves out to the world" that they were running a birth control clinic open to the public, but at the same time they were claiming that the right of privacy of unnamed married couples taking advantage of the clinic's services was being violated. In addition, the right of privacy was invoked for three married women who voluntarily testified that they had received contraceptive services at the New Haven Center. Second, he raised the point stressed in his brief that the appellants had not presented their constitutional claims in either a timely or an appropriate fashion in the Connecticut courts below. The justices chose not to follow up these points.

Clark was finally able to return to his prepared remarks. He recommenced by addressing the point raised by Tom Emerson in oral argument the previous day that the Connecticut anticontraception statute had become a "dead letter" through its nonenforcement. Clark's response to this was that the law must have some life because it had survived regular biennial challenges in the state general assembly since the 1920s. Clark then noted that the assembly was considering yet another repeal bill in the current session. He followed this by restating another point prominently raised in his brief, namely, that contraception is not a medical matter but a social issue. The purpose in advancing this point, he indicated, was to discount the statements in support of contraception in the amicus briefs of Planned Parenthood and the 138 distinguished physicians. No matter how overwhelming was the medical community's endorsement of the safety of contraception, and no matter how many authorities advocated the spacing of children for married couples by the means of artificial birth control, Clark reiterated his position that it still fell within the state of Connecticut's police power to ban the use of contraceptives.

Near the end of his presentation, Clark characterized the 1879 anticontraception law as a piece of economic regulation, which, if challenged constitutionally on due process grounds, should be held to a lower-level standard of "reasonableness," as opposed to the higher level of "strict scrutiny" that the Court has reserved since the late 1930s for laws affecting fundamental liberties. If Clark could establish this point, he might well prevail on due process grounds, because the Supreme Court had upheld almost every law it identified as a piece of economic regulation since the years of the Depression. When challenged to explain how a law forbidding contraception could be economic, Clark pointed to the fact that some women were charged as much as $15 for contraceptives by the Center. With that exchange, Clark's time at the podium was over and Tom Emerson was recalled to complete his reserved time.

The Case Is Submitted

After taking a minute or two to address the issue of standing, Emerson spoke to what he felt was the real impact of the anticontraception legislation on the people of Connecticut. Emerson acknowledged that the law was not being enforced against private physicians counseling their patients, nor against individuals who went to a drugstore or grocery and purchased packages of condoms. But in a highly publicized fashion, it had twice been enforced (in the *Nelson* case and the current case) against birth control clinics. This selective enforcement effectively prevented other birth control clinics from operating in the state.

Before Emerson could move on to another point, he was asked to comment on the difference between *Sanger v. People of New York* (1918) and *Gardner v. Commonwealth of Massachusetts* (1938) on the one hand and the Connecticut birth control decisions on the other. He noted that in the New York case the person being prosecuted,

Margaret Sanger, was not a physician like Dr. Buxton, and in the Massachusetts case the issue was the sale of contraceptives as opposed to the use of such articles as in the current appeal from Connecticut. Emerson was then asked whether his adversary, Joseph Clark, was correct in characterizing the Planned Parenthood Center of New Haven as a "business institution." He pointed out that the charges to the clients were minimal, that Dr. Buxton served without fee, and that Mrs. Griswold worked at the center as part of her duties as the executive director of the PPLC, for which she received a salary.

Finally Emerson was able to get back on track. He spoke for a few minutes about the need for the justices to render a broad decision in the case, not just to find that the statute as administered in this instance was inappropriate. He then fielded questions from the Court on whether the advice rendered at the Center was protected speech. A couple of the justices appeared concerned that the prescription of contraceptives by Dr. Buxton was conduct and not speech. And, following this logic, because the use of contraceptives was a criminal act in Connecticut, Buxton's conduct was also proscribed. Emerson's response was that if the "use" statute was found unconstitutional on the basis of due process or privacy grounds, Dr. Buxton's counseling — whether termed speech or conduct — could not be judged to be a crime either.

Justice Black then raised a matter with Emerson that neither side had addressed in its briefs or oral argument. He asked: "Would your argument, concerning these things you've been talking about relating to privacy, invalidate all laws that punish people for bringing about abortions?" Emerson, perhaps not realizing the full import of Black's question, responded that the practice of birth control takes place in the privacy of the home, whereas abortion generally occurs in a doctor's office or a medical facility. Justice Byron White chimed in: "Well, apart from that, Mr. Emerson, I take it abortion involves killing a life in being, doesn't it? Isn't that a rather different problem from conception?" Emerson readily agreed. Black then put the question starkly: "Are you saying that all abortions involve killing or murder?" Emerson said that he would not "characterize it that way" and went on to point out that Connecticut statutes permit abortion to save the life of the mother, but that Section 53–32 prohibits the use of contraceptives without exception. Drawing back from the explosive issue of abortion,

Emerson's final moments at the podium were occupied by a few quick responses to procedural questions.

The oral argument of *Griswold and Buxton v. Connecticut* concluded about 10:45 AM, and the case was submitted for decision. The press accounts of the *Griswold* oral argument emphasized that the justices constantly interrupted Joseph Clark and Tom Emerson. The stories mentioned different aspects of the give and take between the justices and the attorneys, such as questioning whether the liberty of unmarried women was protected by the right of privacy that Emerson was recommending, and why Connecticut needed a ban on contraceptives when it also had on its statute books laws against adultery and fornication. A fact surprisingly not mentioned by the press was the conspicuous silence over the two days of arguments by the Court's leading advocate of privacy, Justice William O. Douglas.

CHAPTER 8

Confidential Discussion and Public Decision

The Conference

At the conclusion of an oral argument in a case before the U.S. Supreme Court, it is almost as if a veil of silence falls over the matter. The parties, their attorneys, and the amici breathe a collective sigh of relief that their heavy lifting is finally at an end. The media usually place the issues on the back burner and move on to other timely and more visible concerns. Those directly involved in the litigation, together with the larger legal community and the general public, learn nothing more about a case until the decision is released to the media in a public Supreme Court session sometime later in the term. All they can do is wait and worry.

Periodically, the nine justices gather in their private conference room within the Supreme Court Building to discuss cases that they have recently heard. The conference room is beautifully paneled, with a fireplace, a chandelier, and a complete set of *U.S. Reports* (the official volumes containing the Court's decisions) in one of the walled bookcases. Generally, twice a week during a term the Court conducts a conference. Early in the term, review of petitions for certiorari and probable jurisdiction is the main item on the docket. Later in the term, discussion of cases that have recently been argued becomes the focus of the conference.

When it is time for a conference to commence, a buzzer summons the justices from their offices elsewhere in the building. As the justices file into the conference room, they shake hands with each other. Although there are strong intellectual and occasionally personal disagreements among the justices, the ritual of handshaking before conferences (as well as before oral arguments) is maintained in an attempt to preserve harmony on the Court. Under a painting of Chief Justice John Marshall and around a handsome table, the justices seat themselves in high-backed leather chairs. The chief justice is ensconced at one end of the table; the senior associate justice occupies the other end; the remaining justices sit in assigned places on the long sides of the table. No clerks, secretaries, aides, or visitors ever attend conferences of the Supreme Court. The most junior associate justice guards the door, dispatching and receiving any messages.

Supreme Court tradition holds that discussion on a case at the conference begins with comments of the chief justice and then proceeds in descending order from the most senior associate justice down through the Court's most recent appointee. By allowing the discussion to progress in order of seniority, the most experienced justices are able, if they wish, to establish the tone, direction, and even content of what is said. Earl Warren's reign on the Court as chief justice was loose enough, however, to permit some unstructured give-and-take discussion independent of seniority. After expending as much time as is needed to address all the points about a case that the justices wish to raise, a tentative vote is taken. The votes are cast orally in reverse order of seniority (most recent appointee first), so that junior justices will not be swayed by the votes of their senior colleagues or the chief justice. Each justice normally keeps a tally sheet of the voting on a case. After the votes have been cast, if the chief justice is in the majority, he assigns the writing of the "opinion of the Court" to one of those in the majority (himself included). If the chief is not in the majority, the senior associate justice in the majority makes the assignment from the justices voting with him (himself included). During the course of its yearly term, an effort is made by the chief justice to balance the workload of opinions of the Court somewhat evenly among the justices. Justices in the majority are free to write "concurring opinions" — opinions agreeing with the decision of the majority for different reasons than those specified in the opinion of the Court. Justices not in the majority may, if they choose, write dissenting opinions.

After the conference ends, the real work of the justices begins. The justice assigned to write the opinion of the Court prepares a draft, frequently benefiting from the advice, research, and writing skill of one or more of his or her law clerks. The law clerks are normally recent law school graduates with outstanding academic records. When the draft is completed, it is circulated to other members of the Court, including those not in the tentative majority, to see how many of them will "join" the opinion. At the same time, any justices who elect to produce concurring or dissenting opinions will similarly prepare drafts, circulate them, and solicit the votes of colleagues. Justices may change their votes on a case until the decision is announced in open court. Occasionally, the ebb and flow of votes may transform a concurrence or even a dissent into an opinion of the Court. Aside from their clerks and secretaries, the confidentiality of the how the justices voted and how a case will be decided is maintained until the decision is publically announced. On only a handful of occasions in the Court's history has word of a pending decision been leaked. However, years after the fact, as justices release their judicial papers, scholars are permitted to probe the notes, memoranda, and draft opinions on cases of interest to them. Through this review, details about the Court's decision making on a particular case, unknown to the public or the media at the time of decision, can be disclosed.

The Votes Are Tallied

The Supreme Court discussed *Griswold v. Connecticut* at its conference on Friday, April 2, 1965. Chief Justice Warren, in line with the traditions of the Court, spoke first. Warren had taken the time in advance of the conference to jot down notes on what he would say to his associates. He began by confessing that he was "bothered" by this case. Although he did acknowledge that the petitioners (that is, the appellants) had standing to bring their case "as aiders and abettors," Warren expressed the hope that the whole dispute would simply go away: "I would give [the] legisl[ature] a chance to dispose of it by waiting, if possible, to adjournment."

If forced to make a decision on the merits, Warren said that he was prepared to vote to reverse the Connecticut Supreme Court of Errors and strike down the anticontraception law. But he noted for his colleagues a number of possible legal grounds for reversal with which he had no sympathy: "I cannot say that it affects the 1st Amend[ment] rights of doctors; I cannot say the state has no legitimate interest — that would lead me to trouble on abortions; I cannot balance the interest of the state against that of the individual; I cannot use the substantive due process approach; I do not believe the equal protection argument is sound; and I do not accept the privacy argument." The comment on abortion is especially interesting. Warren's resignation from the Court took effect in 1969, four years before the nation's highest court confronted the legal issue of abortions squarely in *Roe v. Wade*. But Warren hinted here as to what his position would have been had he still been a member of the Supreme Court at the time of the *Roe* decision, that is, that state governments should have some say over when and under what circumstances abortions may be legal. What Warren had in mind when he mentioned "the substantive due process approach" was probably the argument proposed by John Marshall Harlan in *Poe v. Ullman*, to the effect that the Connecticut law violated "liberties" under the Fourteenth Amendment of those married couples choosing to use contraceptives. For Warren, the reliance on unnamed and ambiguous "liberties" was too close to the judicial fiat of *Lochner v. New York* (1905) and economic due process cases of that ilk.

Warren did indicate in his comments that he found two positions which he could possibly accept to justify reversal of the Connecticut Supreme Court — a "*Yick Wo* theory" and an argument that the statute was not tightly drawn. Reliance on *Yick Wo v. Hopkins* (1886) had been suggested as a possible basis for the decision by Warren's clerk, John Hart Ely. In the memorandum that had been circulating around the chambers of the justices for about a month, Ely had argued that the enforcement of the Connecticut anticontraception law targeted the class of married women but spared the sellers and manufacturers of contraceptives. Thus it denied married women equal protection. The "not tightly drawn" argument Warren had in mind was that the statute swept too broadly in its regulation of birth control and had the unsatisfactory effect of restricting the intimate right of association of married couples.

Hugo Black, the senior associate justice, presented his views next. Black began by stating that he could not vote to reverse the Connecticut statute on "any ground." He was critical of a contention by the appellants that the Connecticut law violated the "right of association" stemming from the right of assembly mentioned in the First Amendment. Black stated: "[T]he right of a husband and wife to assemble in bed is a new right of assembly to me." He also maintained that he would have "a hard time" applying the overbreadth doctrine to the statute because, as bad a law as it might be, it was, nevertheless, "pretty clear and carefully drawn." Then he qualified his stance. He indicated that he might be able to vote for reversal if the opinion of the Court was based on protecting the free expression rights of physicians to render advice to their patients about birth control. Black acknowledged that he could have supported a more finely tailored law that would have permitted physicians' counseling on birth control if made subject to reasonable restrictions. He finally stated that he was not at all comfortable with the kind of open-ended due process approach, urged on the Court by Tom Emerson and found in Justice Harlan's dissent in *Poe v. Ullman*, that would have permitted the creation of rights — like privacy — not found in the Bill of Rights. It appeared likely that Black would be writing a strong dissenting opinion.

William O. Douglas tersely noted that he supported reversing the Connecticut Supreme Court. In opposition to Justice Black, Douglas maintained that the right of association of a married couple is more than a right of assembly. It is a right protected on the "periphery" of the First Amendment, analogous to the right of association established by past Supreme Court decisions that permit a child to attend a private school or for an American citizen to travel abroad. Douglas did not, apparently, feel the need to remind his colleagues that he was on record in his dissent in *Poe* as not sharing the broad due process argument of Justice Harlan.

Tom Clark expressed agreement with Douglas. He mentioned that the Bill of Rights must be construed so as to protect "a right to marry, to have a home, to have children." Clark's position marked a switch from his support of the majority opinion of Felix Frankfurter in *Poe v. Ullman* four years earlier. Clark then stated that "this [marriage and birth control] is an area where I have the right to be left alone" and indicated that this is the basis that he would prefer for reversal.

There was no mystery as to the position that John Marshall Harlan would take on *Griswold*. He declared that he would reverse the Connecticut Supreme Court on the basis of his due process analysis in *Poe v. Ullman*. He indicated that he was critical of the Connecticut law because it was a "use statute," unlike most other state contraception laws still on the books that regulated the manufacturing, sale, or advertising of extrinsic birth control articles. He was also troubled that the law did not provide an exception for married couples in the use of contraceptives. Harlan did not take this opportunity to confront the several justices who had just made critical references to his open-ended view of "liberty" under the Fourteenth Amendment.

William J. Brennan expressed agreement with some of the views of the justices who had already indicated their wish to strike down the Connecticut law. He encouraged placing an emphasis on the right of privacy in crafting the opinion of the Court. In addition, Brennan ventured a cryptic comment to the effect that privacy should not be the exclusive province of a husband and wife. Of the justices who had spoken to this point in the conference, Brennan was the fifth to endorse reversal. Thus, unless votes later shifted, the 1879 Connecticut anticontraceptive statute was on the way out.

Potter Stewart took a position close to that of Hugo Black. For him, there was "nothing in the Bill of Rights that touches this." Disputing Tom Emerson's contention that selected provisions of the Bill of Rights "embody separate aspects" of a right of privacy, he declared, "I can't find anything in the First, Second, [Third?], Fourth, Fifth, Ninth, or other amendments, so I would have to affirm." As much as he might be skeptical of the wisdom and sweep of the Connecticut anticontraception law, Stewart indicated that the petitioners should seek relief in the state general assembly, not in the courts. Stewart's position was a bit surprising, given his cryptic statement in his *Poe* dissent. Often the enigma, Stewart had apparently changed his views from 1961 and was now on the opposite side of the birth control dispute from Douglas and Harlan.

Finally, the two newest appointees to the Court had a chance to express their views. Byron White simply indicated that he would vote to reverse. Arthur Goldberg was a bit more expansive. He supported reversal, he said, because he did not see any compelling reason that the state could justify such a sweeping statute as Section 53–32. Alluding to cases in which the Supreme Court had permitted freedom of association in education and cases in which the Court had held that past membership in the Communist Party did not imperil certain individual rights, he stated that he saw similar associational rights in the Connecticut case: "If one can form a club, he can join his wife and live with her as he likes."

The alignment of votes was thus seven in favor of reversing the

Connecticut Supreme Court on the birth control appeal (Warren, Douglas, Clark, Harlan, Brennan, White, and Goldberg) and two supporting its affirmation (Black and Stewart). After the oral argument, Tom Emerson in fact predicted to his clients that the vote would be 7–2 in their favor. He did not, however, specify the breakdown by justice. Had he done so, given the votes of the justices in *Poe*, he probably would have reversed the positions of Clark and Stewart.

A few days after the conference at which *Griswold v. Connecticut* was discussed, Chief Justice Warren distributed to all the judicial chambers copies of the assignment list for the next spate of majority opinions that the justices would be writing. Perhaps to the disappointment of Justice Harlan, who felt that he had placed his personal stamp on privacy with his dissent in *Poe*, the chief justice had assigned the *Griswold* opinion to William Douglas. Although Douglas was not as patient or as meticulous a judicial writer as Harlan, his view that a right of privacy could be gleaned from the emanations of particular portions of the Bill of Rights appeared to be closer to the doctrinal center of the Court than was Harlan's more ethereal liberty analysis under the Fourteenth Amendment. Also, Douglas was on record in favor of a constitutional right of privacy with as much vehemence as Harlan, as noted in the dissenting opinions from his "privacy spring" of 1952, *Beauharnais v. Illinois, Public Utilities Commission v. Pollak*, and *On Lee v. U.S.* Finally, some members of the Court and their clerks saw the whimsy of the chief justice in the assignment of this opinion: Douglas, with his failed marriages and numerous extramarital affairs, was now being asked to prepare a paean to the sanctity of marriage as the key foundation for a constitutional right of privacy.

Negotiating Language

The selection of William Douglas to write the opinion of the Court in *Griswold* sparked a bit of off-color kidding of "Wild Bill" by a couple of his colleagues. In an undated memo to Douglas, Byron White suggested four possible grounds for an opinion striking down the Connecticut anticontraception law: (1) the Fourth Amendment — "because the Conn. law would authorize a search for an intra-uterine coil"; (2) the Fifth Amendment — "the right to counsel — from a Dr.";

(3) the Eighth Amendment — "since there is an obvious addiction to sex involved & it is cruel & unusual punishment to deprive one of it or to permit it only at the cost of having children. A grizzly [sic] choice"; and (4) an allusion to the Court's recent reapportionment decisions — "one man, one child." It is possible, however, that it was Tom Clark who first suggested the "one man, one child" principle to Douglas. In an undated memo that Douglas sent to Clark, he complimented him: "I think your 'one man one child' formula is a flash of genius." Clark responded in a note back to Douglas that it "should be patentable."

Douglas's opinion of the Court in *Griswold v. Connecticut*, destined to be perhaps the most important majority opinion that he would write in his record-long tenure on the Court, was framed in the justice's typically hurried fashion. He had set to work promptly after receiving his assignment, and in just over a week had fashioned a first draft. It was a six-page, double-spaced effort, scrawled in blue ink on a yellow legal pad. After offering a terse statement of the facts and an explanation as to why the appellants had standing to bring the case to the Supreme Court, Douglas launched into his argument. This was not a substantive due process case, Douglas explained: "Overtones of some arguments suggest that *Lochner* . . . should be our guide. But we decline that invitation. . . . We do not sit as a super-legislature to determine the wisdom, need, and propriety of laws that touch economic problems, business affairs, or social conditions. . . . This case . . . has no commercial aspect or any marketing aspect. It deals with an intimate relation of husband and wife." The purpose of this statement was, no doubt, twofold: on the one hand, it would serve as a response to the likely dissent that would be coming from Hugo Black, and on the other, it would differentiate the opinion of the Court from the more abstract due process analysis that John Marshall Harlan had proposed in *Poe v. Ullman* and would likely be reprising in a concurrence in *Griswold*.

Douglas conceded in the face of the impending dissent from Black (and perhaps Stewart) that the word *privacy* is not mentioned in the Bill of Rights, nor is the "association" of husband and wife. However, he maintained, because education cases from the 1920s and civil rights cases from the 1950s had established that the First Amendment included "peripheral rights" of association, it was not much of a stretch to bring the relationship between husband and wife within this ambit. "Marriage," Douglas wrote, "does not fit precisely any of the categories of First Amendment rights. But it is a form of association as vital in the life of a man or woman as any other, and perhaps more so. . . . We deal with a right of association older than the Bill of Rights. . . . It is a coming together for better or for worse, hopefully enduring, and intimate to the degree of being sacred." What the Connecticut anticontraception law did, in Douglas's rhetoric, was to threaten this sacred and intimate association and thus run afoul of the spirit of American liberties: "The prospects of police with warrants searching the sacred precincts of marital bedrooms for telltale signs of the use of contraceptives is repulsive to the idea of privacy and of association that make up a goodly part of the penumbra of the Constitution and Bill of Rights."

The draft contained much of the stirring language that would make it into the final version of Douglas's opinion. But it was short on supporting analysis, particularly in regard to the concept of privacy. Privacy, as we have seen, had a substantial history on the fringes of constitutional interpretation, including in Douglas's own dissent in *Poe v. Ullman*. In fact, Douglas's only clerk in the 1964–65 term, James S. Campbell, a Stanford Law School graduate, encouraged the justice to infuse his draft with more of the privacy analysis from his *Poe* opinion. Douglas acquiesced somewhat to this suggestion and, after the opinion was set in type, sent a copy to the chambers of William Brennan, the justice whom Douglas believed came closest to sharing his views on this case. As a cagey judicial politician, Douglas wanted Brennan's thoughts on his draft before he sent it to all the justices' chambers.

Brennan, who took more advantage of the intelligence and legal skills of his law clerks than Douglas, gave the draft of Douglas's majority opinion in *Griswold* to S. Paul Posner, one of his 1964–65 clerks, for a reaction. Posner was not impressed with the Douglas draft and said so bluntly in a three-page memorandum to Brennan. Making only a few changes in Posner's memo, and adding some language flattering to his longtime colleague, Brennan had the memo retyped and sent to Douglas on April 24, 1965, over his own signature. The Posner/Brennan suggestions to Douglas were substantial. Brennan stated at the outset of the letter that he agreed with a great deal of Douglas's draft. He indicated that Douglas was "absolutely right" for rejecting *Lochner* as a basis for the opinion and that he was also correct that the lack of specific mention of the "association of husband and wife" in the Bill of Rights is "the obstacle we must hurdle to effect a reversal in this case." However, he indicated that he wanted to propose a "substantial change in emphasis for your consideration."

The Posner/Brennan letter argued that it would not be a good idea for the opinion of the Court in *Griswold* to attempt to bring the marriage relationship under the rubric of the right to association in the context of the First Amendment. To place language in the opinion suggesting that "the family unit is a sacred unit, that it is unreachable by the State . . . may come back to haunt us just as *Lochner* did." Instead of the narrow husband-wife rubric, Posner and Brennan encouraged Douglas to adopt the larger and more protective umbrella of privacy. Under the right of privacy, they maintained, could be subsumed the "associational rights" of individuals in groups. Members of associations such as the NAACP have constitutional rights because of something more fundamental than legal incorporation in a group's bylaws: "Instead of expanding the First Amendment right of association to include marriage, why not say that what has been done for the First Amendment can also be done for some of the other fundamental guarantees of the Bill of Rights? In other words, where fundamentals are concerned, the Bill of Rights guarantees are but expressions or examples of those rights, and do not preclude applications or extensions of those rights to situations unanticipated by the Framers." This was vintage Brennan: the diminutive jurist from New Jersey was the Court's leading exponent of the view that the spirit of liberty in the Constitution should be allowed to flourish as changing times demanded and not be circumscribed by the eighteenth-century experiences of the framers.

Brennan indicated that he would support Douglas's opinion, whether it expanded the guarantees of specific amendments in the Bill of Rights to include privacy or if it used the Ninth Amendment's "certain rights . . . retained by the people" language as a tool to move privacy within the orbit of the Bill of Rights. Using either of these approaches, the Posner/Brennan letter maintained, would find the Connecticut statute "run[ning] afoul of a right to privacy." In the Posner/Brennan view, the Connecticut law breached privacy as protected by the Third, Fourth, and Fifth Amendments. They did not recommend that Douglas lay out all the boundaries and particulars of a right of privacy: "All that is necessary for the decision of this case is the recognition that, whatever the contours of a constitutional right to privacy, it would preclude application of the statute before us to married couples." Brennan concluded the letter by declaring that the approach just proposed "would be attractive to me because it would require less departure from the specific guarantees and because I think there is a better chance it will command a Court."

Douglas may not always have been a careful legal draftsman, but he was generally astute enough to take good advice on his opinions when it was offered. On April 27, 1965, within three days after he had received the Posner/Brennan letter, Douglas produced another draft of the *Griswold* opinion. This version emphasized the right to privacy. The April 27 draft, in fact, was very close to the final iteration of Douglas's opinion in which he would declare that the each of the first eight amendments casts shadows, what he termed "penumbra," within which the Bill of Rights protections shade into other rights not specifically enumerated in those amendments. Brennan showed this draft to Posner. In a note to Brennan, Posner characterized the second Douglas draft as "a signal victory." He continued: "The approach is, I think, substantially in accord with your note of April 24. The only changes I would suggest now are in emphasis." Among the minor changes that Posner proposed, through Brennan to Douglas, was a "beefing up" of the "penumbra stuff." This, he felt, would take some of the steam out of the attacks on the vagueness of Douglas's analysis that was likely to issue from the dissenting justices, Hugo Black and Potter Stewart. He also asked Brennan to encourage Douglas to bolster his Ninth Amendment argument. Finally, he recommended that Douglas consider acknowledging that there are some limitations to the constitutional right of privacy. After offering these suggestions on emphasis and tone, Posner had the temerity to propose to Brennan tactics for negotiating the opinion with Douglas: "I think points 4 & 5 [the most weighty points mentioned in his memo] can be made to Justice Douglas directly, without offending him, if you point out that they may be helpful in getting a Court. I can probably take care of 1, 2, and 3 [the narrow, more technical points raised by Posner], by speaking to his law clerk after the opinion has circulated, if he hasn't taken care of them by then."

The difference between how Brennan dealt with his clerks and how Douglas did is instructive. Douglas, as his Supreme Court papers on *Griswold* indicate, had his 1964–65 clerk, James Campbell, checking citations and finding cases. Many years later, in an interview with a Douglas biographer, Campbell indicated that his justice "wouldn't let me near" a majority opinion as important at *Griswold*. Douglas's clerks wrote countless memos on certiorari petitions, brought him research materials for his travel books and legal writings, and searched out answers to any questions, no matter how strange, that Douglas had for them. Occasionally, especially in Douglas's later years on the Court, they helped him prepare his dissents and footnotes. In the 1970s Douglas told a new colleague, Justice Harry Blackmun, not entirely tongue in cheek, that "law clerks are the lowest form of human life." Douglas's law clerks dreaded the sound of the buzzer that the justice would press incessantly, summoning them to his beck and call. Once, when a new law clerk who had not been properly schooled in the protocol of the Douglas chambers had the effrontery to make a substantive suggestion, without being asked, in the margins of a draft opinion, Douglas buzzed him angrily into his inner office. He berated the young man: "Were you nominated by the President for a seat on the Supreme Court? Were you confirmed by the Senate?" Had Douglas known that Brennan was serving as the conduit for suggestions to him from a mere clerk, it is unlikely that he would have been so accommodating in making the changes that Brennan proposed.

John Hart Ely, the clerk who had already had influence on the chief justice with a preoral argument memorandum on *Griswold*, was not as enamored of the second draft of the Douglas opinion in the case as were Justice Brennan and his clerk. Still believing that the Constitution should not be stretched to create a right of privacy, he discouraged Earl Warren from signing on with Douglas. "This opinion," he wrote in a memo to the Chief Justice, "incorporates an approach to the Constitution so dangerous that you should not join it." He urged Warren to "wait and see what is written" in other chambers. If nothing better should materialize, Ely mentioned to his justice that "I do not think it would be much trouble for us to write a brief concurrence." The use of the pronoun "us" by Ely suggests that his relationship with the chief justice was more akin to that of Posner and Brennan than Campbell and Douglas.

The period beginning in late April and running through the month of May 1965, coming as it did near the end of the 1964–65 term of the Court, was a typically busy time for the justices and their clerks. *Griswold v. Connecticut* was just one of many pending cases, but it was proving more troublesome to find closure than most of the term's cases. Yes, the justices had voted 7–2 to support reversal of the Connecticut Supreme Court of Errors and strike down the 1879 anticontraception law. But Douglas's assigned opinion of the Court was not attracting much support. Besides Chief Justice Warren, Byron White was up in the air about whether he would be writing a separate opinion. He would eventually decide to do so. Initially, John Marshall Harlan had requested that Douglas simply add a statement at the end of the opinion of the Court indicating that he, Harlan, "concurs in the judgment of reversal on the grounds stated in his dissenting opinion in *Poe v. Ullman.*" However, Harlan would later ask that this language be removed; he would submit a separate concurring opinion. Arthur Goldberg wrote to Douglas on April 29 that he was "very glad to join your fine opinion." Goldberg, however, announced two weeks later that he would be submitting a separate concurrence stressing the Ninth Amendment as the basis for a right of privacy. In Goldberg's words: "I have added some of my views about the 9th Amendment which, as I recall the Conference discussion, you are not free to do as reflecting the views of all in the majority." Ultimately Goldberg's long concurrence would draw the support of Warren and Brennan. Hugo Black had been committed to preparing a separate dissent for some time. On April 29, Potter Stewart wrote the Court that he would be circulating a dissenting opinion himself. Only Tom Clark seemed firmly in line with Douglas's draft on all particulars. On April 28 he wrote to Douglas: "Bill, Yes I like all of it — it emancipates femininity and protects masculinity — TC."

So as of about the middle of May 1965, it appeared that there would be six opinions in *Griswold.* Douglas would still command the opinion of the Court — assuming that he could find four justices to agree with him. If not, perhaps one of the concurring opinions — the opinion of White, or Harlan, or Goldberg — would change clothes and become the opinion of the Court. The two dissenting opinions of Black and Stewart were taking shape. Because drafts of dissenting opinions are circulated around the Court just as other opinions, occasionally a dissent can influence the way an opinion of the Court or a concurrence is written. Or a dissent can have the further effect of splintering a tentative Court majority.

Many years after the fact, some of the individuals who were Supreme Court clerks in 1965 talked to interviewers about the assembly of opinions in *Griswold* during the last six weeks of the 1964–65 term of the Court. They indicated that the April 27, 1965, draft of Douglas's opinion was not well received in various justices' chambers. Some of the clerks were shocked by how weak an opinion was taking shape in this important case. A few made jokes about Douglas's talk about "emanations" and "penumbras." Drawing on what he was hearing from the other clerks, Jim Campbell offered gentle suggestions in the form of short memos to his justice about how his *Griswold* opinion might be made more palatable to the Court's majority.

In particular, Campbell was hoping that a more finely tuned opinion by Douglas could attract the votes of Warren and White. One of the memos written by Campbell attached "a rider" that highlighted a passage from Louis Brandeis's classic dissent in *Olmstead v. U.S.* (1928), which in turn included allusions to the celebrated "right to be let alone" phraseology of Thomas Cooley and the famous 1890 *Harvard Law Review* article by Brandeis and Samuel Warren. Campbell hoped that Douglas's invocation of one of Brandeis's classic civil liberties dissents would move the chief justice and Byron White to Douglas's side. Campbell also offered another rider to Douglas that sought to counter some of the language in Hugo Black's dissent accusing Douglas, for the Court, of trying to elevate a common law right of privacy to constitutional status. But Douglas, true to his reputation as a loner, turned a deaf ear to most of his clerk's advice. Although he did delete a sentence near the end of the opinion as a courtesy to Tom Clark, the final version of his opinion would be very close to the second draft that he had written in late April.

What ultimately allowed Douglas to command a five-person majority for his opinion were not the entreaties of James Campbell or Douglas's own rhetorical brilliance. It was a tactical choice made by Chief Justice Warren. John Hart Ely, Warren's assertive clerk, thought that the best draft opinion emerging out of the fog of *Griswold* was a concurrence written by Byron White that featured the *Yick Wo* equal protection argument for which Ely had lobbied in his February memorandum. Despite Ely's plea that he join the White opinion, Warren finally decided in early June that he would sign another concurrence — the one that had been prepared by Arthur Goldberg. Much of the research for Goldberg's opinion had been accomplished by one of Goldberg's clerks, Stephen Breyer. Unlike the White or Harlan concurrences, the Goldberg opinion was directly linked to Douglas's opinion of the Court. At the outset of his opinion, Goldberg wrote: "I agree with the Court that Connecticut's birth-control law unconstitutionally intrudes upon the right of marital privacy, and I join in its opinion and judgment. . . . In reaching the conclusion that the right of marital privacy is protected, as being within the . . . penumbra of specific guarantees of the Bill of Rights, the Court refers to the Ninth Amendment. . . . I add these words to emphasize the relevance of that Amendment to the Court's holding." Besides the chief justice, William Brennan signed the Goldberg concurrence.

Chief Justice Warren's reluctant acquiescence to Goldberg's opinion meant that there were now five justices — Douglas, Clark, Goldberg, Brennan, and Warren — who were willing to accept Douglas's opinion as the official statement of the Court in *Griswold*, with the latter three of these also subscribing to Goldberg's Ninth Amendment codicil. The Harlan and White concurrences would represent their agreement in the judgment of the Court striking down the Connecticut anticontraception law, but their reasoning would be unique to each of them individually. Justices Black and Stewart would be submitting separate dissents, and they would concur in each other's opinion. Having finally reached closure on *Griswold* on June 4, the six opinions were sent to the Court's print shop, and the Court prepared to announce its long-awaited decision in the Connecticut birth control case.

The Shadows of the Constitution

After fifty years of fruitless legislative efforts to modify or repeal the Connecticut anticontraception law, and after twenty-five years of abortive judicial challenges to Sections 53–32 and 54–196 of the Connecticut General Statutes by the Planned Parenthood League of Connecticut (PPLC), finally — in the last public session of the 1964–65 term of the U.S. Supreme Court — the nation's highest court relieved the country of an eighty-six-year-old vestige of Comstockian prudery. The opinions in *Griswold v. Connecticut* were distributed to the media and interested Court watchers on Monday, June 7, 1965. They shared billing that day with a 5–4 Supreme Court decision that ruled that the criminal trial of Texan Billy Sol Estes had been fatally contaminated by the presence of television coverage in the courtroom. The next day, some newspapers led with the TV coverage story; others featured the Connecticut birth control case. Given the years of effort in lobbying legislators and thousands of hours preparing and delivering legal arguments, Justice Douglas's terse six-and-a-half page opinion might have seemed to the Connecticut activists as an anticlimax. But the true sweep of Douglas's opinion establishing a constitutional right of privacy and its potential significance in a variety of legal contexts was apparent to those who took the time to read and study his argument. The views of the other justices, presented in five additional opinions, also offered much to ponder.

Douglas devoted only a page in his opinion to a statement of the facts in the case and the route it took to arrive in the Supreme Court. His summary placed in italics the fact that the Planned Parenthood League of Connecticut's New Haven Center offered birth control services only to *married persons.* On the second page of the opinion, Douglas confronted the matter of whether the appellants, Estelle Griswold and Lee Buxton, possessed the necessary standing to raise constitutional issues in their own right and also on behalf of unnamed married couples. He distinguished this case from the declaratory judgment case of *Tileston v. Ullman* (1943). By being themselves found guilty of counseling married persons about contraception, Douglas held on behalf of the Court that Griswold and Buxton may assert the rights of unnamed individuals. In his words: "Certainly the accessory should have standing to assert that the offense which he is charged with assisting is not, or cannot constitutionally be, a crime." In support of this proposition he cited several cases, many of which had been touched on by Thomas Emerson in his brief for the appellants. To nail down standing for the unnamed individuals, Douglas wrote: "The rights of husband and wife, pressed here, are likely to be diluted or adversely affected unless those rights are considered in a suit involving those who have this kind of confidential relation to them." Joseph

Clark, the state prosecuting attorney, had argued the standing issue at great length in his Supreme Court brief; Douglas had brushed it off in two short paragraphs. None of the other five opinions in *Griswold* even mentioned the standing issue.

At the bottom of the second page of his opinion Douglas began his discussion of the merits of the birth control case. He noted that the appellants had raised "a wide range of questions that implicate the Due Process Clause of the Fourteenth Amendment." In fact, this had been the heart of Emerson's brief, occupying almost sixty pages. Rather than confronting each of Emerson's many points and subpoints regarding the law's numerous putative due process failings, Douglas sidestepped the issue by writing the following: "Overtones of some arguments suggest that *Lochner v. New York* . . . should be our guide. But we decline that invitation. . . . We do not sit as a super-legislature to determine the wisdom, need, and propriety of laws that touch economic problems, business affairs, or social conditions."

Saying no more about due process, Douglas moved nimbly to the privacy issue: "This law . . . operates directly on an intimate relation of husband and wife and their physician's role in one aspect of that relation." He indicated that neither the Constitution nor the Bill of Rights protects by direct language "the association of people." But the First Amendment, as made applicable to the states by the Fourteenth Amendment, he argued, protects the right to educate children in schools chosen by their parents (*Pierce v. Society of Sisters*) and the right to study German in a private school (*Meyer v. Nebraska*). In broader terms, Douglas declared, "the State may not, consistently with the spirit of the First Amendment, contract the spectrum of available knowledge." He cited several cases — some mentioned in the briefs of Emerson and Clark, some not — that established what he termed "peripheral rights" under the First Amendment. Among the peripheral rights flowing from the freedom of expression were the following: the right to distribute, the right to read, the freedom to teach, and the "freedom to associate and privacy in one's associations."

In addition to "privacy" and "periphery," in this context Douglas introduced another, more obscure, "p" word — *penumbra*: "[T]he First Amendment," he wrote, "has a penumbra where privacy is protected from government intrusion." According to the *Oxford English Dictionary* (*OED*) the word *penumbra* came into English usage about the middle of the seventeenth century. Its origin is Latin, a conjoining of two words, *paena*, "almost," and *umbra*, "shadow." Its most common usage over the last three centuries has been in the field of astronomy; there the penumbra is defined by the *OED* as "the partially shaded outer region of a shadow when the light comes from a source of some size, especially that of the shadow cast by the moon or the earth in an eclipse." Figuratively, the term *penumbra* is generally understood to be "a surrounding area of uncertain extent." Sometimes it is used synonymously with the word *peripheral*. That, judging from context, is what Douglas had in mind. Douglas was not the first justice to enlist the word *penumbra* in aid of a critical point in a Supreme Court opinion. Before *Griswold*, the word had found its way into Supreme Court opinions twenty-four times, usually in cases involving statutory interpretation. Justice Holmes used it first in a 1916 case and then enlisted the word on four other occasions. Douglas used it in eight cases before 1965. Curiously, Douglas had not used the term *penumbra* in his dissent in *Poe v. Ullman*.

Douglas then proceeded to refer to instances in the past where the Supreme Court had seen fit to protect penumbral, or derivative, First Amendment rights. One such case was *Schware v. Board of Examiners* (1957), in which a penumbral right of association within the Communist Party was deemed not a permissible ground to exclude a lawyer from the practice of his trade. Another case Douglas alluded to was *DeJonge v. Oregon* (1937), in which the right of attending a meeting conducted by a radical group was deemed to fall within the peripheral freedom of association under the First Amendment. Association may not be explicitly listed among the First Amendment's protected freedoms, but, according to Douglas, "its existence is necessary in making the express guarantees [of the First Amendment] fully meaningful."

Having argued that the Court has extended First Amendment protections to peripheral activities, Douglas then posited that other "specific guarantees in the Bill of Rights have penumbras, formed by emanations from those guarantees that help give them life and substance." In support of this proposition, he cited his dissenting opinion in *Poe*. Then Douglas followed with a rapid listing of what he felt were some of the "zones of privacy" protected by provisions of the Bill of Rights. The freedom of association under the First Amendment, he reiterated, falls within one of the protected zones. Another "facet of that privacy" is the Third Amendment's prohibition against quartering soldiers in a private home in time of peace without the owner's permission. The Fourth Amendment's protection of individuals against unreasonable searches and seizures and the Fifth Amendment's privilege against self-incrimination also fall within such protected zones. Finally, the "rights . . . retained by the people" language of the Ninth Amendment, Douglas suggested, could be read as to permit a right of privacy. Curiously, Douglas did not cite any cases or analysis to support his assertions about penumbral rights in the context of the Third and Ninth Amendments. His Fourth and Fifth Amendment examples were bolstered only by brief allusions to the old case of *Boyd v. United States* (1886) and the recent search and seizure decision of *Mapp v. Ohio* (1961), and to two law review articles. He also cited without specific comment a few opinions — mainly those that Douglas himself had written — that reinforced, as he put it, the "rights of privacy and repose."

Then, in the penultimate paragraph of his opinion, Douglas returned to the facts of the case before the Court. He ruled, on behalf of the five justices signing his opinion, that the relationship between physicians and patients falls within the constitutionally protected zone of privacy, and that Connecticut, in proscribing the use of contraceptives to married couples, has acted in a fashion that has "maximum destructive impact" on the doctor-patient relationship. A state may have the legal right to regulate the sale or manufacture of contraceptives, Douglas held, but a law such as Section 53-32 that attempts to punish the mere *use* of contraceptives "sweep[s] unnecessarily broadly and thereby invade[s] the area of protected freedoms."

Douglas concluded his opinion with several sentences, closely tracking those in his previous drafts, defending the fundamental nature of privacy in a marriage. He asked rhetorically: "Would we allow the police to search the sacred precincts of marital bedrooms for telltale signs of the use of contraceptives? The very idea is repulsive to the notions of privacy surrounding the marriage relationship." He continued to voice this point in the final paragraph of the opinion: "We deal with a right of privacy older than the Bill of Rights. . . . Marriage is a coming together for better or worse, hopefully enduring, and intimate to the degree of being sacred. It is an association that promotes a way of life, not causes; a harmony in living, not political faiths; a bilateral loyalty, not commercial or social projects. Yet it is an association for as noble a purpose as any involved in our prior decisions." The irony of the Supreme Court's most profligate adulterer extolling the sanctity of marriage was presumably missed by the large but unknown number of young couples in the late 1960s and early 1970s who included language from the final paragraph of Douglas's *Griswold* opinion in their wedding vows.

In spite of the polite entreaties from his clerk, James Campbell, nowhere in the opinion of the Court in *Griswold v. Connecticut* did Douglas pay deference to Louis Brandeis's classic dissenting opinion defending privacy in *Olmstead v. U.S.* (1928). Nor did he refer to the well-known "The Right to Privacy" essay, published by Brandeis and Samuel Warren in 1890. As several Court watchers would later observe, Douglas's opinion of the Court in *Griswold* was considerably shorter and less pithy than his dissenting opinion in *Poe*. Those justices offering concurrences and dissents went to much greater lengths than Douglas to defend their particular views of the constitutionality of Sections 53–32 and 54–196 of the General Statutes of Connecticut.

Goldberg's Ninth; and Harlan's and White's Fourteenth

In late April 1965, at about the time Goldberg had indicated to Douglas that he would be writing a concurrence in *Griswold*, the Court's most junior justice had charged one of his clerks, Stephen Breyer, with performing research on the origins and purpose of the Ninth Amendment. Breyer, who would be appointed to the Supreme Court himself in 1994, also wrote the initial draft of Goldberg's concurrence. In mid-May, the Goldberg/Breyer draft was circulated around the eight other chambers. In one sense, the final version of Goldberg's concurrence, which also bore the signatures of Chief Justice Warren and William Brennan, was proffered as merely an extended footnote to Douglas's opinion of the Court. Near the beginning of his opinion, Goldberg noted that he agreed with Douglas's view that the guarantees of liberty are not confined to the specific terms of the Bill of Rights but include rights that may be termed "fundamental" in the American constitutional system. Following from that precept, Goldberg expressed agreement with Douglas that the right of marital privacy falls within the protective penumbra of various general guarantees of the Bill of Rights. He emphasized that one of the specific protections that Douglas claimed to possess a penumbra was the Ninth Amendment's promise that "[t]he enumeration in the Constitution, of certain rights, shall not be construed to deny or disparage others retained by the people." To carry forward Douglas's figure of speech, one thing that Goldberg was attempting to accomplish in his concurrence was to illuminate the Ninth Amendment that Douglas had not taken the time to drag from the constitutional shadows. In addition, by attempting to infuse the Ninth Amendment — what one scholar in the middle 1950s had termed "the forgotten amendment" — with content from the nation's historical experience, Goldberg was adding a new chapter to the legal discussion about privacy. Not surprisingly, striving for these two goals took more than a few paragraphs. In fact, Goldberg's opinion ended up being over thirteen pages, about twice the length of Douglas's opinion of the Court.

As the research of Breyer and Goldberg illustrated, the framer primarily responsible for drafting the Ninth Amendment was James Madison, the principal architect of the Constitution as a whole. Madison's text of the amendment was approved by the two houses of Congress with little debate and almost no change from Madison's original language. Madison's purpose in introducing the Ninth Amendment in Congress was to allay the concerns of members of the legislative branch who feared that the specific guarantees in the Bill of Rights would not be comprehensive enough to secure the rights and liberties of Americans. He also wanted to make clear that the first eight amendments were not meant to be the last words on the "rights . . . retained by the people." Joseph Story, perhaps the greatest legal scholar of the early republic, agreed with Madison that there was a need for such a strong statement of rights retained by the people and saw the Ninth Amendment as ably filling this void. The research of Breyer and Goldberg, however, disclosed only a handful of references to the Ninth Amendment in over 180 years of U.S. Supreme Court opinions. Nevertheless, Goldberg contended that the Ninth Amendment provided on important prop for the right of privacy. Goldberg was quick to add that he did not see the Ninth Amendment as an independent source of rights to be guaranteed against transgression by the states or the federal government. "Rather," he wrote, "the Ninth Amendment shows a belief of the Constitution's authors that fundamental rights exist that are not expressly enumerated in the first eight amendments and an intent that the list of rights included there not be deemed exhaustive."

Goldberg noted in his opinion that he supported the "selective incorporation theory" of the Bill of Rights, namely, the view that holds that the due process clause of the Fourteenth Amendment serves as a lever to bring key liberties to individuals in the face of state as well as federal infringement. For him, thus, the Ninth Amendment "lends strong support" to the incorporation view that the "liberty" mentioned in the Fourteenth Amendment is not limited to the rights specifically laid out in the first eight amendments. Judges cannot decide which rights are key or "fundamental" by exercising their own value preferences. Instead, according to Goldberg, they must attempt to identify only those rights that are firmly embedded in the "traditions and collective conscience of our people." For Goldberg, the right of privacy passed this test of being sufficiently rooted in American history as to be judged a "fundamental personal right." To bolster this viewpoint, he quoted the famous passage from Louis Brandeis's dissent in *Olmstead v. U.S.* that Douglas had chosen not to include in the opinion of the Court: "The protection guaranteed by the [Fourth and Fifth] Amendments is much broader in scope. . . . [The founders] sought to protect Americans in their beliefs, their thoughts, their emotions and their sensations. They conferred, as against the Government, the right to be let alone — the most comprehensive of rights and the right most valued by civilized men." And, like Douglas, Goldberg cited *Meyer v. Nebraska* and *Pierce v. Society of Sisters* in support of the proposition that marriage and family life are "particularly important and sensitive area[s] of privacy."

The draft dissenting opinions of Hugo Black and Potter Stewart in *Griswold* made their rounds of the justices' chambers at about the same time that Goldberg's draft concurrence was being circulated. Both of the dissenting opinions accused Goldberg of falling prey to the danger of imposing his own personal views to determine what constitutes liberty within the Bill of Rights. Goldberg responded in his concurrence that the Black/Stewart charge was unjustified. For Goldberg, the Connecticut anticontraception law violated the intensely personal and intimate rights of married couples. Such personal liberty, according to Goldberg, could only be encroached on by demonstrating a "compelling" state interest. To the state argument that the banning of the use of contraceptives by the Connecticut legislature discourages sexual relations outside of marriage, Goldberg had no sympathy. Even if the discouraging of sexual relations was considered a compelling basis for the law, the Connecticut statute falls prey to the attack that it is not finely enough tailored. Then existing Connecticut laws forbidding adultery and fornication, Goldberg maintained, better target extramarital activity than universal state proscriptions on the use of contraceptives. Moreover, Goldberg argued, forbidding the use of contraceptives among married couples had no impact on sexual activity outside of marriage. Goldberg closed his opinion by quoting with approval a passage from Justice Harlan's dissent in *Poe v. Ullman:* "It is one thing when the State exerts its power either to forbid extra-marital sexuality . . . or to say who may marry, but it is quite another when, having acknowledged a marriage and the intimacies inherent in it, it undertakes to regulate by means of the criminal law the details of that intimacy."

Justice John Marshall Harlan's concurrence was shorter and more focused than Goldberg's. It was also an opinion in which no other justice on the *Griswold* Court expressed agreement. Shortly after the conference on *Griswold,* Harlan had asked Douglas to append a short note to his opinion of the Court indicating that he, Harlan, concurred for the reasons expressed in his dissenting opinion in *Poe v. Ullman.* Eventually, however, Harlan was stirred to compose a slightly longer opinion because of arguments presented by Black and Stewart in dissent that were circulating through the Supreme Court chambers during May 1965. To the surprise of no one familiar with the positions of Harlan, Black, and Stewart, their differences in constitutional philosophy raged once again in the pages of the *U.S. Reports* containing the opinions in *Griswold v. Connecticut.*

Hugo Black had argued in opinion after opinion for almost two decades that the due process clause of the Fourteenth Amendment incorporated all of the protections of the Bill of Rights to safeguard the rights of individuals against state legislative infringements. Further, Black's position was that there were no other individual liberties that could be found to be protected by the Bill of Rights than those explicitly enumerated in the first eight amendments. By contrast, Harlan was a strong believer in the selective incorporation theory of the Fourteenth Amendment. For Harlan, the best expression of the standards for which liberties of the Fourteenth Amendment should be held as binding on state governments was enunciated by Justice Benjamin Cardozo in *Palko v. Connecticut* (1937). In that opinion, Cardozo held that only those liberties that constituted "the very essence of a scheme of ordered liberty, . . . principles of justice so rooted in the traditions and conscience of our people as to be ranked fundamental" should be held to protect individuals against state infringement. Consistent with this position, Harlan did not see protected liberties being limited to the enumerated items in the Bill of Rights. The right of privacy was one such unenumerated protected liberty, as Harlan had argued at length in dissent in *Poe*. Hence, a law like Connecticut's old anticontraception statute, which intruded into the realm of marital privacy, drew the wrath of Harlan. Black, in his dissent, also accused Harlan of abandoning his traditional adherence to judicial self-restraint in his *Poe* and *Griswold* opinions. This charge clearly bothered the aging Harlan, who, in return, accused Black of peddling a "historically unfounded incorporation formula" through his alleged misreading of the positions of key congressmen involved in the drafting and passage of the Fourteenth Amendment.

Byron White, shortly after offering William Douglas the risqué advice for his opinion of the Court in *Griswold*, set to work on his own concurring opinion in the case. Like other opinions written in favor of reversing the Connecticut Supreme Court, White relied on *Meyer v. Nebraska* and *Pierce v. Society of Sisters* to support the argument that liberties protected by the due process clause of the Fourteenth Amendment include the right to "marry, establish a home and bring up children." Having erected this constitutional platform, it was but a short further climb for White to reach the position that marital privacy was also a liberty entitled to protection. For White, the most serious problem with the 1879 Connecticut law was its effect on low-income married women. As a consequence of the closing of the PPLC's New Haven Center in November 1961, Connecticut women without the means to receive counseling on family planning from private physicians found themselves unable to obtain birth control services anywhere in the state. In White's view, this was class discrimination, unconstitutional under both the due process and equal protection clauses of the Fourteenth Amendment. In support of this position, White cited *Yick Wo v. Hopkins* (1886) and *Skinner v. Oklahoma* (1942). Such a law could be held constitutional, White submitted, only if it served a "compelling state interest" as determined by the Supreme Court's "strict scrutiny" standard.

White also failed to perceive any relationship between Connecticut's ban on the use of contraceptives by married couples and the state's avowed policy of discouraging all forms of promiscuous or illicit sexual behavior. The state had seldom, if ever, prosecuted individuals for the mere use of contraceptives. On the basis of the reasoning of decisions in nearby Massachusetts, White ventured that the sale of contraceptives to prevent disease was effectively legal in Connecticut. Given this social reality in Connecticut, the only reason White could see behind a statute denying married people the use of contraceptives is that such individuals, as a result of not having ready access to contraceptives, would be less tempted to engage in extramarital relationships. Of course, any Connecticut residents engaging in fornication or adultery could have a free pass under the law if they used contraceptives for the prevention of disease. The legislative purpose of discouraging extramarital sex, White concluded, could be better realized by the enforcement of existing fornication or adultery statutes than by the nonenforcement of a statute forbidding the use of contraceptives. Thus, for White as well as some of the other justices on the Court, Section 53–32 ran afoul of the doctrine of overbreadth.

———

Beware the Platonic Guardians

The longest opinion in *Griswold* was a twenty-page dissent by Hugo Black. It bore many of the distinctive features of Black's jurisprudence: it emerged out of a literal reading of the Bill of Rights; it drew from historical as well as legal sources; it was argued passionately; and it proved to be eminently quotable. Early in his opinion, Black made clear his position on the Connecticut anticontraception law as a matter of public policy and the separate issue of its constitutionality: "[T]he law is every bit as offensive to me as it is to my Brethren . . . who, reciting reasons why it is offensive to them hold it unconstitutional. There is no single one of the graphic and eloquent strictures and criticisms fired at the policy of this Connecticut law either by the Court's opinion or by those of my concurring Brethren to which I cannot subscribe — except their conclusion that the evil qualities they see in the law make it unconstitutional."

As perhaps the Supreme Court's most passionate defender of free expression, Black insisted that, if the question presented in this case was whether Mrs. Griswold and Dr. Buxton had been denied the right to voice their opinions on birth control, he would have easily found in their favor. But, in Black's words, "speech is one thing; conduct and physical activities are quite another." Griswold and Buxton were prominent members of an organization that provided contraceptive services to Connecticut women. The fact that some speech was instrumental in carrying forward their conduct did not, in Black's view, prevent the state from punishing that conduct.

Then Black launched into his objections to the majority's creation of a constitutional right of privacy. He acknowledged that there are specific provisions of the Bill of Rights that afford protection to privacy in certain contexts, such as the Fourth Amendment's guarantee against unreasonable searches and seizures. But to jump from that clause to claim a general right of privacy is a leap that Black categorically rejected. In his words: "One of the most effective ways of diluting or expanding a constitutionally guaranteed right is to substitute for the crucial word or words of a constitutional guarantee another word or words, more or less flexible and more or less restricted in meaning." Black much preferred, he wrote, to "stick to the simple language" of the amendments rather than "invoking multitudes of words substituting for those the Framers used." Then, employing strong language directed at Douglas's particular formulation of a constitutional right of privacy, Black stated: "I get nowhere in this case by talk about a constitutional 'right of privacy' as an emanation from one or more constitutional provisions. I like my privacy as well as the next one, but I am nevertheless compelled to admit that government has a right to invade it unless prohibited by some specific constitutional provision." In a footnote, Black accused Douglas of sloppy jurisprudence by attempting to elevate the tort of privacy into a constitutional doctrine.

Having dealt rather summarily with Douglas's opinion of the Court, Black directed even greater fire against the concurring opinions of Goldberg, Harlan, and White. Black treated these three opinions together because he felt that the Fourteenth Amendment due process arguments advanced by Harlan and White and the Ninth Amendment argument proposed by Goldberg "turn out to be the same thing." By that he meant that all three arguments were predicated on the view that the Connecticut anticontraception law violated standards of what he called "natural justice." In a footnote, he cataloged from past Supreme Court opinions examples of what he termed the "catchwords and catch phrases" of the natural justice. Among them were the following: "shocks the conscience," "decencies of civilized conduct," "deeply rooted feelings of the community," "fundamental notions of fairness and justice," "rights . . . basic to our free society." In all cases when the justices used phrases such as these they were, in Black's view, substituting their own standards concerning the wisdom of a statute for those of a legislative body. Black put it this way: "I do not believe that we are granted power by the Due Process Clause or any other constitutional provision or provisions to measure constitutionality by our belief that legislation is arbitrary, capricious or unreasonable, or accomplishes no justifiable purpose, or is offensive to our own notions of 'civilized standards of conduct.'" Black pointed out in yet another footnote that, during the Constitutional Convention of 1787, a proposal was introduced to grant federal judges the power to veto unwise Congressional legislation; this proposal was defeated, not once but twice. If the Framers had intended for justices to use their own standards of what is arbitrary or capricious in reviewing legislation, they would have supported proposals to this effect introduced at the Philadelphia Convention.

Notwithstanding the protests of Douglas and the concurring justices, Black saw the dreaded specter of *Lochner v. New York* (1905) behind the majority finding that the Connecticut anticontraception law violated "fundamental notions of fairness and justice." Even the decisions of *Meyer v. Nebraska* and *Pierce v. Society of Sisters*, relied on by several of the opinions in *Griswold*, were predicated, Black argued, on the same natural justice philosophy that infused the Court in *Lochner.* In addition, the majority opinions in both *Meyer* and *Pierce* were written by Justice James McReynolds, a politically conservative member of the Court in the 1920s, hardly revered by civil libertarian justices like Douglas and Brennan (and Black himself). Since the late 1930s, the Supreme Court had looked askance at the judicial fiat in an economic regulation case such as *Lochner.* In fact, Black in large part owed his 1937 appointment to the Supreme Court by President Franklin Roosevelt to his hostility to the now disgraced doctrine of economic substantive due process epitomized by *Lochner.*

Why, Black asked rhetorically, should the practice of justices substituting their own judgment for that of legislators be more palatable in cases concerning individual liberties? Black, of course, had no hesitancy about voting to strike down a state law that violated the explicit language of a clause in the federal Constitution. But he took his constitutional injunctions literally, not liberally. Later in the opinion he cited language from the dissent of Justice Oliver Wendell Holmes in *Tyson v. Banton* (1927) to make this point: "I think the proper course is to recognize that a state legislature can do whatever it sees fit to do unless it is restrained by some express prohibition in the Constitution of the United States or of the State, and that Courts should be careful not to extend such prohibitions beyond their obvious meaning by reading into them conceptions of public policy that the particular Court may happen to entertain."

Turning directly to Goldberg's attempt to breathe life into the Ninth Amendment, Black expressed disdain for his junior colleague's confidence in ascertaining the "traditions and [collective] conscience of our people." The Court does not possess the machinery to conduct Gallup Polls, Black pointed out. Moreover, is there a better indication of the traditions and conscience of a nation than the enactments of duly elected legislative bodies? Furthermore, Black assailed Goldberg for what he saw as a misreading of the views of the men who wrote and voted for the Ninth Amendment. In his words: "That Amendment was passed, not to broaden the powers of this Court or any other department of 'the General Government,' but, as every student of history knows, to assure the people that the Constitution in all its provisions was intended to limit the Federal Government to the powers granted expressly or by necessary implication." Black went on to assert that since the passage of the Ninth Amendment there had been "no serious suggestion . . . ever made" that this portion of the Constitution could be wielded as a weapon to keep state legislatures from enacting statutes that, in their judgment, they believed at the time of passage to be reasonable. To find that the Ninth Amendment could be used to strike down laws that a majority of the Supreme

Court found offensive, Black wrote, would place in danger the separation of powers at the federal level and the principle of federalism that allowed states and the federal government to share power.

Black then took a shot at loose constructionists on the Court like Douglas and Brennan: "I realize that many good and able men have eloquently spoken and written, sometimes in rhapsodical strains, about the duty of this Court to keep the Constitution in tune with the times. . . . For myself, I must with all deference reject that philosophy. The Constitution makers knew the need for change and provided for it." Black was alluding here to the process of proposing and ratifying constitutional amendments. Although that view of government might appear too cumbersome or old-fashioned to some, Black averred "it is good enough for me."

Black concluded his stinging dissent in the Connecticut birth control case with additional verbiage on the folly of judges and justices imposing their own standards of what is best for the people of a state in passing on the constitutionality of a challenged law. He quoted with enthusiasm a statement from a 1958 book by longtime Circuit Court of Appeals Judge Learned Hand: "For myself it would be most irksome to be ruled by a bevy of Platonic Guardians, even if I knew how to choose them, which I assuredly do not."

The other dissent in *Griswold* was written by Potter Stewart. It tracked many of the same points as Black had advanced. In fact, Stewart and Black officially concurred in each other's dissents. In his opinion, Stewart expressed a hostility to substantive due process almost approaching the fervor of his intellectual compatriot, Hugo Black. Stewart found the 1879 Connecticut statute to be an "uncommonly silly law" and, in a practical sense, unenforceable against married couples and single individuals. Stewart stated that he agreed, as a matter of public policy, that professional medical advice on birth control should be widely available to a state's population. "But," he wrote, "we are not asked in this case to say whether we think this law is unwise, or even asinine. We are asked to hold that it violates the United States Constitution. And that I cannot do."

Stewart referred to the six different constitutional amendments mentioned by Justice Douglas in the opinion of the Court: the First, Third, Fourth, Fifth, Ninth, and Fourteenth. Then he pointed out that Douglas never stated directly which if any of these amendments had been infringed by the Connecticut law. As a constitutional literalist, Stewart found no language in the six amendments cited in the opinion of the Court that could be brandished to find the Connecticut law unconstitutional. In looking at the facts of *Griswold* in terms of the First Amendment, Stewart found no abridgment of the religion clause, the free speech clause, the right of assembly, or the right to petition the government for redress of grievances. Under the Third Amendment he did not find that any soldiers had been quartered in any house. Regarding the Fourth Amendment, he noted that there was no search or seizure at issue. And he did not find anyone being compelled to give evidence against himself, contrary to the Fifth Amendment. To attempt to tease a general right of privacy out of the express and clear language of these amendments offended Stewart's philosophy of constitutional interpretation. He wrote: "With all deference, I can find no such general right of privacy in the Bill of Rights, in any other part of the Constitution, or in any case ever before decided by this Court."

Like Black, Stewart read the Ninth Amendment, as ratified in 1791 and as construed by the courts for over 150 years, as being a restriction on the federal government, not a provision of the Constitution granting carte blanche to a group of activist judges to strike down a state law that violated their sense of the "traditions and [collective] conscience of our people." In Stewart's view, "to say that the Ninth Amendment has anything to do with this case is to turn somersaults with history." If the anticontraception law is not in line with current community standards, as the appellants contend, then Griswold, Buxton, and the PPLC should once again seek to persuade the Connecticut legislature to repeal the law. "That," Stewart concluded, "is the constitutional way to take this law off the books."

CHAPTER 9

Reactions and Repercussions

Patting Themselves on the Back

Because the case bore her name, Estelle Griswold was obviously a focus of media attention in the immediate aftermath of the ruling in *Griswold v. Connecticut*. Interviewed by various newspapers and magazines, the executive director of the Planned Parenthood League of Connecticut (PPLC) said essentially the same thing time and time again in early June 1965: Yes, she was very pleased with the Court decision; and, no, it did not come as a surprise. She gave principal credit for bringing the successful constitutional challenge to the nineteenth-century anticontraception law to Lee Buxton and to the attorneys for the PPLC. Buxton, who was caught by reporters just before getting on a plane for a medical conference in France, characterized the decision as "a great advance for married couples in our state to be able to live a normal life without breaking the law." He accorded the majority of the credit for winning the case to the PPLC attorneys, Fowler Harper, Catherine Roraback, and Thomas Emerson. A friend of Buxton's, quoted in a newspaper profile published the day after the announcement of the *Griswold* decision, quipped "now maybe . . . [Lee will] be able to go to a party without someone asking . . . how he feels being out of jail."

Buxton and Griswold also indicated in their postdecision comments to the press that the League was planning to reopen the Planned Parenthood Clinic on Orange Street "within six weeks." When asked if the PPLC had an advertising campaign planned for the Clinic's reopening, Buxton joked: "After this case I don't think we need to be publicized." PPLC board members contacted by the press were effusive in their praise of Estelle Griswold and for those who carried the torch for the League in its championing of birth control since the 1930s.

Thomas Emerson, who had accurately forecasted the 7–2 vote (if not the exact alignment of the justices) of the Supreme Court in *Griswold*, conferred foremost credit for carrying the case successfully to the Supreme Court to his associate, Catherine Roraback, and his late friend and law school colleague, Fowler Harper. Emerson also told reporters that he applauded Justice William Douglas and the Court majority for providing a "bold innovation" in the crafting of a constitutional right of privacy. He cautioned that the Court had only promulgated a *marital* right of privacy; unmarried individuals would have to wait and hope for another day for a decision favorable to their privacy rights.

Fowler Harper had been personally acquainted with Justice Douglas. On the day after the announcement of the *Griswold* decision, Harper's widow, Miriam, wrote a heartfelt longhand note to Douglas. It read in part: "Having lived with Fowler through almost every facet of the Birth Control case . . . I cannot refrain from writing to tell you how pleased Fowler would have been with your opinion this week. It is one of the great sadnesses of life that he could not see his work come to fruition." In conclusion, she added: "As you know, . . . Fowler's cause was . . . for the civil rights of people, and in this case to keep the sanctity of the home and the marital relationship. I feel the outcome of this case is a fitting memorial to Fowler and will have widespread effects."

The New Haven birth control clinic did not reopen as quickly as Estelle Griswold and Lee Buxton had hoped. The "within six weeks" that they had initially predicted turned into a little more than three months. Finally, on the evening of Monday, September 20, 1965, the Planned Parenthood League of Connecticut conducted its first birth control counseling sessions since its brief ten-day run in November 1961. There were no disruptive incidents. Clinic sessions at the New Haven site continued to be conducted several times a week. Within a year, the PPLC had opened birth control clinics in two other Connecticut cities. Two and a half years after the Supreme Court decision in *Griswold*, according to responses to questionnaires prepared by Buxton, there were six PPLC birth control clinics operating in the state. In addition, by 1968, fourteen of Connecticut's thirty-four hospitals offering obstetrical services also provided family planning information and contraceptive prescriptions. Nevertheless, some hospitals reported that they had not yet begun to provide birth control services because "the local environment was averse to the establishment of this type of clinic." Buxton estimated that only about 8,400 of the 40,000 indigent married women in Connecticut were receiving contraceptive counseling at the time of his survey. Notably, no state, county, or municipal family planning clinics had been established in Connecticut as of early 1968. Perhaps Connecticut's pervasive Catholicism — at that time just shy of 50 percent of the state's population — still had a negative effect on the acceptance of birth control services in all parts of the state. Legal change was one thing; social change was something else.

At the time of the Supreme Court decision in *Griswold*, Lee Buxton was a sick man. Clinical depression, coupled with alcoholism, had taken a toll on his health. He was forced to accept a leave of absence from his position at Yale in the fall of 1965. Over the next three years he was hospitalized on several occasions. He died in July 1969. Before his death, however, Buxton confided to Thomas Emerson and other friends that he regretted that his fragile health kept him from being able to devote himself to what he saw as the next great issue for reproductive reform: liberalizing abortion laws.

Although Estelle Griswold would outlive her friend Lee Buxton, she withdrew from the birth control cause before he did. The day after the announcement of "her" Supreme Court decision, she celebrated her sixty-fifth birthday. Even before the June 1965 decision, she had resolved to leave her position as executive director of the PPLC. The tension she had experienced for several years in dealing with the New Haven birth control activists — tensions that had been responsible for her earlier threats to resign — had never fully abated, even with the success of the appeal to the Supreme Court. Griswold communicated her decision to the PPLC board in midsummer 1965. The board once again tried to smooth things over, but it only served to postpone the inevitable. Griswold remained in her administrative position only until the end of 1965. Sometime after her retirement took effect, Griswold relocated to Fort Myers, Florida, where she died in 1981.

The Fourth Estate

The early press response to the ruling in the *Griswold* decision was generally of a cursory, nonjudgmental nature. The major national papers carried "day one" stories that mentioned the issues in the Connecticut birth control case and noted the main points raised in the six opinions. A few offered quotations from some of the participants, lawyers, or public figures knowledgeable about the controversy. Because the decision in *Griswold* came down on the same day as the Court's ruling in a case involving the effect of extensive TV coverage on the trial of Texas financier Billy Sol Estes, it shared billing with that case.

Outside of the Connecticut papers, the most weighty journalistic treatment of the *Griswold* decision was in the *New York Times*. On June 8, the *Times* featured the Connecticut birth control case on its front page in an article written by the paper's legal correspondent, Fred Graham, titled "High Court Bars Curbs on Birth Control; Finds Connecticut Law Invades Privacy." A picture of Justice Douglas accompanied the story. The *Times* also published on June 7 a front-page story on the status of a bill in the New York legislature designed to liberalize that state's ban on the sale and advertising of birth control devices. That story not only treated the pending legislative action in New York, but it also surveyed some reactions of religious leaders to the decision in *Griswold*. The June 8 issue of the *Washington Post* offered only a few summary paragraphs on Griswold on an inside page; the *Post* gave more attention to the Billy Sol Estes case. The *Christian Science Monitor*, in a June 9 inside page story on the 1964–65 term of the Supreme Court, discussed first the Billy Sol Estes case and a decision concerning the rights of members of the Communist Party to serve as union officers before mentioning the Connecticut birth control case. *Newsweek*'s treatment of the case, in its June 21 issue, focused mainly on the reopening of the Planned Parenthood clinic in New Haven.

After about a week, the print media began to offer editorial commentary on *Griswold*. Here the perspectives varied widely. Once again the *New York Times* provided the most comprehensive coverage. The *Times* published an unsigned editorial, titled "Right of Marital Privacy," on June 9. Calling the *Griswold* decision "a milestone in the judiciary's march toward enlarged guardianship of the nation's freedoms," the *Times* editorial acknowledged that the dissenters, Hugo Black and Potter Stewart, had presented a strong argument that the infringements on civil liberties presented by the Connecticut anti-contraception law would have been better dealt with by a legislative repeal than a splintered decision by the Supreme Court. "But," the editorial intoned, "the fact is that . . . [the problems presented by the Connecticut law] were not corrected. To what forum but the Supreme Court could the people then repair, after years of frustration . . . ? Once again, as in the school desegregation cases and in state reapportionment, the failure of the states to protect individual liberties has impelled the Court to move onto untrod ground." The *Washington Post* editorialized in much the same vein as the *Times*. It identified the protection of privacy as a "central purpose" of the Bill of Rights and criticized Justices Black and Stewart for taking judicial restraint "to the point of abdication."

The two dissenters in *Griswold*—Black and Stewart—drew plenty of support from newspaper editorialists around the country. The *Richmond* (Virginia) *Times-Dispatch* had this to say in its June 10 editorial: "On Monday, Justice Hugo Black issued a dissenting opinion that ought to be emblazoned on the walls of the chamber in which members of the United States Supreme Court deliberate. . . . The Supreme Court, Black says, should declare a law invalid *only* if the law is unconstitutional. The fact that members of the court simply *don't like* a law is no basis for throwing it out" (italics in original). Similarly, in a syndicated column that appeared, among many places, in the *Oregon Journal*, Lyle Wilson wrote: "The stability of this institution (Supreme Court) ultimately depends not only in its being alert to keep other branches of government within constitutional bounds, but equally upon recognition of the limits of the court's own functions in the constitutional system."

Justice Black, by the way, stuffed in his Supreme Court papers a small file of newspaper articles and editorials favorable to his dissenting opinion in *Griswold* that had been mailed to him by sympathetic Court watchers. He also retained a myriad of fan letters that he received from private citizens who agreed with his dissenting opinion. One correspondent scrawled the following note to Black on a copy of a newspaper editorial that lauded the justice's *Griswold* dissent: "I agree with you, but this same idea [judicial restraint] should have been adhered to in *Brown v. Bd. of Ed.* in 1954."

A number of newspapers were critical of Justice Douglas's opinion of the Court for the looseness of its legal reasoning. Best epitomizing this view was an editorial from the *Waterloo* (Iowa) *Daily Courier* of June 9, 1965: "Douglas' choice of the word [penumbra] may have been unfortunate, for the Constitution goes into full eclipse when the Supreme Court makes an addition to the Bill of Rights simply because the justices think it is needed." After submitting that the Connecticut anticontraceptive law would "in due time" have been repealed by the state legislature, the Iowa editorialist continued: "The 'right of privacy' which the majority of justices enunciated in this case was made up out of whole cloth. References to some items in the Bill of Rights were merely made to satisfy the legal niceties. The Supreme Court . . . was not intended to be an agency for correcting any practice which the justices conceive to be wrong. But the present court has made itself a legislature beyond the reach of the people."

Commentaries on *Griswold* by news magazines and journals of opinion were varied but generally supportive of the decision. *U.S. News & World Report* stressed the creative use of the Ninth Amendment by Justice Arthur Goldberg. Similarly, James Carroll, writing in a September 1965 issue of the *Nation*, argued that "[t]o the student of constitutional history, perhaps the most interesting aspect of the birth control case is the Court's recognition of the Ninth Amendment as a mechanism for the expression of 'the collective conscience of our people' against both federal and state action." *Life* magazine, even after granting that the two dissenters in *Griswold* "made the clearest juridical sense," concluded that the majority's position was superior public policy: "When legislatures fail to keep our laws in tune either with the elementary requirements of democracy or (as Jefferson urged) 'with the progress of the human mind,' it is surely better that the Court should fill the gap than that nobody should." The *New Republic*, in accepting that the Court had indeed engaged in "legislating" in *Griswold*, emphasized that the decision was hardly a sign that the apocalypse was just around the corner: "[The Court] held only that a statute directed at the use of contraceptives could not stand in a state that does not prohibit manufacture or effectively forbid sales; and a state that did not trouble to treat married couples at all differently from frolicking teen-agers. All kinds of regulation of the production, distribution and even use of contraceptives remains [*sic*] possible."

Render unto Caesar . . .

Several journalists assigned to write about the impact of the Supreme Court decision in *Griswold* sought out the opinions of religious figures. The church officials and clergymen contacted appeared quite willing to provide their thoughts on the Connecticut birth control decision. Archbishop Henry J. O'Brien of Hartford, for example, expressed a view held by a number of Catholic leaders: "Catholics, in common with our fellow citizens, recognize this decision of the court as a valid interpretation of constitutional law. However, I must emphasize that this is a juridical opinion, and in no way involves the morality of the question. Artificial contraception remains immoral by the law of God." Contacted by reporters in early June 1965, Richard Cardinal Cushing reiterated his previously announced hands-off position: "I do not see where I have the obligation to impose my will on those who do not accept the faith I do." In the summer of 1965, Cardinal Cushing also appeared on a Massachusetts radio show and fielded questions from listeners. One female caller asked if Catholics who had not followed the Church's teaching against the use of artificial contraceptives were guilty of a "mortal sin." The Cardinal replied: "Only God knows that, my dear."

Patrick J. Crowley, a lawyer and a member of Pope Paul VI's commission studying birth control, declared "I suspect it's a good decision. In a pluralistic society like ours, this type of law is obsolete." One Catholic priest who was quite familiar with the PPLC-sponsored litigation that led to the June 1965 Supreme Court decision was Father Robert Drinan, dean of the Boston College of Law. When asked for his reaction to the decision in *Griswold*, Father Drinan responded: "I agree with the majority that the Connecticut law is in fact an invasion of the right to privacy, but I share dissenting Justice [Hugo] Black's misgivings about the scope and thrust of the majority opinion with respect to the alleged constitutional basis for the right to privacy."

During 1965, some of country's leading religious journals of opinion published essays on the *Griswold* decision and the right of privacy.

America, a magazine that bears the imprimatur of the Society of Jesus (Jesuits), characterized the Supreme Court's voiding of the Connecticut anticontraceptive law as "a small loss." Several editorials and articles addressing issues raised in the Connecticut birth control case appeared in *Commonweal,* the country's leading journal of Catholic lay opinion. In a June 25 issue of the publication, an editorialist referred to *Griswold* as a "muddy" decision in which the justices "had some difficulty locating an amendment which would provide a clear constitutional basis for the decision." The *Christian Century,* billing itself as "a magazine that believes the Christian faith calls people to a profound engagement with the world — an engagement of head and heart," kept readers up to date in the early 1960s on the Connecticut birth control controversy. Written from the orientation of liberal Protestantism, *The Christian Century* had long been on record as a critic of restrictive state contraceptive laws. Accordingly, in its June 23, 1965, issue, it lauded the ruling in *Griswold v. Connecticut* for reversing a law that for years had been "farcically ineffective and the butt of numerous coarse jokes." In addition, the publication went so far as to declare that "[t]he decision rescued marriage in Connecticut from desecrating implications and honored it in words comparable to those . . . in church manuals affirm[ing] the sacredness of the married state."

———

Legislative Aftershocks

Although the Supreme Court's announcement of a constitutional right of privacy in *Griswold* portended, in the eyes of many legal experts, to sweep expansively into a number of areas of American life, the immediate effect on state laws regulating contraception was the most pronounced. The convictions of Estelle Griswold and Lee Buxton under the Connecticut accessory statute, Section 54–196, were reversed, and the application of Connecticut's ban on the use of contraceptives, Section 53–32, was ruled unconstitutional as applied to married couples. Connecticut Governor John Dempsey, a Catholic, declared that the "rulings of the nation's highest court [in *Griswold v. Connecticut*] become . . . the law of the land, and we accept this decision as such."

Laws in twenty-eight other states regulating the manufacturing or sale of contraceptives, however, were not immediately disturbed. Nine states still had laws on their statute books prohibiting the advertising of drugs or devices for preventing conception or on the dissemination of certain kinds of birth control information. Ten other states only permitted the disbursal of contraceptives by physicians, pharmacists, and other licensed distributors. The remaining nine states maintained miscellaneous other restrictions on birth control. In addition, federal law prohibited the mailing and transportation of contraceptive devices and information, except when done so for the purpose of preserving life and health. Even given the complex web of state and federal contraceptive restrictions that persisted after the ruling in *Griswold*, Dr. Alan F. Guttmacher, the national director of the Planned Parenthood Federation of America, called the Court's decision in the Connecticut case "a tremendous step toward elimination of all restrictions on the right of parents to plan their families with the help of competent medical guidance."

To confirm Guttmacher's optimism, on the same day that the *Griswold* decision was handed down, a bill to liberalize New York's nineteenth-century statute (which severely limited the sale of contraceptives and information about them) was favorably reported out of the state's Senate Rules Committee. The proposed New York modification, cosponsored by state senators George Metcalf and Howard Thompson, was written so as to permit the sale or distribution by pharmacists of "any instrument or article or recipe or drug or medicine for the prevention of conception." The Metcalf/Thompson bill continued the prohibition on the open advertising of contraceptives and their distribution to minors in New York.

The New York legislature spared the courts of its state the trouble of dealing with the constitutionality of the nineteenth-century anti-contraception law. On June 14, the state Senate conducted a brief but spirited debate on the Metcalf/Thompson reform bill. Senator Metcalf stated that the law he drafted was designed to "set up a private right [for contraceptive services], one that should not be interfered with by law." He also referred to the Supreme Court's *Griswold* decision as evidence that the mood of the country supports keeping government out of the private lives of its citizens. Critics of contraceptive law reform in New York saw the proposed law as "sanctioning sexual promiscuity" because it permitted the sale of contraceptives to unmarried as well as married individuals. Despite this opposition, the bill passed the Senate by an overwhelming vote of 41 to 13 and was sent to the state assembly. A few days later, the measure was reported out of the assembly by an 85-to-50 vote. Governor Nelson Rockefeller signed the legislation in early July, and it went into effect on September 1, 1965.

The summer of 1965 proved to be a halcyon period for contraceptive reform in the country. Two weeks before the *Griswold* ruling, Minnesota had repealed its law banning the sale of contraceptive materials. Then came Justice Douglas and his "penumbra," striking down the timeworn Connecticut law. This was followed by heated but abbreviated debate in the legislatures of New York and Massachusetts, leading to the abandonment of those states' nineteenth-century laws proscribing contraception. Thus, is less than three months, some of the oldest, least enforced, but still most troubling anticontraception statutes had met their demise.

Playing Charades with the Constitution?

Law professors and law students pay close attention to leading decisions of the U.S. Supreme Court. Their reactions to these decisions are, of course, discussed in law school lecture halls and seminar rooms. But, more importantly, commentary on high-profile Supreme Court decisions regularly finds its way into the pages of legal periodicals, generally called "law reviews" or "law journals." Virtually every American law school publishes a law review; some law schools issue several. Law review articles provide a good insight into the way the legal community responds to decisions of the Supreme Court.

Griswold v. Connecticut was, in some ways, a dream case for the academic legal community. It presented law professors and even law students with the opportunity to score points by picking at the opinions of members of the nation's highest court, identifying the difficulties, frustrations, and contradictions voiced by the justices in dealing with a law that was unenforced and virtually unenforceable. Out of the more than thirty legal scholars and law students writing in the law reviews on *Griswold* in the two years after the decision, it was hard to find a single commentator who felt that even one of the six members of the Court writing opinions in *Griswold* "got it right."

190   { *Griswold v. Connecticut* }

One of the first published law review comments on *Griswold* appeared in the November 1965 issue of the *Harvard Law Review*. In its annual recapitulation of the previous term of the U.S. Supreme Court, the nation's oldest law review referred to *Griswold* as "immediately recognizable as [a] constitutional landmark" for bringing privacy officially within the ambit of the Constitution. The editors of the Harvard publication found Justice Douglas's "penumbra" theory and Justice Harlan's "ordered liberty" approach to "differ more in tone than in the results to which they lead." What surprised the editors about *Griswold*, however, was Justice Goldberg's "injection of the ninth amendment into this controversy." According to them, the Ninth Amendment, since its ratification in 1791, had never served as the basis for a Supreme Court decision. The editors speculated that Douglas's opinion commanded the Court because it furnished the narrowest ground that the majority could utilize to rule the objectionable Connecticut law unconstitutional.

Among the first wave of *Griswold* articles, most of the points of analysis that would be advanced in the 1965–66 period can be found in a set of essays prepared by leading constitutional scholars for the December 1965 issue of the *Michigan Law Review*. Among the academic luminaries represented in this legal periodical were the following: Robert G. Dixon Jr., professor of law at Georgetown University; Paul G. Kauper, professor of law at the University of Michigan; Robert B. McKay, professor of law at New York University; Arthur E. Sutherland, professor of law at Harvard; and, perhaps most intriguingly, Thomas I. Emerson, professor of law at Yale and the principal author of the appellants' Supreme Court brief in *Griswold*. An examination of the essays in this issue of the *Michigan Law Review* thus provides a good sample of the legal community's early reactions to the Connecticut birth control decision. A surprising number of common points were raised by the essayists.

All of the essayists in the *Michigan Law Review* were pleased that the Court had cobbled together a constitutional right of privacy. Thomas Emerson, writing as a law professor as well as the lawyer for Estelle Griswold and Lee Buxton, perhaps put it best: "The precise source of the right of privacy is not as important as the fact that six Justices found such a right to exist, and thereby established it for the first time as an independent constitutional right. It was a bold innovation." Arthur

Sutherland observed that he had long believed that "some 'right of privacy' ought to be guaranteed by the due process clauses" and that "[t]he Supreme Court was clearly right in the *Griswold* result."

Most of these essayists, however, were troubled by the loose "emanations and penumbras" approach to the Bill of Rights proffered by Justice Douglas. Paul Kauper, for example, used the following adjectives to describe the reasoning in Douglas's short opinion: "curious," "puzzling," "confusing," "uncertain," and "ambiguous." He posed a series of complex rhetorical questions to illustrate the fuzziness of Douglas's formulation of the right of privacy: Did Douglas's right of privacy fall within the penumbra of selected portions of the Bill of Rights? Or was Douglas saying that the intimate marriage relationship is found within the zone of privacy of home and family? Or was the justice arguing that the Connecticut anticontraception law used means that violated a right of privacy derived from certain language in the first ten amendments? Robert Dixon wrote that *Griswold* "stands as a decision without a satisfying rationale." All of the *Michigan Law Review* essayists, as well as most of those writing on *Griswold* in other legal publications, would probably have agreed with the concluding sentence of Dixon's article: "The actual result of *Griswold* may be applauded, but to reach this result was it necessary to play charades with the Constitution?"

Another point agreed on by authors of the essays in the *Michigan Law Review* was that Douglas had not done a good job of identifying the elements or the scope of a right of privacy. Robert McKay noted that the *tort* of privacy had developed with slow, hesitant steps since its first serious mention in the famous 1890 article by Louis Brandeis and Samuel Warren, but that the *constitutional* right of privacy sprang with very little previous judicial grounding from Douglas's opinion in *Griswold*. For Dixon, Douglas's opinion "does little . . . to clarify the conceptual dimensions of the privacy concept." Thomas Emerson, although delighted with Douglas's ruling, was troubled that the "source," "standards," and "scope" of the right of privacy were not clearly articulated. McKay suggested that, as promising as a right of privacy may be for the protection of civil liberties, the "judicial experiment" in *Griswold* might be discarded as "unworkable" unless future Supreme Court decisions do a better job of defining the right than Douglas had done. Perhaps one of the reasons that Douglas did not do a better job of explaining what he meant by privacy is that he did not receive much help from the briefs submitted to the Supreme Court in the case. Privacy was almost an afterthought to Thomas Emerson, and, for obvious reasons, it was not an issue addressed at all by Joseph Clark in the brief for the state of Connecticut. Several of the *Michigan Law Review* essayists commented on the fact that the appellate lawyers in the case, particularly Emerson, stressed the due process problems with the Connecticut anticontraception law rather than the need for a constitutional right of privacy.

As problematic as Douglas's opinion might have been, the writers in the *Michigan Law Review* recognized that the Court's most idiosyncratic justice had, in this instance, probably staked out the narrowest ground on which the case could have been decided. Robert McKay noted that the "ordered liberty" approach to identifying a right of privacy, emphasized in Justice Harlan's concurring opinion in *Griswold* and in his dissenting opinion in *Poe v. Ullman*, would not have been attractive to any five-person Court majority. To McKay, Harlan's opinion smacked too much of the loathed substantive due process approach of early twentieth-century economic regulation cases like *Lochner v. New York* (1905) and was therefore the source of scorn by the *Griswold* dissenters, Hugo Black and Potter Stewart. Likewise, Emerson saw Douglas's treatment of the right of privacy "as the narrowest and most precise formula available" to the justices. Kauper posited in his essay that Douglas had backed off from the due process analysis that he had stressed in his *Poe* dissent when faced with the prospect of writing an opinion for a majority in *Griswold*.

The Scholars Continue to Weigh In

After flaying Douglas for his "emanations and penumbras," the law professors writing in the December 1965 *Michigan Law Review* found other aspects of *Griswold* on which to comment. For example, the Ninth Amendment approach of Justice Goldberg that had so enamored some lay writers was not well received in the legal community. Dixon, for example, did not believe that the Goldberg approach offered any assistance to judges interested in a tight legal definition of privacy. McKay agreed with Justice Black that the Ninth Amendment's "retained rights" approach, like the "flexible due process" concept of Harlan, reeked of fuzzy natural law jurisprudence. A similar line of analysis led Emerson to conclude that he had "grave doubt that the ninth amendment has a significant future" because it "does not seem to open any really new possibilities."

Several of the *Michigan Law Review* essayists argued that Goldberg's emphasis on the rights "retained by the people" in the Ninth Amendment and Harlan's "ordered liberty" approach under the Fourteenth Amendment were not that different from Douglas's "emanations and penumbras." Kauper, in fact, saw all the opinions of the Court majority as possessing the same essential framework: "For a court to find that these rights are fundamental, whether because they are deeply written in the tradition and conscience of our people [Goldberg], are part of the concept of ordered liberty [Harlan], are implicit in the notion of a free society [White], or emanate from the totality of the constitutional order [Douglas], involves no immodest or startling exercise of judicial power." Thus, he saw the majority opinions in *Griswold* — individually and collectively — as "treading a worn and familiar path."

Justice Black's lengthy dissent in *Griswold* also came in for substantial criticism by the academic legal community. In the view of most scholars who have studied the intentions of the framers of the Fourteenth Amendment, Black's reading of constitutional history was not persuasive. Moreover, in Black's criticism of the four majority opinions for excessively loose analysis, Paul Kauper noted a double standard. Black himself had been more than willing to go beyond the clear meaning of the Constitution in the reapportionment cases of *Reynolds v. Sims* (1963) and *Wesberry v. Sanders* (1964). More specifically, his opinion of the Court in *Brotherhood of Railway Trainmen v. Virginia* (1964) had found an "associational right" under the First Amendment that allowed a railway union to assist and advise injured railway employees in the prosecution of claims against the railroad. Yet Black did not see a right of privacy extending into the penumbra of the First Amendment so as to permit Dr. Buxton and Mrs. Griswold to advise young Connecticut women on birth control. In Kauper's words, for Black "[t]o exclude the privacy of marital association from protection under the Bill of Rights, while using the first amendment as an umbrella for the kind of associational right protected in the *Brotherhood* case, appears to be a case of straining at gnats while swallowing a camel."

Given Thomas Emerson's role as the appellate attorney for Griswold and Buxton, his essay in the *Michigan Law Review*, titled "Nine Justices in Search of a Doctrine," was particularly illuminating. In looking back on his brief, the oral argument, and the six Supreme Court opinions, Emerson was willing to entertain a degree of second-guessing. In his Supreme Court brief, Emerson had not relied on an equal protection argument to challenge the Connecticut anticontraceptive statute. Hence, he was surprised to be asked a number of questions about equal protection in the oral argument by Justice Brennan and other members of the Court. Perhaps, Emerson seemed to be saying, he should have laid more emphasis on this ground for challenging the statute. By contrast, the Yale law professor noted in his essay that his brief for the appellants had "strongly urged" a web of substantive due process arguments. He pointed out that a "basis for lay optimism over the outcome" of the case was the appellants' contention that the Connecticut law was "arbitrary, unreasonable, capricious, and not reasonably related to a proper legislative purpose." However, Emerson noted with some chagrin, only Justice White of the seven justices in the majority was willing to base his opinion on due process concerns. Emerson was most surprised with the Court's reliance on privacy as the principal linchpin for the decision because "no constitutional 'right of privacy' had previously been recognized, at least as an independent doctrine." Although Emerson was uncomfortable with the vagueness of Douglas's articulation of the right of privacy, he considered its creation to be "a step with enormous consequences."

Many legal commentators on *Griswold* were not hesitant about speculating where the newly created right of privacy might take the Court in the future. Today, with the benefit of forty years of hindsight, it is striking to be reminded as to where the experts were right and where they missed the boat. William Beaney, in a *Wisconsin Law Review* article, saw almost no logical limits to the right of constitutional privacy if the Court in the future adheres to Douglas's "penumbras and emanations" approach: "it is a concept capable of almost limitless judicial formulation, since by definition the courts are not encumbered by the historical or analytical meanings associated with specific provisions of the Bill of Rights."

Beaney was one of a number of readers of *Griswold* who predicted that the marital right of privacy enunciated by Douglas might later be broadened to include protection of individuals against wiretapping, electronic eavesdropping, and data gathering by computers. Robert McKay agreed: "[E]ven if it is conceded that wiretapping and electronic eavesdropping are not violations of the fourth or fifth amendments, the Douglas 'penumbra' argument could be advanced to establish that 'emanations' from the Bill of Rights forbid wiretapping and electronic eavesdropping."

Although there have been several federal and state laws passed in the last forty years to regulate electronic intrusions into privacy on the phone, in the office, and on the computer, the *constitutional* right of privacy has not yet been extended by the courts to cover these situations. To forbid wiretapping and electronic eavesdropping constitutionally would have taken the leadership on the Court of a tenacious presence like a Louis Brandeis to keep the pressure on the other justices. Even Douglas, who would continue to serve on the Court for more than ten years after writing his opinion in *Griswold,* did not write another landmark opinion on privacy. In addition, increases in the crime rate and the election of Republican presidents in 1968, 1972, and 1980 (who were not inclined to nominate justices of the ilk of Douglas, Brennan, Goldberg, and Warren) militated against extending the right of privacy to shield individuals from government surveillance. In the early twenty-first century, in the shadow of the terrorist attacks on September 11, 2001, and the passage of the USA Patriot Act, there has been little support among lawmakers or judges for constitutional restraints on the government's right to engage in high-tech surveillance of individual Americans.

Legal scholars writing in the immediate aftermath of *Griswold* were slightly more prescient when it came to predictions about extending the marital right of privacy to cover situations affecting bodily privacy. Emerson believed that statutes that mandated contraceptive dissemination only through physicians and licensed pharmacists — such as New York's 1965 law — would be upheld if challenged in the courts. He was proven right on this score. McKay predicted — correctly it turned out — that *Griswold* would be judicially construed so as to permit the communication of birth control information through public health clinics and other social welfare programs. Emerson anticipated that the right of privacy would lead to the striking down of state legislation still on the books permitting the compulsory sterilization of residents of mental asylums. He thought it, however, "unlikely that the Court would disturb . . . legislation relating to adultery, fornication (commercial or otherwise), and homosexuality." He followed this statement with an important qualification: "It is conceivable that sometime in the future, as mores change and knowledge of the problem grows, all sexual activities of two consenting adults in private will be brought within the right of privacy." It would take thirty-eight years for this prediction to be borne out.

Thomas Emerson was one of the few constitutional experts in the immediate aftermath of *Griswold* to mention the implications of the Connecticut birth control decision on the constitutionality of abortion. In his *Michigan Law Review* essay, Emerson offered a single sentence on the matter, suggesting that the right to privacy might leave a path "open for an attack upon significant aspects of the abortion laws." In 1973, the leading abortion decision, *Roe v. Wade*, used the constitutional framework of privacy to protect a woman's right to an abortion in the first trimester of a pregnancy. In retrospect, it is surprising that so few legal experts anticipated that the Supreme Court would later rule that a woman's right to an abortion would be predicated on the constitutional right of privacy established in *Griswold v. Connecticut*. Justices Black and White had asked Emerson in the final minutes of the oral argument in the Connecticut birth control case about the implications of the right of privacy for the constitutionality of state abortion laws. So it is understandable that Emerson himself would refer to abortion, albeit cryptically, in writing about *Griswold* a few months after the decision was announced. Yet few other scholars in the 1960s and early 1970s mentioned abortion at all in the context of the right of privacy. For example, Emerson's Yale law school colleague and friend, Charles Black, delivered a series of three lectures in 1970 titled "The Unfinished Business of the Warren Court." Black devoted one of the three lectures to the significance and consequences of *Griswold v. Connecticut*; in that entire lecture he never once mentioned abortion.

CHAPTER 10

Elaboration of the Constitutional Right of Privacy

A Step . . . and a Bridge

In the oral argument and in the law review commentary that followed the decision in *Griswold v. Connecticut,* an obvious question posed was whether the right to privacy that had just been granted to married couples to use contraceptives would ever be extended to unmarried individuals. That question would be answered in a case from Massachusetts involving the actions of William Baird. This young man had first attracted public attention when he was arrested in a Long Island, New York, community in May 1965 for handing out contraceptives. At the time, his actions did not square with New York law on the proper dissemination of contraceptives. Even under a revision of the New York contraceptive law that was accomplished later in the summer of 1965, Baird's distribution of contraceptives was still not a permissible activity because he was not a licensed physician or pharmacist. Baird, ever the publicity seeker, persisted in his pro–birth control agitation. In the summer of 1966 he attracted press attention by protesting the Catholic Church's opposition to birth control on the steps of New York's St. Patrick's Cathedral. Later that year he was arrested in New Jersey for exhibiting contraceptives in public in defiance of that state's law. His conviction was reversed on appeal because the New Jersey Supreme Court found the law under which he was convicted to be unconstitutionally vague.

In the spring of 1967 Baird finally did something that garnered him a place in constitutional history. On April 6, 1967, he delivered a lecture on overpopulation and contraception before an audience of about two thousand on the campus of Boston University. At the conclusion of his remarks, he invited anyone interested to come to the stage and examine the selection of contraceptives that he had brought with him. In fact, he encouraged some of those who examined the articles to take samples. He personally handed one young woman a jar of Emko vaginal foam. Then he indicated to police officers in the lecture hall that he had probably just broken Massachusetts law and encouraged them to arrest him. The police accepted Baird's challenge and took him into custody.

The Massachusetts law under which Baird was charged permitted only physicians to prescribe means of birth control and then only to married persons. It was not clear from the facts of the case whether the woman who accepted the vaginal foam was married, but it was clear that Baird was not a licensed physician. Baird was convicted in a bench trial in Massachusetts Superior Court on two counts: exhibiting contraceptives and disseminating contraceptives to an unmarried person. He was sentenced to serve three months in prison. The Supreme Judicial Court of Massachusetts set aside the first count of the conviction because it violated Baird's First Amendment rights, but sustained the second count by a vote of 4 to 3. Baird then applied in federal court for a writ of habeas corpus, asking that his state conviction be set aside because, as he contended, the law under which he had been convicted was unconstitutional. The federal district court dismissed his action, but the Court of Appeals vacated the dismissal. The sheriff of Suffolk County, Eisenstadt, appealed the intermediate federal court's decision to the U.S. Supreme Court.

In the 6–1 decision of *Eisenstadt v. Baird*, the High Court upheld the appellate court ruling and vindicated Baird's right to distribute contraceptives to unmarried persons. Just as in *Griswold*, the majority opinion in Baird "relaxed" the Court's general policy against the assertion of third-party rights, thus allowing Baird to represent the rights of the woman to whom he gave the vaginal foam. Justice William Brennan, writing the majority opinion in *Baird*, ruled that the Massachusetts law prohibiting the dissemination of contraceptives to unmarried persons violated the equal protection clause of the Fourteenth Amendment. The state of Massachusetts had argued that the deterrence of premarital sex was a defensible reason to attempt to keep contraceptives out of the hands of unmarried individuals. Brennan found this to be an unreasonable justification because the logical effect of a law banning the sale or gift of contraceptives to unmarried women was to "prescribe pregnancy and the birth of an unwanted child as punishment for fornication." At the time of the *Baird* case, fornication was a misdemeanor in Massachusetts, punishable by a $30 fine or three months in jail; but the violation of the contested statute was a felony, punishable by up to five years in prison. In addition, two years before the Supreme Court decision in *Baird*, Congress had removed birth control devices from the category of obscene materials under what still remained of the nineteenth-century Comstock law. Furthermore, the same contraceptive articles that Baird had exhibited at his lecture were for sale openly in most drugstores in Massachusetts. Thus, to punish someone for providing contraceptives to an adult, even if unmarried, seemed to fly in the face of custom and public policy.

Near the end of his opinion in *Baird*, Brennan linked his ruling to the right of privacy. He accomplished this without revisiting the constitutional ground for the right of privacy that William Douglas had found in the penumbra of selected provisions of the Bill of Rights, but he succeeded in extending the sweep of Griswold to unmarried individuals. "It is true," Brennan wrote, "that in *Griswold* the right of privacy in question inhered in the marital relationship. Yet the marital couple is not an independent entity with a mind and heart of its own, but an association of two individuals each with a separate intellectual and emotional makeup. If the right of privacy means anything, it is the right of the *individual*, married or single, to be free from unwanted governmental intrusion into matters so fundamentally affecting a person as the decision whether to bear or beget a child" (italics in original). Brennan's announcement for the Court in *Baird* that privacy was now a constitutional right possessed by individuals proved to be of important precedential value in the years that followed for disputes involving bodily privacy.

Brennan's majority opinion, however, did not go as far as some advocates of the continually evolving right of privacy would have preferred. Because married individuals had been extended the constitutional right to use contraceptives in *Griswold*, Brennan found in *Baird* that a denial of the same right to unmarried individuals violated the equal protection clause of the Fourteenth Amendment. Brennan did not, however, rule that the right of unmarried individuals to use contraceptives and the right of privacy in general were protected as unenumerated liberties under the due process clause of the Fourteenth

Amendment. The subtle difference between the use of the two clauses of the Fourteenth Amendment did not seem to be a very weighty matter at the time of the *Baird* decision in 1972, but it would loom larger during Supreme Court confirmation hearings in the late 1980s and early 1990s when nominees were grilled about the degree of their commitment to the right of privacy.

The other leading right to contraceptives case in the post-*Griswold* era was *Carey v. Population Services International* (1977). At issue in this case was a New York statute that placed various restrictions on the distribution and sale of contraceptives. Justice Brennan, building on his opinion in *Baird*, wrote the opinion of the Court in *Carey*. He held that the section of the law dealing with the dissemination of contraceptives to individuals over the age of sixteen was an unconstitutional violation on the "right of decision in matters of childbearing." Brennan termed childbearing a "fundamental" right and ruled that "regulations imposing a burden on [this right] may be justified only by compelling state interests, and must be narrowly drawn to express only those interests." Brennan further held that the right of privacy recognized in *Griswold* includes the liberty of individual choice for adults concerning the "decision whether or not to beget or bear a child." To an extent, Brennan's opinion in *Carey* also relied on reasoning of the majority opinion in the Court's leading abortion decision, *Roe v. Wade* (1973).

Privacy, Abortion, and the Ghost of *Lochner*

Establishing privacy as a right possessed by an individual rather than merely a right that resides in a marital unit spanned the constitutional synapse between *Griswold* and the abortion decisions that would follow. The first and most controversial of these decisions, *Roe v. Wade*, was already in the works at the time the Supreme Court considered *Eisenstadt v. Baird*.

Contraception and abortion have endured a long and uneasy relationship in American history. When the birth control movement chose to identify itself under the rubric of "planned parenthood" in the 1940s, abortion was partially pushed out from under the umbrella of groups like the Planned Parenthood Federation of American (PPFA) and the Planned Parenthood League of Connecticut (PPLC). The Connecticut activists, in their polite but persistent campaign to overturn the state's 1879 anticontraception law, sought at every opportunity to divorce themselves from the call to liberalize the state's abortion law. The PPLC did not mention abortion, even in passing, in its appellate brief in *Griswold v. Connecticut*. PPLC attorney, Thomas Emerson, was clearly uncomfortable when he was asked about the linkage between abortion and contraception during the oral argument in *Griswold*. Given the opportunity to reflect further on this issue, Emerson changed his tune. In his December 1965 *Michigan Law Review* article, he expressed sympathy with the view that the Supreme Court might someday decide to subsume abortion under the new constitutional right of privacy.

Although fascinating, the facts, the personalities, the procedural twists and turns, and the emotions stirred in *Roe v. Wade* need not be related here. That story has been well told on many occasions and in numerous publications. What needs to be stressed is how *Roe* stretched the constitutional right of privacy enunciated in *Griswold* and modified in *Baird*. In the majority opinion written by Justice Harry Blackmun, the Court ruled that the Constitution protected a woman's right to an abortion in the first three months of her pregnancy but allowed the state to regulate abortion during the remaining two-thirds of her term. Blackmun grounded this decision in the right of privacy. In a paragraph near the end of his opinion, Blackmun made reference to a long chain of Court decisions and individual justices' opinions involving privacy going back to 1891. "[T]he Court has recognized," Blackmun wrote, "that a right of personal privacy, or a guarantee of certain areas or zones of privacy, does exist under the Constitution."

Blackmun hedged on the constitutional grounding for privacy that the Court was adopting in *Roe:* "The right of privacy, whether it be founded in the Fourteenth Amendment's concept of personal liberty and restrictions upon state action, as we feel it is, or, as the District Court determined, in the Ninth Amendment's reservation of rights to the people, is broad enough to encompass a woman's decision whether or not to terminate her pregnancy." A close reading for the forgoing sentence reveals that Blackman and the Court majority in *Roe* appeared to find the principal basis for the constitutional right of privacy in terms much closer to those expressed by Justice Harlan in his dissenting opinion in *Poe* and his concurring opinion in *Griswold* than in Douglas's "emanations and penumbras" opinion for the *Griswold* majority. Blackmun was also quick to add that, although "the right of personal privacy includes the abortion decision, ... this right is not unqualified and must be considered against important state interests in regulation."

From a legal point of view, much of the criticism of Blackmun's opinion in *Roe v. Wade* that would ensue in the generation after the decision was derived from a statement in the dissenting opinion of Justice William Rehnquist: "While the Court's opinion quotes from the dissent of Mr. Justice Holmes in *Lochner v. New York* . . . , the result it reaches is more closely attuned to the majority opinion of Mr. Justice Peckham in that case. . . . The decision here to break pregnancy into three distinct terms and to outline the permissible restrictions the State may impose in each one . . . partakes more of judicial legislation than it does of a determination of the intent of the drafters of the Fourteenth Amendment."

Taking their cue from Rehnquist in *Roe*, critics of the constitutional basis for a right of privacy began to refer to decisions such as *Griswold v. Connecticut, Eisenstadt v. Baird,* and *Roe v. Wade* as "liberal *Lochner*-ism." The first and still one of the best expressions of this line of criticism came from John Hart Ely, the former law clerk of Chief Justice Warren and, by 1973, a young law professor. The right of privacy, Ely argued in a *Yale Law Journal* article, was not linked to the text of the Constitution and was, thus, created out of the same "whole cloth" as *Lochner*'s economic substantive due process. "The problem with *Roe*," Ely emphasized, "is not so much that it bungles the question it sets itself, but rather that it sets itself a question the Constitution has not made the Court's business." For him, the right to an abortion "lacks even colorable support in the constitutional text, history, or any other appropriate source of constitutional doctrine." In the context of a further comparison of *Lochner* and *Roe*, Ely offered this ominous prediction: "I would . . . like to suggest . . . that although *Lochner* and *Roe* are twins to be sure, they are not identical. While I would hesitate to argue that one is more defensible than the other in terms of judicial style, there are differences in that regard that suggest *Roe* may turn out to be the more dangerous precedent."

It is, perhaps, a truism to say that whether one accepts John Hart Ely's prediction about the dangerousness of the precedent in *Roe v. Wade* depends on the view that one holds about the right to an abortion. But few in American society in 1973, including the justices on the Supreme Court, anticipated the depth and intensity of the reactions to *Roe*. As one legal scholar put it, "the Court elevated the issue of abortion to the national political agenda and invited a larger political struggle within the country."

No Longer a "Fundamental Right"

In *Planned Parenthood of Missouri v. Danforth* (1976), the Court considered a challenge to a state law that, for women seeking early-term abortions, required parental consent for a minor and a husband's consent for a married woman. The *Danforth* Court's majority, now one vote slimmer than in *Roe*, still held that a woman's right to an abortion was protected by the constitutional right of privacy. But all the justices, who lined up in a variety of configurations in *Danforth*, were willing in one degree or another to accept legislative restrictions on that right.

In the 1986 case of *Thornburgh v. American College of Obstetricians and Gynecologists*, the Supreme Court was asked to rule on the constitutionality of an array of Pennsylvania abortion regulations. With just a few exceptions, the Court struck down the regulations as imposing more than minimal burdens on a woman's right of privacy. Justice Blackmun's majority opinion offered an eloquent defense of abortion as covered by the right of privacy: "The Constitution embodies a promise that a certain private sphere of individual liberty will be kept largely beyond the reach of government. . . . Few decisions are more personal and intimate, more properly private, or more basic to individual dignity and autonomy, than a woman's decision — with the guidance of her physician and within the limits of *Roe* — whether to end her pregnancy. A woman's right to make that choice freely is fundamental." Although *Thornburgh* followed, even arguably extended *Roe*, the prochoice majority had shrunk to a bare 5–4.

The Court significantly called into question a woman's right to an abortion in *Webster v. Reproductive Health Services* (1989). This decision involved the constitutionality of another set of restrictions on abortion from the state of Missouri, a hotbed of "right-to-life" activity in the 1980s. *Webster* followed the line of decisions, highlighted by *Maher v. Roe* and *Harris v. McRae*, that held that a state has no constitutional duty to fund abortions. The Court in *Webster* also backed off from the position, held from *Roe* through *Thornburgh*, that abortion was a "fundamental right." Under the reasoning of *Webster*, a state need not defend abortion restrictions under the exacting "strict scrutiny" standard of previous abortion decision but only demonstrate that its regulations were founded on a "rational basis." Finally, a majority of the Court in *Webster* abandoned the rigid but useful trimester framework assembled in *Roe*.

In *Casey v. Planned Parenthood* (1992), the Court reviewed the constitutionality of a Pennsylvania antiabortion statute that placed several restrictions on the right of a woman to seek an abortion. In a complicated set of opinions, the justices upheld most of the state restrictions. In addition, a bloc of justices — William Rehnquist, Byron White, Antonin Scalia, and the Court's most recent appointee, Clarence Thomas — came within one vote of overturning *Roe v. Wade*. The majority made clear in *Casey* that it would continue to follow the "undue burden" test in determining the constitutionality of state regulations of abortion rather than treating abortion as a woman's fundamental right. For the remainder of the 1990s the Court avoided hearing a major case on the constitutionality of abortion.

Notwithstanding the qualifications on the right to abortion propounded in *Casey v. Planned Parenthood*, the majority opinion in that case proffered one crucial sentence that helped to clarify the extent to which the Court was then prepared to go to protect the right to privacy: "[O]ur laws and tradition afford constitutional protection to personal decisions related to marriage, procreation, contraception, family relationships, child rearing, and education." This catalog of subrights of privacy would be recounted in several subsequent Court decisions.

In the late 1990s, the Court accepted certiorari in an action filed by Nebraska doctor Leroy Carhart challenging a state law that prohibited physicians from performing rare late-term abortions. The procedure that the Nebraska legislature sought to ban was generally referred to as "partial-birth" abortion because it involved removing the fetus from the woman's birth canal late in her pregnancy rather than from her uterus. The medical term for the procedure was dilation and extraction, or D&X. In the 1990s Congress had passed bills prohibiting D&X operations, but they had been vetoed by President Bill Clinton. In the 5–4 decision of *Stenberg v. Carhart* (2000), the Court struck down the Nebraska law and placed in jeopardy the partial-birth bans of about thirty other states. The opinion of the Court, written by Clinton appointee Stephen Breyer, held that the Nebraska law swept too broadly. As well as prohibiting late-term abortions by the D&X technique, Breyer found that the statute's language could also be construed so as to prohibit the normally legal dilation and evacuation (D&E) type of abortion. This reading of the statute, Breyer concluded, placed an "undue burden upon a woman's right to make an abortion decision" and therefore violated her right of privacy under the due process clause of the Fourteenth Amendment. For supporters of the right of abortion, *Carhart* was a hollow victory: the undue burden approach was once again used by the Court, rather than treating abortion as a fundamental unenumerated right. In addition, Justice Anthony Kennedy, who had sided with the Court majority in *Casey*, joined the dissenting bloc in *Carhart*. The "essence of *Roe*" — that a pregnant woman's right to privacy in making an abortion decision — may have been preserved in *Carhart*, but it hangs by a thread. President George W. Bush, elected in 2000, pledged to appoint prolife justices should vacancies occur on the Supreme Court during his term of office. Thus, *Carhart v. Stenberg* and even *Roe v. Wade* have been placed in jeopardy.

―――――

Privacy in Family Life and Other Areas

In the immediate afterglow of the Warren Court's pro–civil liberties decisions of the 1960s, some constitutional commentators predicted that the right of privacy would soon be wielded as the constitutional implement for striking down such intrusive law enforcement practices as wiretapping and electronic eavesdropping. But like the "dog that didn't bark" in Arthur Conan Doyle's classic story "Silver Blaze," such rulings did not occur in the generation after *Griswold*. The pro–law enforcement orientation of the Burger and Rehnquist Courts did not lend themselves to an extension of the right of privacy in this direction. In addition, although there have certainly been a number of

Supreme Court decisions dealing with Fourth Amendment searches and seizures of private domiciles since 1965, the gravamen of these cases was almost exclusively traditional Fourth Amendment principles of probable cause and sufficiency of warrants rather than the unenumerated right of privacy. Similarly, although American courts since the 1960s have heard hundreds of personal appearance cases, there have not been any definitive Supreme Court rulings on whether the right of privacy allows governmental restrictions on hair length, body piercings, or tattoos.

Most of the right of privacy decisions that have been issued in the last third of the century, in addition to the birth control and abortion cases just discussed, have involved family life or home-based activities. Take, for example, the right to marry. Well before *Griswold*, the Supreme Court in *Skinner v. Oklahoma* (1942) struck down a state law mandating the sterilization of habitual criminals. For the unanimous Court in *Skinner*, Justice Douglas held that marriage and procreation are "fundamental to the very existence and survival of the race." Similarly, two years after *Griswold*, the Court in *Loving v. Virginia* (1967) ruled unconstitutional an antimiscegenation statute that had made it a felony for a "white" person to marry a "colored" person. In both *Skinner* and *Loving*, the Court applied an equal protection analysis, maintaining that these laws prevented marriage for reasons that were constitutionally suspect. In particular, the Court in *Loving* held that laws establishing racial classifications can only be upheld if subjected by courts to the "most rigid scrutiny." Although the Court in *Loving* did not directly tie the right to marry to the right to privacy or even cite *Griswold*, it did hold that the right to marry is an unenumerated, substantive right secured by the due process clause of the Fourteenth Amendment.

The explicit link between privacy and the right to marry was supplied by *Zablocki v. Redhail* (1977). At issue in this case was a Wisconsin statute that required special court approval to marry for a person who had "minor issue," not in his or her legal custody, for which he or she was paying court-ordered child support. In such a situation, the court order was generally only granted if the applicant could demonstrate compliance with his child support decree and that the children covered by the support order were "not liklely thereafter to become public charges." The opinion of the Court in *Zablocki* stated explicitly that recent decisions relying on *Griswold* had established the right to marry as a subright of the fundamental right of privacy protected by the due process clause of the Fourteenth Amendment. *Zablocki* should also be remembered for the standard of constitutional review it posited for right of privacy: if the regulation in question "significantly inter-fere[s]" with the exercise of the right of privacy (or other unenumer-ated right) or relies on a "quasi-suspect" classification, it will be found unconstitutional. When these special conditions do not attend, all the government needs to do to justify a restriction on the right of privacy is to present a plausible case that the means applied to advance a rea-sonable end are rationally related to that end.

Another category of constitutional privacy cases might be termed "home-based activities." In *Stanley v. Georgia* (1969), the Court re-fused to overturn the conviction of a man who watched allegedly obscene eight-millimeter films in the privacy of his home. The three offensive reels of film had been taken from the appellant's domicile without a warrant. The appellant argued that his right to conduct a home-based activity, namely, watching risqué films, was violated by the police seizure of the articles in question. Without delving into the constitutional basis for a statute banning the possession of obscenity, the Court ruled in *Stanley* that the law did not give law enforcement officials the right to "reach into the privacy of one's home." *Stanley* is not a pure privacy case because of the commingling of privacy and free expression. One commentator characterized the case as one in which a home-based activity "triggered" the right of privacy. In *Rowan v. U.S. Post Office Department* (1970), the Court was asked to uphold a federal law that allowed home owners to direct the federal post office to order certain mailers to cease sending types of mail that recipients found objectionable. In opposition, mass mailers argued that their First Amendment right of free expression was jeopardized by the statute. The Court sided with the home owner, holding that the statute "permits a citizen to erect a wall . . . that no advertiser may penetrate without his acquiescence." Effectively, the *Rowan* decision allowed the home owner, with the assistance of the government, to establish a "zone of privacy" for determining which communications will be allowed to pierce the sanctity of the home. In the early twenty-first century, the *Rowan* precedent may prove relevant in defending federal "do not call" legislation against telemarketers and "do not spam" laws against mass e-mailers.

The right of privacy has also come into play in cases involving what has been termed "associational choice." In *Runyon v. McCrary* (1976), the Court predictably upheld a federal statute that prohibited private, commercially operated, nonsectarian schools from denying admission to students on the basis of race. In a concurring opinion, however, Justice Lewis Powell maintained that there are constitutional limitations on this governmental power to encourage nondiscrimination. He contended that an individual's right of privacy protects certain contractual relationships on the basis of "a close association." The examples Powell mentioned were bargains with private tutors, babysitters, or housekeepers. In *Roberts v. United States Jaycees* (1984), the Supreme Court upheld a Minnesota statute that prohibited discrimination on the basis of sex in places of public accommodation. The Minnesota chapters of the Jaycees were determined by the Court to constitute agencies of public accommodation and thus were subject to the nondiscrimination mandate of the state law. However, the majority opinion, written by Justice William Brennan, did acknowledge that there might be other associational choices that cannot be disturbed by governmental regulation. Without providing examples, Brennan noted that "certain intimate human relationships must be secured against undue intrusion by the State because of the role of such relationships in safeguarding the individual freedom that is central to our constitutional scheme." For Brennan, such hypothetical affiliations needed to be highly individualized, such as the choice of an intimate partner or a dinner guest. Brennan appeared to be saying that such associations were protected as unenumerated liberties by the due process clause of the Fourteenth Amendment. The *dicta* (nonbinding language) in *Runyon* and *Roberts* posit home-based hypothetical situations and may thus be linked to the home-based activity privacy cases of *Stanley* and *Rowan*.

In 1958 the Supreme Court in *NAACP v. Alabama* held that a state could not require the disclosure of the membership lists of a major civil rights organization. The Court based its ruling on confidentiality in the freedom of association as a "necessary attribute" of the freedom of expression guaranteed by the First Amendment. The privacy interest in *NAACP v. Alabama* was recognized only indirectly by the Court. Yet the case was one of those cited by Justice Douglas in *Griswold* to support his claim that the First Amendment possessed a penumbra that shaded into a right of privacy. In two post-*Griswold* cases, *Whalen v. Roe* (1977) and *U.S. Department of Justice v. Reporters Committee* (1989), the Court explicitly identified the nondisclosure of information as a subright of privacy. Although the Court did recognize the constitutional basis for the right of privacy in such nondisclosure situations, it did not clearly identify the level of scrutiny it would apply to test the propriety of demanded disclosures. Some language in these two cases, however, indicates that the Court will henceforth apply a balancing standard in the nondisclosure cases as opposed to the strict scrutiny standard that the Court has generally deployed to evaluate the right of privacy in contraception and abortion cases.

———

Private Sexual Conduct

Sex with a minor, nonconsensual sex, and sex involving compensation (except in the few areas of the country where prostitution is legal) have not been considered protected activities by American courts pursuant to the right of privacy. These activities violate statutory laws and long-standing societal traditions. To claim that the constitutional right of privacy protects sex with minors, sexual assault, or prostitution is tantamount to saying that a claim of privacy can be invoked to defend any form of illegal activity taking place behind closed doors. Selling narcotics, fixing prices, and planning violent crimes cannot be insulated by a right of privacy; nor can pedophilia, rape, and prostitution. The stern laws against these activities trump privacy every time.

Two other forms of private sexual activity—fornication and adultery—generally do not raise privacy issues. Fornication, defined as sexual intercourse between two unmarried persons, was illegal in most states until well into the twentieth century. By 2003, however, only eleven states still had criminal laws penalizing fornication on their statute books. Fornication laws are rarely enforced, and they have not occasioned any recent appellate cases involving privacy. Adultery is defined as sexual intercourse involving a man and a woman when at least one of the sexual partners is married to someone else. A substantial minority of American states still makes adultery a crime, although prosecutions are infrequent and convictions are almost unheard of. "Simple" adultery has not resulted in any recent privacy decisions. Adultery, however, remains a leading ground for divorce in many states.

Sodomy is a different matter. Sodomy is generally defined in the law as oral or anal sex. Thirteen states, as of 2003, still criminalized consensual sodomy for heterosexual couples. In fact, most of the prosecutions for sodomy before the 1970s were for "unnatural sexual acts" involving a man and a woman. However, a number of the sodomy laws that remained on state statute books after 1980 targeted only same-sex couples. In recent years it has been the cases involving same-sex couples that have led to the Supreme Court's major privacy rulings on sexual conduct. In fact, next to the cases on abortion, litigation involving sexual activity between same-sex couples has been the leading battleground for the right of privacy since the *Griswold* decision.

The absence before 1970 of many prosecutions of same-sex couples for sodomy did not denote societal approval or even tolerance of sexual activity between individuals of the same sex. One of the reasons for the lack of prosecutions of this category of sexual activity is that the law, until the late nineteenth century, did not recognize homosexuality as a separate category of personhood. The early laws proscribing sodomy did not target same-sex couples; they sought instead to forbid nonprocreative sexual activity in general. Before 1970, most prosecutions of same sex-couples for sodomy involved predatory sexual acts against minors or sexual assault. In the nineteenth century, a man could not be convicted of sodomy on the basis of the testimony of a consenting male partner because the partner was presumed to have been an accomplice. Only when a partner did not consent to the act, the partner was a minor, or the act took place in public did the law seek prosecution of a man for sodomy with another man. This pattern of prosecution would begin to change in the late twentieth century when a handful of states began to single out same-sex relations for prosecution under criminal statutes.

In 1975 two male homosexuals filed suit against Virginia local and state authorities, requesting an injunction against that state's law which made oral and anal sex felonies. Relying on *Griswold*, the attorneys for the plaintiffs maintained that the Virginia law violated their right of privacy. The three-judge federal panel split 2–1 against the litigants. The federal court's majority opinion refused to extend the right of privacy to this fact situation, holding that *Griswold* only addressed the matter of privacy in a "marital situation." Furthermore, the majority ruled that the state's police power justified passing the legislation in question because homosexual conduct "is likely to end in a contribution to moral delinquency." The dissenting district court judge, Robert Merhige Jr., saw no problem in extending the principle of *Griswold* to cover sex between consenting homosexuals: "To say as the majority does, that the right of privacy, which every citizen has, is limited to matters of marital, home or family life is unwarranted under the law." Merhige argued that the majority "misinterpreted the issue" by stressing morality and decency when they should more properly have focused on the constitutional right of privacy. Without comment, by a vote of 6–3, the U.S. Supreme Court in *Doe v. Commonwealth's Attorney* (1976), summarily upheld the two-person majority opinion of the federal district court.

Ten years later, in the high-profile case of *Bowers v. Hardwick* (1986), the Supreme Court elected to directly confront the issue of whether to extend the right of privacy to homosexuals. The facts giving rise to this litigation took place in 1982. Michael Hardwick, then a twenty-eight-year-old gay man living in Atlanta, was issued a citation for carrying a beer from a bar and drinking it in public. Hardwick paid a fine, but because he failed to appear in court, he was confronted one night in his apartment by a police officer with a warrant for his arrest. A guest had let the police officer into the apartment, where Hardwick and a male companion were engaging in oral sex. The officer observed the sex act and proceeded to arrest Hardwick under the Georgia sodomy law that had been passed in 1968. Although the district attorney did not want to press the case, Hardwick did. The Atlanta man accepted the offer of the ACLU to represent him in a challenge to the constitutionality of the Georgia statute. The federal district judge who heard the case granted the defense's motion to dismiss on the basis of the ruling in *Doe v. Commonwealth's Attorney*. Hardwick appealed and the Supreme Court granted certiorari.

In his brief and at the oral argument, the attorney general of Georgia argued that the protection of a privacy in sexual acts should only be available to married couples. To open the door to homosexual acts, the attorney general argued, would lead down the slippery slope to decriminalizing a long parade of horribles — "polygamy; homosexual, same-sex marriage; consensual incest; prostitution; fornication; adultery; and possibly even personal possession in private of illegal drugs." Georgia, he submitted, was at the ramparts fighting for the right "to maintain a decent society." Liberal Harvard law professor Lawrence Tribe argued the ACLU appeal for Hardwick in the Supreme Court. Tribe maintained that Georgia's outdated moral code should bow to the constitutional right of privacy: "If government is going to tell individuals how to behave and what they can and cannot do in their own homes," Tribe wrote in his brief, "it must have a reason other than the morality of a political majority for it."

By a slender 5–4 majority, the Supreme Court ruled against Hardwick. "The issue," Justice Byron White wrote for the Court majority, "is whether the Federal Constitution confers a fundamental right upon homosexuals to engage in sodomy." White answered his question in the negative. He ruled that sodomy was not a "fundamental liberty . . . implicit in the concept of ordered liberty" under the Fourteenth Amendment, nor was the practice "deeply rooted in this Nation's history and tradition." Hence, in the view of the Court majority, the right of privacy did not extend to the protection of sexual activity engaged in by same-sex couples.

Two dissents were filed in *Bowers*. The first, written by Justice John Paul Stevens, rejected the Court majority's "selective application" of the Georgia law to same-sex couples. Because the Georgia legislature did not single out homosexuals for punishment under this law, neither should the courts. A longer and more substantive dissent was filed by Justice Harry Blackmun and concurred in by the other three dissenters. Blackmun's opinion sought to place the interest of same-sex couples "to be let alone" within the broad tradition of the right of privacy extending back to Louis Brandeis's dissent in *Olmstead v. U.S.* (1928). In Blackmun's view, a proper reading of the Court's past privacy decisions supports the position that privacy is an individual right, not a privilege exclusively reserved to "traditional families" or "stereotypical households." In contrast to Justice White, who found no support in the text of the Constitution to extend the shield of privacy to gays, Blackmun and his dissenting brethren felt differently: "[T]he right of an individual to conduct intimate relationships in the privacy of his or her own home [was] the heart of the Constitution's protection of privacy." The state of Georgia had justified its sodomy law on "traditional Judeo-Christian values," and the Court majority in *Bowers* had accepted this rationale. For Blackmun, however, the Supreme Court's affirmation of that law threatened American values to a "far greater [degree] than tolerance of nonconformity could ever do."

The vast majority of law review commentary on *Bowers v. Hardwick* came down on the side of the dissenters in the case. This was particularly evident in several articles published to commemorate the twenty-fifth anniversary of the Supreme Court's decision in *Griswold v. Connecticut*. The *Ohio Northern University Law Review*, published by the institution from which PPLC attorney Fowler Harper received his law degree in 1923, issued its retrospective on *Griswold* in its 1989 volume. The *Connecticut Law Review* published its forum on *Griswold* and its consequences in the summer of 1991. The failure of the Supreme Court to follow the logic of *Griswold* in its majority opinion in *Bowers* was a common theme of the several essayists in these two special issues. In the longest piece in the law journal of Harper's alma mater, titled "The Right of Privacy: Past, Present, and Future," University of Houston law professor G. Sidney Buchanan maintained that "the *Bowers* holding is unique. Among the various areas to which the right of privacy might plausibly be extended, the area of sexual conduct outside of marriage is the only general area that the Court has expressly placed beyond the right's protection." Accordingly, Buchanan found "that the holding in *Bowers* is inconsistent with the spirit, if not the letter, of the holdings in *Griswold*, *Roe*, and *Carey*."

Despite the laments of academic lawyers and gay activists, *Bowers v. Hardwick* provided constitutional sanction for the principle that the right of privacy does not forbid a state from criminalizing certain types of intimate sexual activity if a majority of its legislature believes such behavior is immoral. In addition, another consequence of *Bowers* was that state laws which explicitly withheld certain protections from gays and lesbians did not need to be subjected to strict constitutional scrutiny; all that was necessary for such legislation to pass constitutional muster was for defenders to demonstrate that enacting legislatures acted pursuant to a "rational basis."

An interesting footnote to the *Bowers* decision concerns Justice Powell. One of the Court's most successful consensus builders, Powell sided with the minority at the conference on *Bowers*. He stated that he believed private homosexual acts should be decriminalized and that private sexual conduct should be drawn under the constitutional umbrella of privacy. Yet before the final votes were cast on the case, Powell changed his mind, wrote his short concurring opinion, and voted with the Court majority. Powell retired from the Court in 1987. In an interview three years later, he admitted that he had "probably made a mistake" in casting his lot with the *Bowers* majority.

Had Powell stuck to his guns, the extension of the right of privacy to cover the sexual conduct of same-sex couples would have been achieved in 1986. As was the case, the Court wouldn't take this step until early in the twenty-first century. The Georgia Supreme Court, however, took matters into its own hands in the 1990s. In 1997 the state's highest court struck down the 1968 state sodomy law that was at issue in *Bowers* as a violation of the *state* constitution's right of privacy. Michael Hardwick, however, would not be around to see the law he had challenged expunged from the statute books. He died of AIDS in 1991.

In the years since the *Bowers* decision, agitation against sodomy statutes has increased. A number of states, like Georgia, decriminalized sodomy. Elsewhere, state supreme courts struck down such statutes as violations of the right of privacy. Gay rights activists became increasingly more visible and, on occasion, were successful in convincing states and localities to extend various civil rights protections to gays and lesbians. In the year 2000, Vermont passed a statute providing for the legality of "civil unions" for gay couples. On the other hand, several heavily publicized acts of violence against gays inflamed the passions of many Americans. Survey research indicates that homosexuality remains a discomforting feature of life to a majority of Americans.

In the early years of the new century, a case with a fact situation very similar to that of *Bowers* arose in the Lone Star State. This case, *Lawrence v. Texas* (2003), presented the Court once again with the question of whether the Fourteenth Amendment protects the privacy rights of same-sex couples. Before analyzing the precedent-shattering

Lawrence decision, a few other portions of the landscape of privacy in the late twentieth century need to be sketched out.

———

The Ultimate Privacy Question

G. Sidney Buchanan's long 1989 essay on the right of privacy in the *Griswold* commemorative issue of the *Ohio Northern University Law Review* referred only in its 763rd and final footnote to a matter that would soon become a hot topic. "The right to die," as it is often termed, involves the question of determining when, if ever, it is appropriate to permit a surrogate to order that heroic medical care should cease for a person who is being kept alive by machines. A related question is what role physicians should have in providing assistance to a person who wishes to die or a person unable to make that decision for himself or herself. These are privacy issues that have generated considerable talk among theologians, ethicists, and academic lawyers. A few cases in the 1990s would offer partial answers to what some have called "the ultimate privacy question."

The first case that the U.S. Supreme Court accepted on the right to die, *Cruzan v. Director, Missouri Department of Health* (1990), was occasioned by an automobile accident in 1983. Nancy Beth Cruzan, then twenty-five years old, lost control of her car on a Jasper County, Missouri, road. She was thrown from her vehicle into a ditch filled with water. Paramedics arrived at the scene of the accident quickly and succeeded in restoring Cruzan's breathing and heartbeat. However, she was determined to have been without oxygen for about fourteen minutes. Cruzan was taken to a hospital but degenerated into a "permanent vegetative state" (PVS). Cruzan's parents, realizing that their daughter's sentient life was over, asked the hospital to withdraw life support. The hospital refused to do so, a lawsuit ensued, and the case ultimately found its way to the U.S. Supreme Court. The opinion of the Court, written by William Rehnquist — now Chief Justice Rehnquist — refused to second-guess a Missouri court's previous determination that Nancy Cruzan had not clearly communicated her wish to be allowed to die if placed in a condition of PVS.

There were four dissenters in *Cruzan:* William Brennan, Harry Blackmun, Thurgood Marshall, and John Paul Stevens. Besides disputing the weight and interpretation of Cruzan's intentions by the Court majority, the dissenters strongly advocated affording more sway to the constitutional right of privacy in a right to die situation. Justice William Brennan made this point forcefully in his opinion: "Because I believe that Nancy Cruzan has a fundamental right to be free of unwanted artificial nutrition and hydration, which right is not outweighed by any interests of the State, I find that the improperly based procedural obstacles imposed by the Missouri Supreme Court impermissibly burden that right. . . . Nancy Cruzan is entitled to choose to die with dignity."

In 1997 the U.S. Supreme Court decided physician-assisted suicide cases from the states of New York and Washington. Both these states, like most other American states, had laws on the books making it a crime for a person to aid another in attempting to end one's own life. In *Vacco v. Quill* (1997), three New York physicians challenged their state's ban on physician-assisted suicide on equal protection grounds. Their argument was that the ban on assisted suicide was legally equivalent to long-standing state law and custom that permitted competent patients to refuse life-saving treatment. Their case ultimately found its way to the U.S. Supreme Court. The unanimous opinion of the Court in *Vacco* was written by Chief Justice Rehnquist. There were two key questions in the case, as the chief justice saw it. The first was whether the right of a terminally ill patient to seek the assistance of a doctor in ending his or her life was a fundamental liberty protected by the Fourteenth Amendment. The second was whether the prohibition on physician-assisted suicide targeted a suspect class of individuals. Rehnquist and the Court majority did not find the right to physician-assisted suicide as falling within the panoply of unenumerated rights identified by the Court in previous decisions, and they accepted the state's argument that there is a clear and constitutionally defensible distinction between physician-assisted suicide ("killing") and the cessation of life-saving procedures ("letting go"). Four justices — Sandra Day O'Connor, Stephen Breyer, David Souter, and John Paul Stevens — wrote concurring opinions. In differing degrees, the dissenters were uncomfortable with the arbitrary line drawn by the chief justice between physician-assisted suicide and the cessation of life support. They argued that there remains room for "further debate" about the constitutional limits of states to proscribe physician-assisted suicide. Justice

Stevens, for example, maintained that the Court should be open to the potential constitutionality of better-drawn physician-assisted suicide statutes that might soon come to the Court. Likewise, Justice Breyer urged the justices not to close the door on the issue of whether the right to retain the help of a doctor in ending one's life is a "fundamental" right.

Decided the same day as *Vacco* was the companion case of *Washington v. Glucksberg* (1997). The state of Washington had enacted a statute in 1975 that authorized criminal prosecution for a person causing or aiding another person to attempt suicide. In 1994, four doctors and a number of terminally ill patients requested a declaratory motion from a federal judge that the 1975 Washington law was unconstitutional because it denied the fundamental liberty interests of the plaintiffs under the due process clause of the Fourteenth Amendment. After an en banc panel of the Ninth Circuit Court ruled in favor of the doctors and patients in *Glucksberg*, the U.S. Supreme Court accepted certiorari and proceeded to reverse the lower court by a unanimous 9–0 vote. As in the companion case, Rehnquist wrote the opinion of the Court. Rehnquist held that the Washington statute did not violate the Fourteenth Amendment's due process clause because the right to commit suicide with the aid of a physician is not a "fundamental liberty interest."

Although agreeing with the result that Rehnquist reached for the Court in *Glucksberg*, four justices — O'Connor, Breyer, Stevens, and Ruth Bader Ginsburg — signed concurrences. The longest and most searching concurring opinion was written by Justice David Souter. Arguing with passion and extensive documentation from scores of right-of-privacy cases, Souter rejected the Rehnquist standard for assessing due process of law under the Fourteenth Amendment as too arbitrary. To Souter, the Rehnquist approach was a crude, lockstep weighing of authority and liberty. Souter was not yet willing to cross the right of physician-assisted suicide off his list of possible fundamental liberties. Focusing especially on John Marshall Harlan's dissent in *Poe v. Ullman*, Souter urged the Court not to irretrievably discard the possibility that physician-assisted suicide might fall within the substantive right of privacy. He implored his colleagues to withhold their ultimate verdict on physician-assisted suicide until more data from state legislative experience — such as Oregon's Death with Dignity Act and, perhaps, yet-to-be-passed statutes in other states — have been assembled. In the concluding paragraph of his opinion, Souter expressed this point simply in a manner that recalled opinions of Louis Brandeis defending state creativity: "[E]xperimentation . . . is entirely proper, as well as highly desirable, when the legislative power addresses an emerging issue like assisted suicide. The Court should accordingly stay its hand to allow reasonable legislative consideration."

"Advice and Consent"

Article II, Section 2 of the U.S. Constitution provides that nominations to the U.S. Supreme Court must be accomplished "by and with the Advice and Consent of the Senate." Since 1939 the "advice and consent" of the Senate has commenced with hearings before the Senate Judiciary Committee in which nominees are questioned by committee members, all of whom are lawyers. In addition, at each confirmation hearing, the committee solicits views on the nominee's credentials from leaders of the American bar and other individuals familiar with the nominee's credentials.

Between 1973 and 1986, four nominations to the Supreme Court reached the Senate Judiciary Committee for confirmation hearings: John Paul Stevens, nominated by President Gerald Ford in 1975; Sandra Day O'Connor, nominated by President Ronald Reagan in 1981; William Rehnquist, nominated by Reagan to move from associate to chief justice in 1986; and Antonin Scalia, nominated by Reagan in 1986. Nominees Stevens and Scalia were not presented with questions on privacy at their hearings. Rehnquist and O'Connor were asked minimal questions about privacy and were confirmed easily.

On June 26, 1987, Justice Lewis Powell, one of the Court's most able consensus builders, announced his retirement from the Supreme Court. The man President Ronald Reagan nominated to replace the conciliatory Powell was Robert Bork, a strongly opinionated appellate court judge, longtime law professor, and former solicitor general of the United States. It was Bork who, after the principled resignations of his two superiors in the Justice Department and at the direct order of President Richard Nixon, had fired special prosecutor Archibald Cox in the infamous "Saturday Night Massacre" in October 1973 that contributed to Nixon's downfall in the Watergate scandal. In his long career as a scholar and judge, Robert Bork had written numerous law review articles, books, and judicial opinions on hot button legal topics, including abortion and the right of privacy.

The public hearing on Bork's nomination took place over twelve days in September 1987. It received extensive coverage on television and in the print media. The U.S. government documents official record of the hearing and attachments run to over 3,500 pages, making it the most voluminously documented Supreme Court confirmation hearing in American history. Unlike the handful of other Supreme Court nominees in the late 1980s and early 1990s, Bork had written extensively in law reviews on the right of privacy. He had also expressed criticism of the line of privacy opinions from *Griswold* to *Roe* in his academic addresses and appellate court opinions. Hence, the members of the Judiciary Committee felt that the door was open to ask this nominee to elucidate his position on these issues. Bork was only too happy to oblige. Bork's subsequent comments on the right of privacy at the Judiciary Committee hearing drew criticism from other witnesses and sparked scores of letters from members of the legal community. Bork, refusing to tailor the views that he had expressed in his past writings and speeches, derisively termed privacy, "as defined or undefined by Justice Douglas, . . . [to be] a free-floating right that was not derived in a principled fashion from constitutional materials." After listening to Bork testify for several days, Chairman Joseph Biden (Democrat, Delaware) observed that "[b]ased on your own standard . . . it seems to me that the entire line of privacy decisions would be in some jeopardy. . . . If you think that you should reconsider the rationale . . . in *Griswold*, it worries the devil out of me. If you mean you think you should reconsider the rationale in *Roe*, it worries a lot of other people."

All the Democratic senators on the Judiciary Committee assisted Biden in assailing Bork's position on privacy. But Senator Edward Kennedy of Massachusetts was the most insistent — and the most hostile. Kennedy began his questioning of Bork with a statement of his own that included this language: "I believe, Mr. Bork, that in your world, the individuals have precious few rights to protect them against the majority and I think this is where the Bill of Rights comes in and what the Bill of Rights is all about, that there are some things in

America which no majority can do to the minority or to the individuals." Bork responded strongly that he believed in the Bill of Rights but that he did not believe judges should be called on to enforce a "generalized, undefined right of privacy" that cannot be derived from "the text, the history and the structure of the Constitution." Bork continued: "Aside from the fact that the right was not derived by Justice Douglas, in any traditional mode of constitutional analysis, there is this. . . . [W]e do not know what it is. We do not know what it covers. It can strike at random. . . . [T]he Supreme Court has not applied the right of privacy consistently and I think it is safe to predict that the Supreme Court will not." Then Bork challenged Kennedy: "Privacy to do what, Senator? . . . [P]rivacy to use cocaine in private? Privacy for businessmen to fix prices in a hotel room? We just do not know what it is."

The Senate Judiciary Committee ultimately voted 9 to 5 against Bork's confirmation. The majority report concluded that Bork was "out of the mainstream of constitutional thought" and that, if confirmed, would "disrupt the delicate balance" of the Supreme Court. In spite of those urging him to withdraw his name from consideration, Judge Bork stayed the course. Thus, on October 23, 1987, the Senate had no choice but to vote on Bork's candidacy. The vote, largely on party lines, was 58 to 42 to reject the nomination. Bork would remain on the appellate bench for only a year after the defeat of his nomination for the Supreme Court. He continued in his writings and speeches to point to *Griswold* as an "unprincipled decision." In his book, *The Tempting of America: The Political Seduction of the Law*, published in 1990, Bork referred to *Griswold* as "insignificant in itself but momentous for the future of constitutional law." Justice Stewart had termed the Connecticut anticontraception statute "a silly law." Bork tagged it as "nutty." Yet he reaffirmed statements that he had made at his confirmation hearing to the effect that, had he been a member of the Supreme Court in 1965, he would have allowed the old law to stand pursuant to the same principle of judicial restraint as expressed by Stewart and Hugo Black in their dissenting opinions. Bork declared in his book that *Griswold* should be understood "as an attempt to enlist the Court on one side of one issue in a cultural struggle." He argued that the loose constitutional doctrine spawned by *Griswold* served "to enlist the Court on the side of moral relativism in sexual matters." For Bork, the protection of marriage was not the issue in *Griswold;* it was instead "the creation of a new device of judicial power to remake the Constitution." In the pages of *The Tempting of America*, Bork reaffirmed the linkage of *Griswold* and *Roe* with *Lochner* that he had posited in this writings in the 1970s and 1980s.

In reflecting on the failed nomination of Judge Bork to the Supreme Court, constitutional experts began to recognize that the right of privacy enunciated in *Griswold* and modified by *Baird* and *Roe* enjoyed widespread support as a constitutional value. Bork's refusal to acknowledge or subscribe to this reality meant that his opportunity for a seat on the Supreme Court was scuttled on the shoals of privacy. Moreover, one expert remarked that the Bork hearings had enshrined *Griswold* as a "fixed star in our constitutional firmament" and that the Senate could now use "allegiance to *Griswold* as a litmus test for membership in the 'mainstream of constitutional thought.' "

After the Senate's rejection of Judge Bork, President Reagan nominated Anthony M. Kennedy, a centrist jurist. Kennedy was confirmed in 1988. President George H. W. Bush's nomination in 1990 of a little-known New England jurist, David Souter, was confirmed with only mild opposition. President Bush's other nominee, appellate court judge Clarence Thomas, sparked a great deal of controversy. But Thomas was nevertheless confirmed in 1991. President Bill Clinton's two nominees, Ruth Bader Ginsburg and Stephen Breyer, both federal appellate court judges, were confirmed easily in 1993 and 1994. As different as each of these five nominees were, they shared one experience: each survived a gauntlet of questions at their confirmation hearings on *Griswold v. Connecticut* and the right of privacy.

Privacy and Sexuality at the Dawn of a New Century

The Limits of Privacy

At the time that Estelle Griswold accepted the position as Executive Director of the Planned Parenthood League of Connecticut in 1953, the sale and use of contraceptives was illegal in her state, abortion was permitted only if the life of the mother was in grave jeopardy, and sexual activity by same-sex couples was not an open topic of conversation, let alone protected by the U.S. Constitution. Much transpired in the next half century to change the world with which Mrs. Griswold was familiar when she had began her work at the Planned Parenthood League of Connecticut (PPLC) offices in New Haven. Connecticut's legal proscription of birth control — a statute that was enacted in the late nineteenth century pursuant to the crusading zeal of Anthony Comstock, that was ardently defended on moral grounds by the Catholic Church throughout most of the twentieth century, and that survived the protestations of such advocates of birth control as Margaret Sanger and the Planned Parenthood Federation of America — was finally struck down by the U.S. Supreme Court in a mid-1960s case that bore the PPLC activist's name, *Griswold v. Connecticut*. The constitutional right of privacy, established in *Griswold* to protect contraceptive usage for married couples, was extended over the remainder of the century to cover such important dimensions of human existence as marriage, procreation, family relationships, child rearing, and education. *Griswold* would also provide the major constitutional link to *Roe v. Wade* (1973), the Supreme Court's leading abortion decision that set in motion the most divisive American social controversy of the late twentieth century. Pledging fealty to *Griswold* and *Roe* became a sine qua non for successful confirmation for the handful of men and women fortunate enough to receive nominations to seats on the Supreme Court since the mid-1970s.

The majority opinion in *Griswold*, written by Justice William O. Douglas, remains one of the most idiosyncratic opinions in the two centuries of Supreme Court history. For a decision announcing a major constitutional shift, it is creative but maddeningly cryptic. Douglas's resort to "emanations" and "penumbras" of the Bill of Rights as sources of the right of privacy was criticized by legal experts for sloppiness and facile reasoning almost from the moment the decision was announced. Yet since 1965, many of these same commentators, a majority of the justices who have served on the modern Supreme Court, and most of the general public have come to embrace the substance of a constitutional right of privacy. Justice Douglas may have reached the "proper result" in *Griswold* because the decision is cited constantly as marking the arrival of privacy as a constitutional right. Few, however, defend Douglas's particular — some would say peculiar — reasoning. In fact, it has become almost a parlor game among justices and constitutional experts to come up with new, improved rationales for the "right to be let alone." For a time, Justice Arthur Goldberg's Ninth Amendment "rights retained by the people" analysis had support among the experts as a superior grounding for the constitutional right of privacy. But in the 1980s and 1990s, as witnessed in Supreme Court confirmation hearings and a handful of key Court decisions, privacy as an unenumerated substantive right under the due process clause of the Fourteenth Amendment seemed to have emerged as the preferred constitutional justification for the now almost sacred right of privacy.

At the beginning of the twenty-first century there remained, however, several areas of personal life into which the constitutional right of privacy had not yet taken up residence. Powerfully intrusive law enforcement practices like wiretapping and electronic eavesdropping are regulated but not prohibited by the constitutional right of privacy. The sanctity of records about one's life — medical records, financial accounts, Social Security numbers, credit data — kept by the government and business is the subject of continuing discussion and occasional regulation. But it is unlikely that the privacy of these records will ever be granted constitutional protection. The same is the case for privacy in the workplace. We worry about having on-the-job activities monitored by management. Legislation has been enacted to limit surveillance of employees in private industry, but it is doubtful that there will ever be a *constitutional* shield to prevent bosses from scrutinizing the activities of their employees in office cubicles and on the shop floors. Moreover, given the climate of opinion in America since September 11, 2001, it seems likely that fears about homeland security — as manifested in such legislation as the USA Patriot Act — will continue for the foreseeable future to trump concern for civil liberties.

Recasting the Limits

The constitutional right of privacy has historically had the greatest traction in matters involving sexual activity. Most of the leading privacy cases, as we have seen, have concerned contraception, intimate sexual activity, or reproductive choice. Yet in *Bowers v. Hardwick (1986)*, the Supreme Court struck down a state law proscribing sodomy and refused to extend the constitutional umbrella of privacy to the sexual activities of homosexuals. Despite howls of protest from the academic legal community that the Court had bowed to "homophobia" by not permitting the right of privacy to flow to its logical conclusion, *Bowers* remained the leading case on same-sex constitutional rights as the twentieth century ended.

In 1998, responding to what turned out to be a false report of a "weapons disturbance," police officers entered the Houston, Texas, apartment of John Geddes Lawrence. They found Lawrence and a male companion, Tyron Garner, engaged in a consensual act of anal sex. The police arrested Lawrence and Garner, charging them with violating Texas's "Homosexual Conduct Law," which made it a misdemeanor for a person to engage in "deviate sexual intercourse" with another person of the same sex. The pair was subsequently convicted in a county criminal court and fined $200 each. Lawrence and Garner appealed the decision to the Texas Court of Criminal Appeals, attacking the Homosexual Conduct Law on the ground that it violated the equal protection clause of the Fourteenth Amendment and a parallel clause of the Texas Constitution. The Texas court affirmed the conviction, basing its decision on the Supreme Court precedent of *Bowers v. Hardwick*. Lawrence and Garner then requested that the

U.S. Supreme Court hear their case on a writ of certiorari. In granting certiorari in 2002 the Supreme Court directed that the lawyers for the parties address in their briefs the question of whether *Bowers v. Hardwick* should be overruled. The decision in *Lawrence v. Texas* was announced on June 26, 2003 — the final day of the 2002–3 term. By a vote of 6–3, the Court reversed the convictions of Lawrence and Garner, overruled *Bowers v. Hardwick*, and extended the right of privacy to gay men and lesbian women.

The majority opinion in *Lawrence v. Texas* was written by Justice Anthony Kennedy. Kennedy opened the majority opinion with a bow to *Griswold v. Connecticut* and the principle that substantive but unenumerated liberties reside within the reach of the Fourteenth Amendment. Without endorsing or even mentioning Justice Douglas's "emanations" and "penumbras," Kennedy indicated that *Griswold* stood for the principle of marital privacy. He then noted that the subsequent Court decisions of *Eisenstadt v. Baird* (1972) and *Carey v. Population Services International* (1977) had extended the protection of the right of privacy to unmarried adults. Kennedy next addressed the key question before the Court, namely, whether the right to privacy should now be stretched to shield sexual activity between same-sex individuals.

After summarizing the state of the law of privacy and the procedural course of the Lawrence/Garner litigation, Kennedy challenged the basis for the holding in *Bowers*. In that decision, the Court had identified the central issue as "whether the Federal Constitution confers a fundamental right upon homosexuals to engage in sodomy." Now Kennedy and the *Lawrence* Court concluded that the *Bowers* ruling had "[failed] to appreciate the extent of the liberty at stake." Kennedy made clear the precedent-shattering holding of *Lawrence v. Texas* with this statement: "When sexuality finds overt expression in intimate conduct with another person, the conduct can be but one element in a personal bond that is more enduring. The liberty protected by the Constitution allows homosexual persons the right to make this choice." In words that must have been music to the ears of Justice John Paul Stevens, who had issued a strident dissent in *Bowers*, Kennedy ruled for the Court: "Justice Stevens' [*sic*] analysis, in our view, should have been controlling in *Bowers* and should control here. *Bowers* was not correct when it was decided, and it is not correct today. It ought not to remain binding precedent. *Bowers v. Hardwick* should be and now is overruled." The Texas law was thus ruled unconstitutional because it "[furthered] no legitimate state interest which can justify its intrusion into the personal and private life of the individual." Although the Court did not say so, presumably the remaining handful of state laws singling out same-sex individuals for punishment for sodomy were now null and void.

What's in a Name?

A long and impassioned dissent was filed in *Lawrence v. Texas* by Justice Antonin Scalia. Joined by Justice Thomas and Chief Justice William Rehnquist, Justice Scalia's dissent helped set the terms for the debate over *Lawrence* that would rage in the aftermath of the decision. To Scalia, the specter of gay marriage seemed to be the most upsetting consequence of the *Lawrence* ruling. The opinion of the Court, in Scalia's view, left the constitutional door wide open to the marriage of same-sex couples. Citing the majority's admonition that its decision in *Lawrence* "does not involve whether the government must give formal recognition to any relationship that homosexual persons seek to enter," Scalia responded caustically, "Do not believe it."

Supporters and critics of the Court's ruling in *Lawrence v. Texas* recognized the potentially momentous impact of the decision. In their annual retrospective on the just-completed term of the Supreme Court, the editors of the *Harvard Law Review* had this to say about the opinion of the Court in *Lawrence:* "Far from simply enunciating a circumscribed right for adults to engage in private, consensual sexual activity, *Lawrence* thus embraces the notion of a fundamental right to be gay — a broad liberty to express one's sexuality in myriad ways, including through the formation of meaningful, lasting personal relationships." In terms of specific legal consequences, the *Harvard Law Review* editors argued that the ruling in *Lawrence* means that laws prohibiting same-sex marriage, gay adoption, and service in the armed forces by openly gay men and lesbians "must either be narrowly tailored to further a compelling government purpose or be invalidated."

Fears about the status of marriage on the order of those expressed by Scalia preceded the *Lawrence* decision. In 1995 Utah became the first American state to expressly prohibit same-sex marriage. The next year, however, a Hawaii state court struck down a legislative ban on same-sex marriages in that state. Hawaii's electorate later ratified an amendment to its state constitution overturning the court decision. Sparked in part by the chaotic legal situation in Hawaii, Congress passed and President Bill Clinton signed the "Defense of Marriage Act" (DOMA). This federal law ordained that no state in the nation would be required to give legal effect to a statute of another state that may recognize same-sex marriage. In addition, the DOMA defined the words *marriage* and *spouse* to include only opposite-sex couples for the purposes of federal law. By early 2004 a total of thirty-seven states had enacted laws banning same-sex marriage.

By contrast, Vermont, one of the states that had previously enacted a defense of marriage act, passed in 2000 a law establishing a "civil union" statute for same-sex couples. This law afforded the same rights under the law to same-sex couples as normally enjoyed by married male-female couples, such as inheriting a partner's estate without extra taxes, making medical decisions for each other, and filing joint income tax returns. Internationally, the Netherlands and Belgium recently acted to approve same-sex marriages; such legislation is pending in Taiwan. Same-sex marriage is also permitted in the Canadian provinces of British Columbia and Ontario.

In the aftermath of the ruling in *Lawrence v. Texas*, perhaps triggered by Justice Scalia's apocalyptic vision of homosexual marriage, social conservatives became concerned that courts might strike down state defense of marriage acts, as happened in Hawaii, or even rule the federal DOMA unconstitutional on due process or equal protection grounds. This reasoning led a group of congressional Republicans in the summer of 2003 to propose a constitutional amendment, the Federal Marriage Amendment (FMA). If passed by a two-thirds vote of both houses of Congress and ratified by three-quarters of the states, this measure would extend federal constitutional sanction to a marriage union only if it involves one man and one woman.

Social conservatives have watched with concern and trepidation the rapidly growing numbers of civil unions for same-sex couples in the state of Vermont. By early 2004 Vermont had solemnized more than seven thousand civil unions. About 86 percent of the Vermont-granted civil unions involved nonresident couples. The effect that these unions have in the states where the couples reside, particularly states boasting defense of marriage legislation, is far from clear.

The same-sex marriage issue presented itself most visibly on November 18, 2003, when the Supreme Judicial Court of Massachusetts, that state's highest court, ruled that same-sex couples should be allowed to legally marry under the state's constitution. In *Goodridge v. Department of Public Health*, a 4–3 decision involving seven gay couples from five Massachusetts counties, the court held that "barring an individual from the protections, benefits, and obligations of civil marriage solely because the person would marry a person of the same sex violates the Massachusetts Constitution." The state constitution of Massachusetts, like the federal constitution, contains both due process and equal protection language. However, the Massachusetts Constitution extends greater protections for individual civil liberties than that of the federal document.

The Massachusetts statute at issue in *Goodridge* defined marriage as the union between a man and a woman. The agency charged with enforcing the marriage law, the Massachusetts Department of Public Health, argued in court that heterosexual marriage was mandated on three grounds: (1) that it provided a favorable setting for procreation; (2) that it ensured an optimal setting for child rearing; and (3) that it helped preserve scarce state and private financial resources. The opinion of Chief Justice Margaret Marshall ruled that none of these three grounds survived "a rationale basis review" by the Supreme Judicial Court. She pointed out that many modern marriages are not entered into for procreation and that child rearing is currently taking place in a number of state households headed by same-sex couples. Regarding the economic rationale, Marshall pointed out that the litigants in the case, like many gay parents, are financially comfortable and now simply ask to share with heterosexual couples the pecuniary benefits of a legal marriage. The real reasons for the prohibition of same-sex marriages, the chief justice submitted, was prejudice against homosexuals. She concluded a key portion of her opinion thusly: "The marriage ban [against same-sex couples] works a deep and scarring hardship on a very real segment of the community for no rational reason. The absence of any reasonable relationship between, on the one hand, an absolute disqualification of same-sex couples who wish to enter into civil marriage and, on the other, protection of public health, safety, or general welfare, suggests that the marriage restriction is rooted in persistent prejudices against persons who are (or who are believed to be) homosexuals. The Constitution cannot control such prejudices but neither can it tolerate them." Although her opinion was grounded on the Constitution of Massachusetts, Marshall's analysis was replete with citations from the U.S. Supreme Court's privacy decisions, running the gamut from *Griswold* to *Lawrence.*

The decision of Massachusetts's highest court has spawned a great deal of political debate and public commentary. Massachusetts Republican Governor Mitt Romney, for example, announced that he would push for an amendment to the state constitution overturning the *Goodridge* decision. "I agree with 3,000 years of recorded history," Romney stated, "Marriage is a scared institution between a man and a woman . . . and our constitution and laws should reflect that." Fundamentalist Christians were predictably shocked by the decision and agreed with Governor Romney. On the other side of the issue were the ACLU and virtually all gay and lesbian interest groups. The ACLU urged its membership and other like-minded individuals to e-mail congressional representatives and urge them to oppose the Federal Marriage Amendment. Most of the Democratic aspirants for the presidency in 2004 spoke out against the Federal Marriage Amendment and defended, with varying degrees of intensity, same-sex civil unions and greater constitutional rights for gay persons.

The November 2003 *Goodridge* decision of the Massachusetts Supreme Judicial Court did not strike down the state marriage law. It did, however, declare that the exclusion from access to civil marriage of the seven same-sex couples named in the suit violated the liberty and due process provisions of the Massachusetts Constitution. The Supreme Judicial Court stayed the judgment for six months, so as to afford the legislature time to "take such action as it may deem appropriate." The Massachusetts legislature eventually came up with Senate No. 2175, "An Act Relative to Civil Unions." The legislature transmitted the text of Senate No. 2175 to the Supreme Judicial Court in December 2003, asking that body for an advisory opinion as to whether the bill it had just drafted, "which prohibits same-sex couples from entering into marriage but allows them to form civil unions with all 'benefits, protections, rights and responsibilities' of marriage," complies with the equal protection and due process requirements of the Constitution of the Commonwealth.

On February 3, 2004, the Supreme Judicial Court, by the same 4–3 split as in *Goodridge*, issued a written opinion which held that "[t]he same defects of rationality evident in the marriage ban considered in *Goodridge* are evident in, if not exaggerated by, Senate No. 2175." The difference between Massachusetts's existing civil marriage for male-female units and the proposed "civil union" category for same-sex couples was, in the court's view, more than mere verbiage. Chief Justice Marshall wrote in her advisory opinion that the proposed civil union designation "continues to relegate same-sex couples to a different status. . . . The history of our nation has demonstrated that separate is seldom, if ever, equal."

The same three dissenters in *Goodridge* registered their objection to the February 3 advisory opinion. They maintained that there was no legal difference between the traditional civil marriage and the legislature's proposed "civil union" status. They quoted Juliet's well-known ruminations about nomenclature in Shakespeare's *Romeo and Juliet:* "What's in a name? That which we call a rose by any other name would smell as sweet." If the legislature expressed the intention of treating same-sex marriages in the same legal fashion as male-female marriage, but simply preferred to call the two forms of intimate association by separate names, the dissenters did not see any constitutional problem. The legal problems would occur, the dissenters insisted, when the same-sex partners who had been married in Massachusetts sought the legal and financial benefits and responsibilities of marriage in other states or vis-à-vis the federal government. Their situation would then collide with the Federal Defense of Marriage Act and state laws that prohibited same-sex marriages. The Massachusetts legislature's proposed "civil union" option, according to the dissenters, seemed to offer a way through the legal minefields that might confront same-sex couples united in Massachusetts seeking validation of their relationship in other states or at the federal level. But the court majority's insistence that same-sex couples have a constitutional right to marriage threw down the gauntlet: it flew in the face of the Defense of Marriage Act and laws in the vast majority of states that prohibited the marriage of same-sex persons.

When the Supreme Judicial Court's advisory opinion was read in the Massachusetts Senate on February 4, it was greeted with a mixture of reactions. Because the execution of the *Goodridge* decision had been stayed for six months, pending action by the Massachusetts legislature, and because the legislation's effort to reach a compromise on the issue of same-sex marriage had failed with the Supreme Judicial Court's rejection of Senate No. 2175, the prospect of gay marriage in Massachusetts became a reality in mid-May 2004, when hundreds of same-sex couples took vows of matrimony. Despite doubts about the legality of marriages to same-sex couples from other states, most state officials willingly granted marriage licenses to gay couples attesting that they were Massachusetts residents or expressed a desire to establish residency in Massachusetts. Chagrined by the prospect of Massachusetts becoming the national center for gay marriage, the Bay State legislature in the spring of 2004 debated and passed an amendment to the state constitution that banned gay marriages but provided for civil union status for same-sex couples. To become part of the Massachusetts Constitution, this measure will need to be voted on again by the legislature in 2005 and, if approved, ratified by a majority of the electorate in a referendum at the November 2006 election. In the meantime, Massachusetts will offer legally-sanctioned same-sex marriages.

A few months before the onset of legal same-sex marriages in Massachusetts, an extralegal form of gay marriage emerged on the West Coast. Encouraged in part by the prospect of gay marriage in Massachusetts as well as by exhortations from California gay activists, Gavin Newsom, the mayor of San Francisco, publicly announced in February 2004 that he was of the opinion that the equal protection clause of the California Constitution made denying marriage licenses to same-sex couples illegal. So he ordered city officials to begin issuing marriage licenses to gays and lesbians. Same-sex couples flocked to San Francisco, formed long lines outside City Hall, and patiently waited to receive marriage licenses. In the next few weeks, thousands of marriages between same-sex persons were performed in the City by the Bay. In early August 2004, however, the California Supreme Court, by a vote of 5–2, invalidated these marriages. The court decreed that Mayor Newsom had no authority to grant same-sex marriages in defiance of state law. The larger issue of whether same-sex unions are in fact legal under the state's constitution is scheduled to be decided by California's highest court in 2005. The attention generated by the same-sex marriage issue in Massachusetts and California led to agitation for and against gay marriage across the country. A few mayors and public officials in states as different as New Mexico and New York have begun to issue marriage licenses to same-sex couples.

President George W. Bush, in his January 2004 State of the Union address, indicated that he "stood behind" the federal Defense of Marriage Act. In the immediate aftermath of the February 2004 advisory opinion of the Massachusetts Supreme Judicial Court, the White House released a statement saying that the president viewed the court's pronouncement as "deeply troubling." On February 24, 2004, citing recent developments in same-sex marriage in Massachusetts, California, and other states, President Bush finally took the stand that had been urged on him since the summer of 2003 by conservatives in his party. He announced his support for the Federal Marriage Amendment. In a carefully worded statement, the president declared: "If we're to prevent the meaning of marriage from being changed forever, our nation must enact a constitutional amendment to protect marriage in America. Decisive and democratic action is needed because attempts to redefine marriage in a single state or city could have serious consequences throughout the country." The president, however, appeared to leave the door open to same-sex civil unions by conceding that "state legislatures [should be] free to make their own choices in defining legal arrangements other than marriage." In response to the president's announcement of support for the Federal Marriage Amendment, Massachusetts Senator John Kerry, the Democratic Party's 2004 nominee for the presidency, indicated his support for a "civil union" approach to same-sex relationships and castigated the chief executive for promoting a constitutional amendment as a political "wedge issue" to divide the nation.

Concerns about gay marriage serving as an issue to divide the electorate were borne out by the results of the 2004 election. Eleven states — scattered throughout the South, Midwest and West — had initiatives on their ballots proposing bans on same-sex marriages. Every one of these measures passed. Exit polls and other post mortems on the 2004 election indicated that President Bush's attack upon same-sex marriage and his endorsement of the Federal Marriage Amendment were significant factors in the adoption of the state anti-gay marriage initiatives. In addition, the hostility to same-sex relationships expressed by the Republican Party appeared to resonate with conservative voters and was itself a principal reason for President Bush's own re-election to a second term as the nation's chief executive.

Notwithstanding the electoral results of November 2, 2004, the prospects of ever enacting the Federal Marriage Amendment appear slight. In fact, Congress in the summer of 2004 failed to pass the amendment. Should Congress at some time in the future generate majorities in favor of the amendment, the FMA would still need to be ratified by three-quarters of the states in order to become national policy — a daunting requirement that has condemned to failure all but a handful of the thousands of proposed constitutional modifications in the country's history. Recent public opinion polls have reported that Americans are opposed to same-sex marriage by about a 2 to 1 majority, but these polls also reveal that the public is about evenly divided as to whether a ban on same-sex marriage should be accomplished by a constitutional amendment.

The transforming status of marriage is just the most recent in a long chain of privacy issues set in motion fifty years earlier by Estelle Griswold, Lee Buxton, Fowler Harper, and a small cadre of activists. Their success in *Griswold v. Connecticut* not only legalized the use of contraceptives in Connecticut but it also enabled the right of privacy to achieve a prominent place in the arsenal of American civil liberties. Unsheathed by *Griswold*, the constitutional right of privacy has transformed the nation's legal landscape; its repercussions have touched the most intimate aspects of human life. The diminutive director, the quiet doctor, and the feisty lawyer could not have anticipated the far-reaching consequences that would flow from their successful efforts to dispatch an archaic, "silly law."

1873   Comstock Act — which prohibits sending obscene articles through the mails, including pictures and literature on contraception — passed by Congress.

1879   Connecticut enacts its "little Comstock Act." Section of act banning the use of contraceptives added in a committee chaired by P. T. Barnum. Act also includes a section criminalizing aiding and abetting in use of contraceptives. Thomas Cooley describes privacy as the right "to be let alone."

1890   Louis Brandeis and Samuel Warren's "The Right of Privacy" published in the *Harvard Law Review.*

1916   Margaret Sanger founds first birth control clinic in New York City and is jailed for dispensing contraceptives on the premises.

1917   First legislative attempt to repeal Connecticut's 1879 anticontraceptive law fails.

1920s   More legislative attempts to repeal or modify Connecticut's anticontraceptive law fail.

1928   *Olmstead v. U.S.:* U.S. Supreme Court upholds the practice of wiretapping, but dissents by Louis Brandeis and Oliver Wendell Holmes express support for the constitutional protection of privacy.

1930s   More legislative attempts to repeal or modify Connecticut's anticontraceptive law fail.

1935   Connecticut Birth Control League (CBCL) quietly opens a birth control clinic in Hartford.

1936   U.S. Court of Appeals for Second Circuit rules in *U.S. v. One Package* that the sending of contraceptives through the mails by licensed medical personnel does not violate the Comstock Act.

1938   CBCL opens birth control clinic in lower-class section of Waterbury, Connecticut.

1939   Waterbury Clinic closed by Connecticut law enforcement officials; various contraceptives seized. Proceedings instituted to determine whether Connecticut's anticontraception law can be read so as to afford an

	exception allowing medical personnel to offer birth control counseling and prescriptions for contraceptives.
1940s	More legislative attempts to repeal or modify Connecticut's anticontraceptive law fail.
1940	*State v. Nelson:* Connecticut Supreme Court of Errors refuses to grant a medical exception for two doctors and a nurse to offer birth control counseling and to prescribe contraceptives. All birth control clinics in Connecticut suspend operations.
1943	*Tileston v. Ullman:* In a per curiam opinion, U.S. Supreme Court rules that a Connecticut physician lacked standing to challenge the constitutionality of the state's anticontraception law.
1950s	More legislative attempts to repeal or modify Connecticut's anticontraceptive law fail.
1953	Estelle Griswold accepts position as executive director of Planned Parenthood League of Connecticut (PPLC).
1954	C. Lee Buxton appointed chair of Obstetrics and Gynecology Department in Yale Medical School. Buxton also becomes the Director of the Yale University infertility clinic and is active in various PPLC causes.
Early 1960s	More legislative attempts to repeal or modify Connecticut's anticontraceptive law fail.
1961	*Poe et al. v. Ullman:* U.S. Supreme Court decides that the appeal from Connecticut does not present a "case or controversy" under the U.S. Constitution. Strong dissenting opinions by John Marshall Harlan and William O. Douglas rely on an emerging right of privacy. PPLC opens Planned Parenthood Center of New Haven at 79 Trumbull, Connecticut's first birth control clinic since the 1930s. After ten days of operation, the clinic is raided by New Haven police. Estelle Griswold and Lee Buxton are arrested for violating Connecticut's anticontraception law. PPLC closes clinic.
1962	Griswold and Buxton convicted in New Haven Circuit Court of violating anticontraception law and fined $100 each.
1963	*Connecticut v. Griswold and Buxton:* Appellate Division of Connecticut Circuit Court affirms conviction of Griswold and Buxton.

1964	*Connecticut v. Griswold and Buxton:* Connecticut Supreme Court of Errors upholds the conviction of Griswold and Buxton as justified by the state's "police power." Appealed to U.S. Supreme Court.
1965	Decision in *Griswold v. Connecticut* announced on June 7. By a vote of 7–2, the Court, in an opinion written by William O. Douglas, strikes down the 1879 Connecticut anticontraception law as a violation of the right of privacy as found in the "emanations" and "penumbras" of selected portions of Bill of Rights. A concurring opinion by Arthur Goldberg stresses privacy as grounded in the Ninth Amendment; a concurring opinion by John Marshall Harlan stresses privacy as one of the unenumerated rights protected by the due process clause of the Fourteenth Amendment; and a concurring opinion by Byron White finds equal protection and other Fourteenth Amendment problems with the Connecticut law. Dissents by Hugo Black and Potter Stewart take Court majority to task for creating constitutional rights out of whole cloth.
1972	*Eisenstadt v. Baird:* U.S. Supreme Court extends the right of privacy in the use of contraceptives to unmarried persons. William Brennan, for the Court, bases his ruling on the equal protection clause of Fourteenth Amendment.
1973	*Roe v. Wade:* U.S. Supreme Court upholds a woman's right to abortion in the first trimester of her pregnancy but permits the state regulation of abortion during the last six months of pregnancy. Majority opinion written by Harry Blackmun declares that the right of abortion is guaranteed by the due process clause of the Fourteenth Amendment.
1977	*Carey v. Population Services International:* U.S. Supreme Court rules unconstitutional a New York statute placing various restrictions on the dissemination of contraceptives. Court holds that childbearing is a "fundamental right."
1986	*Bowers v. Hardwick:* U.S. Supreme Court upholds the constitutionality of a Georgia sodomy law.
1987	Robert Bork's nomination to U.S. Supreme Court rejected by the U.S. Senate, largely because nominee refuses to accept existence of a constitutional right of privacy.
1989	*Webster v. Reproductive Health Services:* U.S. Supreme Court decision states that abortion is not a "fundamental right."

1990	*Cruzan v. Director, Missouri Department of Health:* U.S. Supreme Court holds that the "right to die" is subject to a balancing of the liberty interests of the person as set against "relevant state interests." Dissenters argue for affording more weight to the constitutional right of privacy in right to die situations.
1992	*Planned Parenthood v. Casey:* U.S. Supreme Court comes within a single vote of overturning *Roe v. Wade.* Majority follows the "undue burden" test in determining the constitutionality of state regulations of abortion.
1997	*Vacco v. Quill:* U. S. Supreme Court upholds the constitutionality of a New York law banning physician-assisted suicide. Majority holds that the right to physician-assisted suicide does not fall within an individual's unenumerated right of privacy. *Washington v. Glucksberg:* U.S. Supreme Court rules that the right to commit suicide with the aid of a physician is not a "fundamental liberty interest" protected by the Fourteenth Amendment. David Souter's concurrence argues strongly, with citations from many right of privacy cases, that the right to die under some circumstances might be considered an unenumerated fundamental liberty.
2000	*Stenberg v. Carhart:* U.S. Supreme Court strikes down a state law banning "partial-birth" abortions and once again adheres to the "undue burden" test rather than treating abortion as a fundamental unenumerated right under the due process clause of the Fourteenth Amendment.
2003	*Lawrence v. Texas:* U.S. Supreme Court explicitly overrules *Bowers v. Hardwick* and holds that a state law prohibiting sodomy involving consenting same-sex adults violates the unenumerated right of privacy protected by the due process clause of the Fourteenth Amendment. *Goodridge v. Department of Public Health:* Supreme Judicial Court of Massachusetts rules that "barring an individual from the protections, benefits, and obligations of civil marriage solely because the person would marry a person of the same sex violates the Massachusetts Constitution." The Massachusetts court bases its decision on the equal protection and due process protections of the state constitution but cites as authorities numerous U.S. Supreme Court privacy decisions, including *Griswold v. Connecticut.*

Federal constitutional amendment prohibiting same-sex marriage proposed in Congress.

2004   Massachusetts Supreme Judicial Court issues advisory opinion that a proposed civil union status for same-sex couples discriminates against gays on equal protection and due process grounds. Massachusetts, California, and other states begin issuing marriage certificates to same-sex couples. Same-sex marriage becomes an issue in the 2004 presidential election campaign.

BIBLIOGRAPHIC ESSAY

Note from the Series Editors: The following bibliographical essay contains the primary and secondary sources the author consulted for this volume. We have asked all authors in the series to omit formal citations in order to make our volume more readable, inexpensive, and appealing for students and general readers.

Primary Materials

A comprehensive historical study of a major Supreme Court decision like *Griswold v. Connecticut* and the Connecticut birth control cases that led up to it requires the perusal of many different types of original sources. But it should start with the court reports of the key cases themselves. The official court report citations of the Connecticut birth control cases, beginning in 1940 and running until 1965, are as follows: *State of Connecticut v. Roger B. Nelson, William A. Goodrich and Clara L. McTernan,* 126 Conn. 412 (1940) [Connecticut Supreme Court of Errors]; *State of Connecticut v. Certain Contraceptive Materials,* 126 Conn. 428 (1940) [Connecticut Supreme Court of Errors]; *Wilder Tileston v. Abraham S. Ullman,* 129 Conn. 84 (1942) [Connecticut Supreme Court of Errors]; *Tileston v. Ullman,* 318 U.S. 44 (1943) [U.S. Supreme Court]; *C. Lee Buxton, Paul Poe, Harold Hoe, Jane Doe v. Abraham S. Ullman,* 147 Conn. 48 (1959) [Connecticut Supreme Court of Errors]; *David M. Trubek v. Abraham S. Ullman,* 147 Conn. 633 (1960) [Connecticut Supreme Court of Errors]; *Poe et al. v. Ullman,* 367 U.S. 497 (1961) [U.S. Supreme Court]; *State of Connecticut v. Estelle T. Griswold and C. Lee Buxton,* 151 Conn. 544 (1964) [Connecticut Supreme Court of Errors]; and *Griswold et al. v. Connecticut,* 381 U.S. 479 (1965) [U.S. Supreme Court].

The official citations — U.S. Supreme Court unless otherwise indicated — of the most important right of privacy cases discussed in these pages are *Weeks v. U.S.,* 232 U.S. 383 (1914); *Meyer v. Nebraska,* 262 U.S. 390 (1923); *Pierce v. Society of Sisters,* 268 U.S. 510 (1925); *Buck v. Bell,* 274 U.S. 200 (1927); *Olmstead v. U.S.,* 277 U.S. 438 (1928); *U.S. v. One Package,* 86 F2d 737 (1936) [Second Circuit Court of Appeals]; *Skinner v. Oklahoma,* 316 U.S. 535 (1942); *NAACP v. Alabama,* 357 U.S. 449 (1958); *Mapp v. Ohio,* 367 U.S. 643 (1961); *Loving v. Virginia,* 388 U.S. 1 (1967); *Eisenstadt v. Baird,* 405 U.S. 438 (1972); *Roe v. Wade,* 410 U.S. 113 (1973); *Carey v. Population Services International,* 431 U.S. 678 (1977); *Zablocki v. Redhail,* 434 U.S. 374 (1977); *Moore v. East Cleveland,* 431 U.S. 494 (1977); *Bowers v. Hardwick,* 478 U.S. 186 (1986); *Webster v. Reproductive Health Services,* 492 U.S. 490 (1989); *Michael H. v. Gerald D.,* 491 U.S. 110 (1989); *Cruzan v. Director, Missouri*

Department of Health, 497 U.S. 261 (1990); *Planned Parenthood v. Casey*, 505 U.S. 833 (1992); *Lee v. State of Oregon*, 107 F3d 1382 (1997) [Ninth Circuit Court of Appeals]; *Vacco v. Quill*, 521 U.S. 793 (1997); *Washington v. Glucksberg*, 521 U.S. 702 (1997); *Stenberg v. Carhart*, 530 U.S. 914 (2000); *Lawrence v. Texas*, 123 S.Ct. 2472 (2003); and *Goodridge v. Department of Public Health*, 440 Mass. 309 (2003) [Supreme Judicial Court of Massachusetts]. Those interested in consulting one or more of the scores of other decisions mentioned in this book should seek out the text of opinions desired via the online search capabilities of Lexis-Nexis or Westlaw.

Published case reports only scratch the surface of what goes into the making of a major Supreme Court decision like *Griswold v. Connecticut*. Philip B. Kurland and Gerhard Casper, eds., *Landmark Briefs and Arguments of the Supreme Court of the United States* (Arlington, VA: University Publications of America, 1975), found on microfiche and/or paper volumes in most law schools, contains the transcript of the record in *Griswold* that accompanied the appeal to the U.S. Supreme Court. This record includes copies of the various motions by the attorneys in the Connecticut courts; the factual findings of the Connecticut circuit court judge at the trial of Griswold and Buxton held on January 2, 1962; the Supreme Court briefs of the Planned Parenthood League of Connecticut (PPLC), the state of Connecticut and the four amicus curiae; and a transcript of the March 29–30, 1965, oral argument before the U.S. Supreme Court.

The Supreme Court Papers of several justices serving on the Court at the time of *Griswold v. Connecticut* are available for examination by scholars in the Manuscript Division of the Library of Congress in Washington, D.C. Most of the material for my reconstruction of the April 2, 1965, conference on *Griswold* was gleaned from the Papers of Earl Warren (Boxes 267 and 520), the Papers of William O. Douglas (Box 1347), the Papers of Hugo Black (Box 383), and the Papers of William Brennan (Boxes I:118 and I:130). The papers of Byron White and Arthur Goldberg proved less useful than those of the above-named justices, but interesting memoranda from White and Goldberg on *Griswold* can be retrieved from the Douglas Papers. In addition, many of these collections of Supreme Court Papers provide insights as to the behind-the-scenes negotiations on the six opinions that would ultimately be produced for the Court's June 7, 1965, decision. Edited summaries of Supreme Court conferences in selected cases are provided in Del Dickson, ed., *The Supreme Court in Conference (1940–1985): The Private Discussions Behind Nearly 300 Supreme Court Decisions* (New York: Oxford University Press, 2001). Besides the excerpts from the conference in *Griswold*, Dickson's volume contains conference materials on a number of other privacy cases, namely *Tileston v. Ullman* (1943), *Poe v. Ullman* (1961), *Eisenstadt v. Baird* (1972), *Roe v. Wade* (1973), and *Bowers v. Hardwick* (1986). The terrible handwriting and cryptic abbreviations of the justices make many of the conference notes hard to decipher. Hence, different scholars' reconstructions of what was said by the justices at particular Supreme Court conferences frequently do not agree.

Newspapers generally provide useful information and commentary on cases as they make their way through the courts and in the aftermath of important decisions. This was certainly the case for the Connecticut birth control controversy. Such Connecticut papers as the *New Haven Journal-Courier*, the *New Haven Register*, the *Hartford Courant*, the *Hartford Times*, and the *Bridgeport Herald* covered the birth control cases, particularly at the time of the 1961 arrest of Griswold and Buxton. In addition, such national papers as the *Boston Globe* and the *New York Times*, as well as the major press services, also provided fairly ample coverage of the PPLC challenge to the Connecticut anticontraception law. The media frequently used *Griswold* as a jumping-off point to deal with particular contraceptive issues in geographic regions served by the papers. The *New York Times* and the *Boston Globe*, for example, focused on then-pending legislation to liberalize New York and Massachusetts contraceptive laws. In the aftermath of *Griswold*, many papers around the country carried press service reports on the Court decision or excerpted portions of the six justices' opinions. In the week or so following the June 7, 1965, decision, editorials commenting on the wisdom of the *Griswold* holding and the future of the right of privacy appeared in the *New York Times*, the *Washington Post*, the *Boston Globe*, the *Christian Science Monitor*, and myriad papers around the country, just a small sample of which are quoted in my account. Popular magazines, including *Time*, *Newsweek*, *U.S. News & World Report*, and *Look*, carried stories on *Griswold* during the summer of 1965. In addition, the nation's major religious periodicals—*America*, *Commonweal*, and the *Christian Century*—weighed in on the Supreme Court's birth control decision in June and July 1965.

Government documents constitute another important category of primary sources for those interested in *Griswold* and the right of privacy. The voluminous congressional materials on Robert Bork's abortive nomination to the Supreme Court are especially interesting. See Senate Committee on the Judiciary, *Hearings on the Nomination of Robert H. Bork to be an Associate Justice of the Supreme Court of the United States*, 100th Congress, First Session, 1987, 5 vols.; and Senate Committee on the Judiciary, *Committee Report on the Nomination of Robert H. Bork to be an Associate Justice of the United States Supreme Court*, 100th Congress, First Session, 1987. Bork's most important statement of his views on Griswold are found in his essay, "Neutral Principles and Some First Amendment Problems," *Indiana Law Journal* 47 (Fall 1971): 1–17. Bork's caustic reactions to his failed nomination are found in Robert Bork, *The Tempting of America: The Political Seduction of the Law* (New York: Free Press, 1990). The Senate Judiciary Committee's hearings and reports on persons nominated to the Supreme Court since Robert Bork — Anthony Kennedy (1987–88), David H. Souter (1990), Clarence Thomas (1991), Ruth Bader Ginsburg (1993), and Stephen G. Breyer (1994) — are also quite revealing about the politics of the right of privacy.

———

Selected Secondary Materials

This is my third book-length study of a major U.S. Supreme Court decision. Neither of the previous studies, however, came close to posing the bibliographical challenges of this one. The scholarly literature on privacy and sexuality — produced by law professors, judges, historians, social scientists, and philosophers — is substantial and wide-ranging. What follows is a selected list of the secondary works I found most helpful in constructing my account of *Griswold v. Connecticut* and the right of privacy.

On the history, technology, and politics of contraception in the United States, see the following books: Linda Gordon, *The Moral Property of Women: A History of Birth Control Politics in America* (Urbana: University of Illinois Press, 2002; 2 vols.); Andrea Tone, *Devices and Desires: A History of Contraception in America* (New York: Hill and Wang, 2001); Janet Farrell Brodie, *Contraception and Abortion in Nineteenth-Century America* (Ithaca: Cornell University Press, 1994); Carole R. McCann, *Birth Control Politics in the United States, 1916–1945* (Ithaca: Cornell University Press, 1994); James Reed, *From Private Vice to Public Virtue: The Birth Control Movement and American Society Since 1830* (New York: Basic Books, 1978); and David M. Kennedy, *Birth Control in America: The Career of Margaret Sanger* (New Haven: Yale University Press, 1970). See also the following articles: Joshua Gamson, "Rubber Wars: Struggles over the Condom in the United States," *Journal of the History of Sexuality* 1 (1990): 262–82; Esther Katz, "The History of Birth Control in the United States," *Trends in History* 4 (1988): 81–101; and C. Lee Buxton, "Family Planning Clinics in Connecticut," *Connecticut Medicine* 32 (February 1968): 122–24.

Alan Westin, *Privacy and Freedom* (New York: Atheneum, 1967), is a pathbreaking survey of privacy from many angles — historical, legal, philosophical, technological, and policy-oriented. Although dated, Westin's tome is still essential reading for anyone interested in privacy in the American experience. The most complete survey of pre-*Griswold* tort opinions on privacy is William L. Prosser, "Privacy," *California Law Review* 48 (1960): 383–423. The classic article on privacy, years ahead of its time and serving ipso facto as an important moment in the history of the right of privacy, is Louis Brandeis and Samuel Warren, "The Right to Privacy," *Harvard Law Review* 4 (December 1890): 193–220. Commentary on the Brandeis/Warren article can be found in James H. Barron, "Warren and Brandeis, 'The Right to Privacy,' 4 *Harv. L. Rev.* 193 (1890): Demystifying a Landmark Citation," *Suffolk University Law Review* 13 (Summer 1979): 875–922; and Dorothy J. Glancy, "The Invention of the Right to Privacy," *Arizona Law Review* 21 (1979): 1–39. A short but insightful book on privacy and the law is Philippa Strum, *Privacy: The Debate in the United States Since 1945* (Fort Worth: Harcourt Brace, 1998). The most readable examination of the intersection of law and the philosophy of privacy, albeit now dated, is Richard F. Hixson, *Privacy in a Public Society: Human Rights in Conflict* (New York: Oxford University Press, 1987). Other useful books on privacy — some legal in emphasis, some more philosophical — include Jeffrey Rosen, *The Unwanted Gaze: The Destruction of Privacy in America* (New York: Random House, 2000); Adam Carlyle Breckenridge, *The Right to Privacy* (Lincoln: University of Nebraska Press, 1970); Judith Wagner DeCew, *In Pursuit of Privacy: Law, Ethics, and the Rise of Technology* (Ithaca: Cornell University Press, 1997); David M. O'Brien, *Privacy, Law, and Public Policy* (New York: Praeger, 1979); Darien A. McWhirter and Jon D. Bible, *Privacy as a Constitutional Right: Sex, Drugs and the Right to Life* (New York: Quorum Books, 1992); and David J. Seipp, *The Right to Privacy in American History* (Cambridge: Center for Information Policy Research, 1978). See also Toby Lester, "The Reinvention of Privacy," *Atlantic Monthly* (March 2001): 27–39. Although out of the historical period covered by this book, a classic legal and social history of privacy in early American history deserves mention: David H. Flaherty, *Privacy in Colonial New England* (Charlottesville: University Press of Virginia, 1972).

The most extensive scholarly treatment of the case of *Griswold v. Connecticut* is found in the first third of a truly monumental volume, David J. Garrow, *Liberty and Sexuality: The Right to Privacy and the Making of Roe v. Wade* (Berkeley: University of California Press, 1998), 1–269. As the subtitle hints, Garrow treats *Griswold* as the lead-in to the well-known abortion decision, *Roe v. Wade*. However, his lengthy examination of *Griswold* stands on its own as a major contribution to the study of privacy and the law. Garrow's work is particularly distinguished by a prodigious bibliography and an adroit use of interview material from innumerable participants in the Connecticut birth control cases. Readers familiar with *Liberty and Sexuality* will recognize that my account of the internal legal history of *Griswold* departs somewhat from Garrow's. In addition, I have placed my study of the Connecticut birth control cases in a broader historical and legal context. However, it should be apparent to readers of both books that I have leaned heavily on *Liberty and Sexuality* for details on the Planned Parenthood League of Connecticut and its key personnel. A short, well-written book on the Connecticut birth control dispute, intended for students rather than legal scholars or historians, is Susan C. Wawrose, *Griswold v. Connecticut: Contraception and the Right of Privacy* (New York: Franklin

Watts, 1996). Wawrose's book also contains some fascinating photographs of key figures in the struggle for contraceptive reform in Connecticut.

The author of the principal Supreme Court opinion in *Griswold v. Connecticut* — William O. Douglas — wrote a great deal off the bench, including two autobiographical volumes: *Go East, Young Man: the Early Years: The Autobiography of William O. Douglas* (New York: Random House, 1974) and *The Court Years, 1939–1975: The Autobiography of William O. Douglas* (New York: Random House,1980). Unfortunately, Douglas's autobiographies are devoted mainly to spinning myths that the justice constructed around his own life; they contain almost nothing of interest on *Griswold*. The most recent biography of Douglas is also the best, Bruce Allen Murphy, *Wild Bill: The Legend and Life of William O. Douglas* (New York: Random House, 2003). Murphy paints Douglas as an unscrupulous, sad, brilliant, ambitious, and enigmatic legal figure; his *Wild Bill* is truly a "warts and all" biography. Another useful account of Douglas's life is James Simon, *Independent Journey: The Life of William O. Douglas* (New York: Penguin Books, 1980). Short but thoughtful biographical treatments of Douglas and the other justices on the Supreme Court at the time of *Griswold* can be found in Melvin I. Urofsky, ed., *The Supreme Court Justices: A Biographical Dictionary* (New York: Garland, 1994); following the essays on each justice are useful bibliographical entries.

Over the years since 1965, *Griswold* has served as a frequent source of comment for members of the academic legal community. It is best to group the many law review articles on *Griswold* and related subjects in chronological subcategories. First of all, for law review treatments of pre-*Griswold* birth control cases in Connecticut, see Mary L. Dudziak, "Just Say No: Birth Control in the Connecticut Supreme Court Before *Griswold v. Connecticut*," *Iowa Law Review* 75 (May 1990): 915–39; Peter Smith, "The History and Future of the Legal Battle over Birth Control," *Cornell Law Quarterly* 49 (1964): 275–303; Irwin R. Harrison, Connecticut's Contraceptive Statute: A Recurring Problem in Constitutional Law," *Connecticut Bar Journal* 35 (1960): 310–19; and Richard J. Regan, "The Connecticut Birth Control Ban and Public Morals," *Catholic Lawyer* 7 (Winter 1961): 5–10, 49. Perhaps the most important law review article dealing with pre-*Griswold* birth control issues and ultimately proving instrumental in Thomas Emerson's brief for the appellants and Justice Arthur Goldberg's concurring opinion, is Norman Redlich, "Are There 'Certain Rights . . . Retained by the People'?," *New York University Law Review* 37 (November 1962): 787–812.

The most insightful analyses in the immediate aftermath of the *Griswold* decision include "The Supreme Court, 1964 Term: Anti–Birth Control Statute," *Harvard Law Review* 79 (1965): 162–65; William Beaney, "The *Griswold* Case and the Expanding Right to Privacy," *Wisconsin Law Review* 1966 (Fall 1966): 979–95; Robert G. Dixon Jr., "The *Griswold* Penumbra: Constitutional Charter for an Expanded Law of Privacy?" *Michigan Law Review* 64 (December 1965): 197–218; Thomas I. Emerson, "Nine Justices in Search of a Doctrine," *Michigan Law Review* 64 (December 1965): 219–34; Paul G. Kauper, "Penumbras, Peripheries, Emanations, Things Fundamental and Things Forgotten: The *Griswold* Case," *Michigan Law Review* 64 (December 1965): 235–58; Robert B. McKay, "The Right of Privacy: Emanations and Intimations," *Michigan Law Review* 64 (December 1965): 259–82; and Arthur E. Sutherland, "Privacy in Connecticut," *Michigan Law Review* 64 (December 1965): 283–88. The essays in the *Michigan Law Review* were later republished in *The Right of Privacy: A Symposium on the Implications of Griswold v. Connecticut* (New York: Da Capo Press, 1971). Few of these commentators were enamored of Douglas's opinion of the Court, but most seemed to recognize the path-breaking significance of the ruling.

The twenty-fifth anniversary of *Griswold v. Connecticut* provided the occasion for Fowler Harper's law school alma mater, Ohio Northern University, to conduct a symposium in memory of the attorney who initiated the appeal to the Supreme Court in the famous Connecticut birth control case. Some of the papers presented at the symposium, along with eulogies to Harper and a copy of his jurisdictional statement in the case, were published in a special edition of the *Ohio Northern University Law Review*. Included among the published papers were the following: Stephen C. Veltri, "*Fowler v. Harper* and the Right of Privacy: Twenty-five Years," *Ohio Northern University Law Review* 16 (1989): 359–63; Catherine G. Roraback, "*Griswold v. Connecticut:* A Brief Case History," *Ohio Northern University Law Review* 16 (1989): 395–401; G. Sidney Buchanan, "The Right of Privacy: Past, Present, and Future," *Ohio Northern University Law Review* 16 (1989): 403–510; Lackland H. Bloom Jr., "The Legacy of *Griswold*," *Ohio Northern University Law Review* 16 (1989): 511–44; Richard Green, "*Griswold*'s Legacy: Fornication and Adultery as Crimes," *Ohio Northern University Law Review* 16 (1989): 544–49; Bruce Fein, "*Griswold v. Connecticut:* Wayward Decision-Making in the Supreme Court," *Ohio Northern University Law Review* 16 (1989): 551–59; and Jerome H. Skolnick, "Constitutional Privacy, Community, and the Individual: An Essay in Honor of Fowler V. Harper," *Ohio Northern University Law Review* 16 (1989): 561–81. The best of these essays is Buchanan's 100+ page tracking of the journey of the right of privacy since *Griswold*. The silver anniversary of *Griswold* also generated a special issue of the *Connecticut Law Review*. The essays in this issue — found at *Connecticut Law Review* 23 (Summer 1991): 853–999— are not as good as those in the commemorative issue of Fowler Harper's alma mater.

The holding in *Griswold* continues to attract comments — usually critical — in the nation's law reviews. See especially Edward Thomas Mulligan, "*Griswold* Revisited in Light of *Uplinger*," *Review of Law and Social Change* 13 (1984–85): 51–82; Burr Henly, " 'Penumbra': The Roots of a Legal Metaphor,"

Hastings Constitutional Law Quarterly 15 (Fall 1987): 81–100; Henry T. Greely, "A Footnote to 'Penumbra' in *Griswold v. Connecticut*," *Constitutional Commentary* 6 (Summer 1989): 252–65; and Mark Tushnet, "Two Notes on the Jurisprudence of Privacy," *Constitutional Commentary* 8 (1991): 75–85. Other articles that place *Griswold* in the general sweep of the development of the law of privacy include Brian DeBoice, "Note: Due Process Privacy and the Path of Progress," *University of Illinois Law Forum* (1979): 469–546; J. Harvie Wilkinson III and G. Edward White, "Constitutional Protection for Personal Lifestyles," *Cornell Law Review* 62 (1977): 563–625; and J. Braxton Craven Jr., "Personhood: The Right to Be Let Alone," *Duke Law Journal* (1976): 699–720.

Predictably, major law of privacy decisions following *Griswold* sparked published comment by the legal community. The literature on *Roe v. Wade* and the right of privacy is immense. See especially the final two-thirds of Garrow's *Liberty and Sexuality*, 270–741; N. E. H. Hull and Peter Charles Hoffer, *Roe v. Wade: The Abortion Rights Controversy in American History* (Lawrence: University Press of Kansas, 2001); and John Hart Ely, "The Wages of Crying Wolf: A Comment on *Roe v. Wade*," *Yale Law Journal* 82 (April 1973): 920–49. See also Sarah Weddington, "The Woman's Right of Privacy," *Perkins Journal* 27 (Fall 1973): 35–41; Janice Goodman et al., "*Doe* and *Roe*: Where Do We Go from Here?," *Women's Rights Law Review* 1 (Spring 1973): 2–38; Catharine MacKinnon, "The Male Ideology of Privacy: A Feminist Perspective on the Right to Abortion," *Radical America* 17 (July–August 1983): 23–35; Helen Garfield, "Privacy, Abortion, and Judicial Review: Haunted by the Ghost of *Lochner*," *Washington Law Review* 61 (April 1986): 293–365; and Darin P. Wipperman, *Extremism Triumphant: The Politics of Slavery and Abortion* (Parkland, FL: Brown Walker Press, 2003). Bob Woodward and Scott Armstrong, *The Brethren: Inside the Supreme Court* (New York: Avon Books, 1979) offers an account of confidential discussions of the Supreme Court in *Roe v. Wade* and other reproductive rights cases in the early 1970s; regrettably, the authors' version of the justices' conferences and backstage negotiations is unreliable.

On the right-to-die cases, see Melvin I. Urofsky, *Lethal Judgments: Assisted Suicide and American Law* (Lawrence: University Press of Kansas, 2000); and Edward A. Lyon, "The Right to Die: An Exercise of Informed Consent, Not an Extension of the Constitutional Right to Privacy," *Cincinnati Law Review* 58 (1990): 1367–95. And on a potpourri of privacy cases, see Howard Ball, *The Supreme Court and the Intimate Lives of Americans: Birth, Sex, Marriage, Childrearing, and Death* (New York: New York University Press, 2004). Numerous articles on homosexuality and the right of privacy were written in the wake of *Bowers v. Hardwick* (1986). See, for example, Nan D. Hunter, "Life After *Hardwick*," *Harvard Civil Rights–Civil Liberties Law Review* 27 (Summer 1992): 531–54. The 2003 Supreme Court decision in *Lawrence v.*

Texas, overruling *Bowers*, changes everything on the law of privacy and same-sex intimate relations. No doubt there will soon be a spate of law review articles on the impact of *Lawrence* on the law of privacy. Readers interested in identifying other law journal treatments of right of privacy cases should take advantage of the search capabilities of Lexis-Nexis or Westlaw.

Historical research on American legal subjects is expedited by an array of reference works, many of which are found in public libraries as well as law school and university libraries. Kermit L. Hall, ed., *The Oxford Companion to the Supreme Court of the United States* (New York: Oxford University Press, 1992) is an excellent source of information on Supreme Court procedures and many of the best-known cases decided by the Court. More focused on cases themselves is Kermit L. Hall, ed., *The Oxford Guide to United States Supreme Court Decisions* (New York: Oxford University Press, 1999). Slightly longer accounts of several key right of privacy cases, along with selective bibliographies, can be found in John W. Johnson, ed., *Historic U.S. Court Cases: An Encyclopedia*, 2nd ed. (New York: Routledge, 2001), 2 vols. A narrative historical context for the development of the constitutional right of privacy and other recent civil liberties issues is provided by Melvin I. Urofsky and Paul Finkelman, *A March of Liberty: A Constitutional History of the United States*, 2nd ed. (New York: Oxford University Press, 2002). More general legal histories of America that touch on privacy are Lawrence M. Friedman, *American Law in the Twentieth Century* (New Haven: Yale University Press, 2002); and Kermit L. Hall, *The Magic Mirror: Law in American History* (New York: Oxford University Press, 1989). On the history of civil liberties as broadly defined, see Samuel Walker, *In Defense of American Liberties: A History of the ACLU*, 2nd ed. (Carbondale: Southern Illinois University Press, 1990).

INDEX

ABCL. *See* American Birth Control
League
Abortion, 3, 5, 9, 75, 122, 153, 154,
197
contraception and, 202
controversy over, 10, 19, 149–50,
205
health issues and, 33, 223
late-term, 205, 206
partial-birth, 205–6, 238
privacy and, 201–4, 206, 207, 210
regulation of, 202, 205, 237
right to, 132, 203, 204, 205
Abortion laws, liberalizing, 183, 202
Abstinence, 32, 43, 47, 95, 106, 121,
124, 146
problems with, 109–10, 111
ACLU. *See* American Civil
Liberties Union
Act of Congress (1792), 56
Act of Congress (1934), 69
"Act Relative to Civil Unions,
An" (Massachusetts, Senate
No. 2175), 230
"Act to Amend an Act Concerning
Offences Against Decency,
Morality, and Humanity, An"
(Connecticut, 1879)
challenging, 34, 35, 38, 40, 77,
80, 82, 94–95, 96, 124, 126,
137, 195, 236
civil liberties and, 185
Comstock Act and, 8
constitutionality of, 48, 50, 86,
94, 112, 117, 120, 189
defending, 33, 41, 92
enforcing, 20, 35, 36, 50, 85
equal protection and, 136
exceptions to, 26, 30, 42
modification of, 17, 18, 19–20,
29, 35, 36, 43, 90, 235, 236
repeal of, 15, 16, 26–27, 38, 92,
163, 180, 189–90, 202, 235,
236, 237

violation of, 15, 23, 24, 28, 37,
80, 81, 86, 95–96, 101, 236
Adultery, 27, 62, 95, 112, 115, 146,
197, 213
contraceptives and, 173
laws against, 147, 150, 175, 211
privacy and, 52, 210–11
Advice and consent, 219–22
AMA. *See* American Medical
Association
America, on anticontraceptive law,
188
American Birth Control League
(ABCL), 11, 16
American Civil Liberties Union
(ACLU), 136
brief by, 45, 120, 123
Hardwick and, 212, 213
Harper and, 44
same-sex marriage and, 230
American Institute for Public
Opinion, 20
American Medical Association
(AMA), 11, 14
Amicus curiae briefs, 33, 34, 41–42,
116, 136
described, 119, 120
filing, 44, 121
Anti-birth control movement, 29,
36
Anticontraception law. *See* "Act to
Amend an Act Concerning
Offences Against Decency,
Morality, and Humanity, An"
Antimiscegenation statute, 207
Appellate Division of the Sixth
Connecticut Circuit Court,
appeal to, 88, 90–91, 236
Aptheker v. Secretary of State (1964),
134, 142
Article I (U.S. Constitution), 131
Article II (U.S. Constitution),
Section 2 of, 219
Article III (U.S. Constitution), 47

Associational rights. *See* Freedom of association

Atlanta Constitution, 61–62

Avery, Christopher, 33

Baird, William, 198–99

Baker v. Carr (1962), 132

Baldwin, Raymond E., 42, 43

Barnum, P. T., 8, 235

Barrows v. Jackson (1953), 99–100, 107

BCFA. *See* Birth Control Federation of America

Beaney, William, 195–96

Beauharnais v. Illinois (1952), 72, 157

Berg, Harold, 81, 82, 86, 89

Berger, Rauol, 129

Berkman, Alexander, 9

Biden, Joseph, 220

Bill of Rights, 71, 129, 159, 186, 194, 200

    emanations and penumbras approach to, 168, 171, 192, 224

    liberties and, 64, 174

    literal reading of, 175

    marriage and, 160

    privacy and, 2, 54, 55, 56, 63, 113, 114, 143, 155, 156, 158, 168, 169, 170, 174, 176, 180, 185, 220, 221

    protection of, 65, 131, 165, 174

    selective incorporation theory of, 172

Birth control, 3, 8, 13, 29

    banning, ix, 15, 54, 90, 101

    battle over, 90, 92

    contraception and, 146

    practicing, 10, 12, 13, 183

    privacy and, 207

    regulation of, 154, 189

    research on, 12

    safe/effective, 121

    social benefits of, 99, 109

    strategies for, 5

    support for, 19–20, 109, 110, 144

Birth control advocates, x, 9, 11, 29, 30, 38–39, 53, 223

Birth control clinics, 6, 46, 122, 148

    closing, 28, 137

    opening, 10, 20, 21, 47, 50, 79, 81, 182–83, 235

    operating, 77, 117

Birth Control Federation of America (BCFA), name change for, 29

Birth control movement, 18, 78, 81, 201

Birth Control Research Bureau, 14

Birth Control Review, 10

Black, Charles, 197

Black, Hugo L., 44, 47, 132, 156, 157, 187

    on abortion, 149

    appointment of, 178

    dissent in *Griswold* by, 161, 163–65, 172–76, 179, 185–86, 193, 194

    First Amendment and, 154

    freedom of expression and, 176

    jurisprudence of, 129

    liberty and, 178

    Lochner and, 177

    Ninth Amendment and, 178–79, 180, 193–94

    oral argument in *Griswold* and, 141, 142, 197

    Poe and, 128–29

    privacy and, 155, 158, 176

Blackmun, Harry

    abortion and, 202, 237

    Bowers and, 213–14

    Cruzan and, 216

    law clerks and, 162

    Roe and, 203

Blazi, John, 81, 82, 86

Bork, Robert

    Nomination to Supreme Court of, 219–21

    privacy and, 220, 221–22, 237

Bourke, Vernon J., 110

Bowers v. Hardwick (1986), 212, 225, 226–27, 238

    dissents in, 213

    Griswold/Roe/Carey and, 214

Douglas, William O., *continued*
  concurrence by, 174
  criticism of, 193
  dissent by, 52, 53, 130
  due process and, 167
  First Amendment and, 167, 210
  Goldman and, 71
  law clerks and, 130, 162
  lecture by, 51
  on liberty, 72
  marriage and, 159, 207
  Ninth Amendment and, 161, 171
  opinion in *Griswold* by, 63, 129,
    157–59, 161, 163–64, 166, 167,
    169–70, 186, 224, 237
  oral argument and, 140
  penumbras and, 168, 190, 191,
    194, 195, 196, 200, 203, 226
  Poe and, 51, 94, 100, 102, 115,
    130, 159, 168
  Posner/Brennan letter and,
    159–60, 161
  precedent and, 129–30
  privacy and, 51, 71–73, 159, 171,
    193, 195, 220, 221, 236
Doyle, Arthur Conan, 206
Drinan, Robert, 187
Due process, 31, 34, 99, 108,
  110–11, 147, 148, 149
  argument for, 143
  economic, 142, 154, 178, 203
  flexible, 194
  substantive, 154, 178, 193, 203
Due process clause, 106, 114, 123,
  167, 172, 173, 174–75, 177
  marriage and, 208
  protection by, 50, 51, 65, 66
  violation of, 45, 206, 207
  See also Fourteenth Amendment
Durning, Jean and Marvin, 40, 41

Eavesdropping, 56, 58, 62, 137,
  196
  prosecution of, 54
  regulating, 224
Ecobedo v. Illinois (1964), 134
Economic regulation, 70, 108
Eighth Amendment, 158

Eisenhower, Dwight D., 127, 128,
  131, 132
Eisenstadt, Sheriff, 199
Eisenstadt v. Baird (1972), 199, 202,
  222, 226
  fornication and, 200
  privacy and, 201, 203
Ells, Arthur F., 32
Ely, John Hart, 154, 164, 165
  Douglas opinion in *Griswold* and,
    162
  memo by, 102, 135, 136–38,
    142
  Roe and, 203, 204
Emanations, 164, 168, 171, 192,
  193, 194, 195, 203, 224, 226
Emerson, Ruth, 45, 140
Emerson, Thomas I., 39, 45, 103,
  122, 129, 135, 196–97
  abortion and, 149, 202
  on anticontraception law, 109
  argumentative style of, 104–5
  article by, 191, 195
  on birth control, 109–10, 119
  brief in *Griswold* by, 105, 116, 167
  Douglas and, 182, 193
  due process argument and,
    110–11, 112, 144
  Fourth Amendment and, 113
  Griswold and, 104
  Harlan and, 155
  and Harper compared, 105, 106
  Ninth Amendment and, 194
  opinion and, 157, 166, 181
  oral argument in *Griswold* and,
    43, 120, 140–41, 142, 145, 146,
    147, 148
  privacy and, 112–13, 114–15,
    143, 150, 156, 192, 193, 197
  Third Amendment and, 113
  on White/Goldberg, 102
Equal protection, 136, 141, 154,
  174–75, 199, 225, 228
Ernst, Morris, 14, 29, 33, 41, 123
  brief by, 121–22
  challenge by, 34
Estes, Billy Sol, 166, 184
Eugenics, 11–15, 13, 17